CREATING DELIGHTFUL MASTERPIECES
in

Southern Settings

Moultrie Service League
Moultrie, Georgia

Southern Settings
Published by
Moultrie Service League

Additional copies of **Southern Settings** may be obtained at the cost of $17.95, plus $3.00 postage and handling, each book. Georgia residents add $1.08 sales tax, each book.

Send to:
Moultrie Service League
P.O. Box 1365
Moultrie, Georgia 31776

ISBN: 0-9651477-0-3

First Printing   1996

Printed in the USA by

WIMMER
The Wimmer Companies, Inc.
Memphis

Introduction

Celebrating 50 years of service, the Moultrie Service League was founded in January 1946 by ten young women. Throughout the years, volunteer efforts of the League have greatly impacted the community. One of our major projects resulted in the renovation and conversion of the original Moultrie High School into the Colquitt County Arts Center. The cupola pictured throughout the cookbook symbolizes the Arts Center. Its restoration was the first renovation effort completed, thanks to generous donations of time, supplies, and efforts by many League supporters. Since 1977, Arts Center renovation and promotion of the arts have been main focuses of the League. Over one million dollars has been raised through donations from community supporters and League members for this renovation. A maintenance endowment fund was established in 1988 with a goal of $100,000, which we hope to complete with the sale of this cookbook. Since 1987, League members have participated in "Art in the Schools"—a project to teach art to all fifth graders in Colquitt County. The ultimate aim of this project was to ensure professional art instruction for elementary school children. Through the tireless efforts of our members, this goal became a reality in 1995 when the Colquitt County Board of Education hired an elementary art curriculum director, partially funded by the Moultrie Service League.

Early years in the League saw the development of a free dental clinic for elementary school children and the beginning of a Speech School. Through the ongoing financial and volunteer support of members, the Speech and Hearing Clinic continued to prosper and grow until 1975 when it merged with the Colquitt County Board of Education.

From the beginning, members of this organization have undertaken monumental tasks, never deeming any impossible. As one project ends, another begins. The next 50 years will challenge us as we continue to undertake tasks which will meet our community's future needs. Your purchase of *Southern Settings* will help these dreams become realities. We appreciate your support of the Moultrie Service League.

Celebrating 50 Years of Service

How appropriate to culminate the celebration of Moultrie Service League's 50th anniversary by presenting *Southern Settings*. This project links together the five decades of membership and could not have been accomplished without the combined efforts of all members - active, provisional, sustaining and founding. We hope the pages will be worn from hours of use and that you will share these artistic cuisine combinations with family and friends across the country for the next 50 years! May this book honor your faithful contributions and bring you much pleasure in creating your own *Southern Settings*.

Cheryle Reeves

Cookbook Committee

Co-Chairmen
Judy Mobley   Cheryle Reeves

Art and Format
Jane H. Brown

Research
Cooka Hillebrand

Marketing
Paula Neely

Recipe Collection
Laura Keith

Edit and Production
Mary Campagna
Jessica Jordan
Melanie Rykard

Testing
Gail Qurnell
Sally Tyndall

Index
Carol Aguero

Special Sections
Angela Castellow

Special Thanks
Kelly Denton
Cheryl Friedlander

Barbara Hendrick
Lynwood Hall

Active Members

1995-96 Officers

Jessica Jordan, *President*
Peggy Benner, *Vice President*
Debbie Brown, *Recording Secretary*

Gail Qurnell, *Corresponding Secretary*
Cheryle Reeves, *Treasurer*
Paula Neely, *Ex-Officio*

Karen Willis, *Sustaining Advisor*

Lynn Acuff
Carol Aguero
Carol Bannister
Dora Beadles
Mary Ann Blank
Jane H. Brown
Mary Campagna
Angela Castellow
Mica Copeland
Ava English

Christy Hendrick
Cooka Hillebrand
Sandy Hooks
Polly Jackson
Kim Jarrell
Kelly Jones
Laura Keith
Carolyn Lodge
Donna Marshall
Lorri McCrary

Cathy Mobley
Farolyn Mobley
JoAnne Moss
Sabrina Odom
Nancy Paine
Maureen Price
Martha Reeves
Lanelle Rogers
Pam Rojas
Melanie Rykard

Rhonda Sauls
Jan Smith
Joan Stallings
Amanda Statom
Donna Taylor
Jill Traylor
Sally Tyndall
Cindy Tyus
Patti Wells

Provisional Members

Elizabeth Clark
Mary Ann Creech

Cheryl Friedlander
Patti Garcia

Lisa Plant

Founding Members

Mary Beard
Anne Norman
Jane Perry
Mary Vereen

Deceased:
Wilma Brantley
Carolyn Byron
Gladys Henderson

Margaret Ladson
Catherine Pidcock
Bunny Vereen

Sustaining Members

Beverly Adcock
Sharon Adcock
Ellen Alderman
Kristy Allen
Nadeene Ansley
Joyce Barber
Deryl Beadles
Amanda Beaty
Susan Blanton
Sherry Briggs
Nell Brown
Myra Jane Brown
Debbie Cagle
Carol Ann Cannon
Betty Carithers
Anna Carlton
Ann Carlton
Beth Chastain
Gwen Clements
Jeri Clements
Harvie Ann Cox
Marie Cranford
Pete Darbyshire
Judy Dixon

Becky Duggan
Sandra Edwards
Jennie Estes
Londa Faircloth
Barbara Fallin
Koala Fokes
Priscilla Fowler
Debbie Friedlander
Ann Friedlander
Sue Friedlander
LaDonna
  Funderburk
Lasse Gammage
Julia Gardner
Greer Gay
Betty Godbee
Marilyn Harrison
Doris Harsh
Kathy Heard
Betty Hendrick
Barbara Hendrick
Joan Holman
Lisa Horkan
Lillian Hughes

Jo Jeffords
Fliss Jeter
Rosalind Jeter
Mary Joiner
Maribel Kadel
Kit Kirk
Dianne Klar
Jill Lazarus
Nanci Lewis
Joy Matthews
Alyce McCall
Kathy McCall
Nancy McCalley
Kathryne McDonald
Katrina McIntosh
Jackie McLean
Camila McLean
Marsha McLean
Connie Mobley
Judy Mobley
Diane Moore
Susan Newton
Sandra Plant
Mimi Platter

Elaine Redding
Arlene Schreiber
Gloria Shepard
Anne Smith
Rhett Smith
Reese Smith
Lynne Stone
Mary Jo Stone
Bug Trimble
Jane Tucker
Mary Catherine
  Turner
Barbara Vereen
Betty Vereen
Evelyn Vereen
Anne Vereen
Mary Vines
Catherine Ward
Harriett Whelchel
Cherie Anne
  Whiddon
LeVonne Willis
Karen Willis
Vera Zess

5

Creating the Setting

The beautiful Southern setting on the front cover by Lynwood Hall is an original oil painting of the dining room of Mr. and Mrs. Hoyt Whelchel of Moultrie, Georgia. Mr. Hall, also of Moultrie, is a landscape painter who paints in the impressionistic style. He is acclaimed for painting murals and faux finishes. Awarded Georgia's Artist of the Year in 1992, Hall has exhibited in 16 Georgia cities, as well as New York and Washington D.C. After graduating from the University of Georgia with a degree in art, Hall worked with the U.S. Senate for five years, during which he was commissioned to paint a watercolor of the Capitol for the Vice Premier of China. He later completed a watercolor of the White House for President Anwar Sadat of Egypt. He currently resides outside of Moultrie on his family farm, where his studio is located.

The pen and ink drawing of Colquitt County's Courthouse cupola, featured on the back cover, was designed by the late Mitchell Smith, Sr., of Moultrie. A native of New Orleans, Louisiana, Smith spent the last twenty years of his life in Moultrie. He was active in many areas of community life, including his tenure as President of the Arts Council in 1988. Upon his retirement from C & S Bank in 1987, Smith determined to give painting "a try". That try lead to a love for watercolor, which was enhanced by workshops coast to coast from Arizona to Key West. His memory lives on through the paintings he has left behind. A special thanks to Mrs. Reese Smith, sustaining member of the Moultrie Service League, for sharing the cupola, one of the few pen and ink drawings done by Mr. Smith.

Throughout **Southern Settings**, artwork for divider pages was submitted by local artists associated with the Colquitt County Arts Center. A special thanks to Carolyn O'Neal, and Julie Strickland whose prints do not appear on the dividers, but are dispersed within these pages. We also appreciate our sustainers who created the settings selected by the artists and regret being unable to use all those submitted. Thanks to Mr. and Mrs. Hiller Gammage, Mr. and Mrs. Van Platter, and Mr. and Mrs. Bennett Willis.

Wooden spoons found throughout **Southern Settings** will stir your interest with helpful information about the recipe section which follows.

Table of Contents

Portfolios
Menus

Portfolios

Creating the Setting

Cornelia Pattillo Hardy, a Moultrie native, created this pen and ink drawing of a holiday dining room setting in the home of Dr. and Mrs. Lanny Copeland of Moultrie. Hardy, a mother of four, grandmother to eleven and great-grandmother to three, has enjoyed her hobby of drawing, painting and working with crafts throughout her life. She has worked in pastels, oils, acrylics, pen and inks and watercolors, studying with Peacock, University of Alabama Dothan branch, Lorainne Atchley, Bob Jones and Moultrie's Jane Simpson. As a hobby, art has afforded her many hours of pleasure and gifts to those she loves.

Combined for your Setting

Portfolios collect a sampling of the artist's best. An artist steps back from each canvas and views the whole composition, feasting on his color selection, texture, and subject. Satisfied that his story is told, he relishes in the splendor of each masterpiece. You, the artist, can relish in that experience of developing a portfolio, winning combinations that create the right setting for an intimate family gathering or an elaborate evening of entertaining. Here are a few of our favorites for your enjoyment, but feel free to exercise your creativity.

Moultrie Service League's Fiftieth Anniversary Gala

Bleu Cheese and Apple Salad

Cherry Congealed Salad

Chicken and Artichoke Casserole

Pork Tenderloins

Basiled Green Beans

Wild Rice

Yeast Rolls

~ Sandra Plant ~   ~ Melanie Rykard ~

Gala Dessert Menu

Fresh Fruit and Cream in Cocount Shell

Strawberry Holiday Trifle

Strawberry Bavarian Cream

Chocolate Truffles

Ripple Bars

~ Deryl Beadles ~

Gala menu was prepared to serve 240 people. Over 30 desserts served, but we featured 5 of our favorites.

Bleu Cheese and Apple Salad

2 heads Bibb lettuce
1 head red-leafed lettuce
1 Granny Smith apple, cut
   into small pieces
1 cup walnuts, chopped

½ red onion, thinly sliced
1 package of bleu cheese
1 bottle commercial poppy
   seed dressing

Tear lettuce into bite-sized pieces and combine with other ingredients. Pour poppy seed dressing over salad to taste and toss. Serve immediately.
Yield: 10 servings

Sally Tyndall

Cherry Congealed Salad

2 (3-ounce) boxes cherry
   Jello
1 cup boiling water

1 (24-ounce) jar applesauce
1 (20-ounce) can crushed
   pineapple

Dissolve Jello in boiling water. Add applesauce and pineapple. Congeal overnight.
Yield: 12 servings

Patsy Browning

Chicken and Artichoke Casserole

10 cups chicken (breasts and thighs)
4 large cans artichoke hearts
4 (4-ounce) cans button mushrooms, sliced
3 tablespoons butter
4 to 5 ribs celery
1 medium onion, chopped
5 to 10 peppercorns
3 to 4 tablespoons pale, dry sherry
Parmesan cheese, grated
1½ sticks butter
9 tablespoons all-purpose flour
3 cups half & half
2 small cartons sour cream
1 can cream of mushroom soup
1 can cream of celery soup
1 teaspoon salt
1 teaspoon black pepper
2 dashes Worcestershire sauce
2 dashes Tabasco sauce
Paprika

Cook chicken with celery, onion, and peppercorns until tender. Remove from bones and cut into thin slices. Drain artichoke hearts, and cut into 2 or 3 pieces. Drain mushrooms and sauté 10 minutes in 3 tablespoons butter, adding a little salt and pepper while cooking. Prepare a cream sauce by melting 1½ sticks butter over low heat, then stir in flour. Cook until smooth. Slowly add half & half. Cook until thickened, stirring constantly. Make casserole sauce by mixing together cream sauce, soups, sour cream, salt and pepper, Worcestershire, Tabasco, and sherry. Butter a 4-quart casserole. Arrange alternately slices of chicken and artichokes. Spread sautéed mushrooms evenly on top. Pour sauce over all, pressing mushrooms down into sauce. Sprinkle with Parmesan cheese and paprika. Bake in preheated 350 degree oven about 35 to 40 minutes, until hot and bubbly and slightly browned on top. Do not overcook.
Yield: 20 servings

Sandra Plant

Pork Tenderloins

8 pork tenderloins

Marinade for pork:
½ cup oil
⅓ cup soy sauce
¼ cup red wine vinegar
3 tablespoons lemon juice
2 tablespoons
    Worcestershire sauce

1 clove garlic, crushed
1 tablespoon fresh parsley,
    chopped
1 tablespoon dry mustard
1½ teaspoons pepper

Sauce:
1 jar apricot preserves
⅓ jar pineapple preserves

⅓ cup hot spicy mustard
1 to 2 tablespoons bourbon

Combine all ingredients listed for marinade. Pour marinade over pork, cover and refrigerate overnight. Grill for 30 minutes on medium coals, turning every five minutes. Slice pork in ¼-inch to ½-inch slices to serve. Prepare sauce by combining all ingredients in a saucepan and heat thoroughly. Serve sauce with tenderloin.
Yield: 16 servings

Melanie Rykard

Basiled Green Beans

1 (128-ounce) can green
    beans
¼ cup sugar
1 cup butter, melted
2 teaspoons salt

1 teaspoon pepper
6 teaspoons basil
1 tablespoon garlic powder
Cherry tomatoes

Simmer green beans for 10 minutes and drain. Combine all other ingredients except tomatoes. Pour over beans. Simmer 10 minutes. Lay tomatoes on top of beans. Put lid on and steam until tomatoes are tender but not mushy. Serve with tomatoes on top.
Yield: 15 servings

Joan Gay

14

Fresh Fruit and Cream in Coconut Shell

Coconut Pastry:

1 cup all-purpose flour
¾ cup shredded coconut
6 tablespoons butter

2 tablespoons sugar
1 large egg yolk

Place the above ingredients into a medium bowl. With fingertips, mix until just blended. Press dough onto bottom and up the side of 10-inch tart pan with removable bottom. With fork, prick tart shell in many places and line with foil. Bake 10 minutes at 350 degrees. Remove foil and prick dough again. Bake shell 10 to 15 minutes longer until golden. Cool.

Lemon Custard Filling:

1 large lemon
6 tablespoons butter
⅓ cup sugar

1 tablespoon corn starch
4 large egg yolks
1 cup heavy cream

From lemon, grate 1 teaspoon of peel and squeeze 2 tablespoons of juice; set aside. In heavy saucepan over medium or low heat, heat butter, sugar, and corn starch, stirring constantly until mixture thickens and boils. Boil 1 minute. Beat egg yolks, adding small amount of hot sugar mixture. Slowly pour egg yolk mixture back into sugar mixture in pan, stirring to prevent lumping. Continue to cook and stir constantly until mixture thickens and coats spoon. Remove from heat and stir in lemon peel and lemon juice. Cover custard and refrigerate one hour or until very cold. Whip cream stiff and then fold into cold custard. Spoon into tart shell and top with fresh fruit of your choice.
Yield: 2 dozen

Deryl Beadles

Strawberry Holiday Trifle

Sponge cake:
1 cup sifted all-purpose
    flour
1 teaspoon baking powder
¼ teaspoon salt
½ cup milk

2 tablespoons butter or
    margarine
2 eggs
1 cup sugar
1 teaspoon vanilla

Custard:
⅔ cup sugar
2 tablespoons corn starch
¼ teaspoon salt
2 cups milk
4 egg yolks, beaten

2 tablespoons butter or
    margarine
1 teaspoon vanilla
1 teaspoon almond extract
1 cup whipping cream,
    whipped

Filling:
3 pints fresh strawberries
3 tablespoons sugar
¾ cup strawberry liqueur
    or wine

¾ cup sliced almonds
Powdered sugar
Whipping cream, whipped

Sponge cake: Sift together flour, baking powder and salt. In sauce-pan heat milk and butter until butter melts. Keep hot. Beat eggs at high speed of mixer until thick and lemon-colored, about 3 minutes. Gradually add sugar, beating constantly for 4 to 5 minutes. Add dry ingredients and stir until just blended. Stir in hot milk and vanilla. Blend well. Divide batter between 2 greased and floured 8-inch cake pans. Bake at 350 degrees for 20 minutes or until done. Cool in pans 10 minutes; then remove and cool on rack.

Custard: Combine sugar, corn starch and salt in saucepan. Stir in milk. Cook, stirring over medium heat until thickened and bubbly. Stir some of hot mixture into egg yolks. Return egg yolks to mixture in pan, stirring constantly. Cook and stir 2 more minutes. Remove

(Continued on next page)

(Strawberry Holiday Trifle, continued)

from heat. Stir in butter, vanilla and almond extract. Cover custard with plastic wrap and chill. Fold whipped cream into chilled custard.

Assembly: Set aside about 14 strawberries for garnish. Crush remaining berries to make 2 cups. Stir in sugar and set aside. Split cake layers in half to make 4 layers. Place first layer in bottom of 2½-quart soufflé dish or glass bowl. Sprinkle with 3 tablespoons liqueur. Spread with ⅔ cup crushed berries, cover with ⅓ of the custard and sprinkle with ¼ cup almonds. Repeat sequence 2 more times. Sprinkle last cake layer on cut side with remaining liqueur, and place, cut side down, on top. Cover and refrigerate overnight. Just before serving, sift a heavy covering of powdered sugar over the top. Garnish with whipped cream rosettes and reserved strawberries, halved. For Christmas, tint whipped cream green and simulate a wreath with whipped cream rosettes and strawberries. Makes a very festive dessert.
Yield: 15 servings

Cherie Anne Whiddon

Strawberry Bavarian Cream

1½ pounds strawberries,
   minced
10 ounces sugar
Juice from 1 lemon
Red food coloring as
   needed

2 tablespoons plus 2
   teaspoons unflavored
   gelatin
1 cup hot water
3½ cups heavy cream,
   whipped
Strawberries, sliced

Combine first 4 ingredients until smooth; adjust coloring. Dissolve gelatin in water. Add to strawberry mixture. Fold in whipped cream. Pour into champagne glasses and chill. Garnish with sliced strawberries.

Deryl Beadles

Chocolate Truffles

6 ounces milk chocolate
1 tablespoon butter
2 egg yolks, beaten
2 teaspoons brandy or
    coffee liqueur

2 teaspoons cream
½ cup cocoa powder
Sprigs of mint (optional)

Melt chocolate in a double boiler over simmering water. Stir in butter. Add beaten yolks slowly, stirring well to incorporate. Beat in brandy and cream, then chill until firm, at least one hour. Divide the mixture into about 30 even-sized pieces. Using your hands, form into round balls. Put cocoa on a plate and roll the balls in it. Put the coated truffles into paper candy cases and chill until needed. Serve with little sprigs of mint if desired.
Yield: 30 pieces

Barbara B. Vereen

Ripple Bars

1 (8-ounce) package vanilla
    cookies
½ cup butter or margarine
1 tablespoon brown sugar
⅓ cup plus 1 tablespoon
    cocoa powder

¼ cup dark Karo or maple
    syrup
1 (12-ounce) bag semi-sweet
    chocolate morsels

Crush the cookies into small pieces in a food processor or with a rolling pin. Combine the butter, sugar, cocoa powder and syrup in a sauce pan and melt over low heat, stirring constantly. Combine the cookie crumbs and melted ingredients and mix thoroughly. Press into an 8-inch square pan. Melt the morsels in a double boiler over boiling water. Pour melted morsels over the crumb mixture and cool slightly. Mark the top of the chocolate with the back of a fork. Refrigerate until cold. Cut into squares and store in an airtight container.
Yield: 16 servings

Barbara B. Vereen

A Caribbean Buffet

Indigo's Famous Appetizer

Londa's Spinach Salad

*Grilled Teriyaki Pork Chops
with Pineapple Papaya Relish*

Black Bean Soup

Saffron Rice

French Bread

Key Lime Cheesecake

~ Sally Tyndall ~

Indigo's Famous Appetizer

Soft flour tortillas, warmed
White cheese sauce
   (purchased from local
   Mexican restaurant)

Picadigallo sauce
Julienned zucchini,
   carrots, onions
Red and yellow peppers,
   sliced

Arrange ingredients so guests serve themselves. Place vegetables of choice in warm tortilla. Top with cheese sauce and picadigallo sauce, roll and eat.

Sally Tyndall

Londa's Spinach Salad

2 packages sliced almonds
3 to 4 tablespoons butter or
   margarine
3 bunches fresh spinach

3 to 4 stalks celery,
   chopped
2 green onions, chopped
2 cans mandarin oranges,
   drained

Dressing:
1 cup oil
½ cup sugar
⅓ cup vinegar

1½ teaspoons salt
2 tablespoons
   Worcestershire sauce

Roast almonds in butter or margarine for 2 to 3 minutes in a microwave oven. Drain on paper towels. Wash spinach; pat dry. Tear spinach into pieces and put in serving bowl. Top with celery, onion, mandarin oranges and almonds. Combine dressing ingredients well and toss with salad just before serving. Remaining dressing will keep well in the refrigerator.
Yield: 16 servings

Londa Faircloth

Grilled Teriyaki Pork Chops with Pineapple Papaya Relish

For marinade:
⅔ cup soy sauce
⅓ cup light brown sugar, firmly packed
⅓ cup water
¼ cup rice vinegar
3 garlic cloves, finely chopped

1 (2-inch) piece fresh gingerroot, peeled and finely chopped
6 (1-inch thick) rib pork chops, bones frenched
Accompaniment: pineapple papaya relish

Pineapple Papaya Relish:
2 cups fresh pineapple, finely diced
1 cup fresh papaya (mango may be substituted), finely diced
½ cup red bell pepper, finely diced
½ cup Vidalia or other sweet onion, finely diced

1 garlic clove, minced
1 small, fresh hot green chili (serrano or Thai), seeded and minced (wear rubber gloves)
Salt to taste
2 tablespoons fresh mint leaves, shredded

In a saucepan combine marinade ingredients and bring to a boil, stirring until sugar is dissolved. Cool marinade completely. Put chops in a large resealable plastic bag and pour marinade over. Seal bag, pressing out excess air, and set in a shallow dish. Marinate meat in refrigerator overnight, turning bag once or twice. Pour marinade into a saucepan, and boil 5 minutes. Grill chops on an oiled rack, set about 4 inches over glowing coals. Cook 7 to 8 minutes on each side, or until just cooked through, basting with marinade during last 5 minutes. (Meat may be grilled in a hot well-seasoned ridged grill pan or broiled.) Serve pork chops with relish. To prepare papaya relish, combine ingredients and let stand at room temperature 1 hour.
Yield: 6 servings

Sally Tyndall

Black Bean Soup

1 package black beans
½ gallon water
1 large onion
3 green peppers
1 clove garlic
½ cup olive oil

¼ ham bone or large ham
   hock
3 bay leaves
1 tablespoon salt
1 ounce streak-o-lean
   (white bacon)
½ cup vinegar

Rinse beans thoroughly and soak overnight in water. Reserve this water for cooking beans. Sauté onion, peppers, and garlic lightly in olive oil. Combine all ingredients except vinegar, and cook slowly on low heat until beans are soft and liquid is of thick consistency. Add vinegar to beans when ready to serve.
Yield: 6 to 8 servings

Cherie Anne Whiddon
*Similar recipe submitted by Cooka Hillebrand

Key Lime Cheesecake

1¼ cups graham cracker
   crumbs
2 tablespoons sugar
¼ cup butter, melted
1 teaspoon lime rind,
   grated
3 (8-ounce) packages cream
   cheese, softened

¾ cup sugar
3 eggs
¼ cup key lime juice
1 teaspoon vanilla
2 cups sour cream
3 tablespoons sugar

Combine first 4 ingredients; stir well. Press crumb mixture evenly over bottom and up sides of a 9-inch springform pan. Bake at 350 degrees for 5 to 6 minutes. Let cool. Beat cream cheese until light and fluffy; gradually add ¾ cup sugar, beating well. Add eggs, one at a time, beating well after each addition. Stir in lime juice, and vanilla. Pour mixture into prepared pan. Bake at 375 degrees for 45 minutes or until set. Combine sour cream and 3 tablespoons sugar; stir well, and spread evenly over cheesecake. Bake at 500 degrees for 5 minutes. Let cool to room temperature on a wire rack; chill at least 8 hours. To serve, carefully remove sides of springform pan.
Yield: 9-inch cheesecake

Sally Tyndall

Gentleman's Dinner Choice

Tomato Juice

Fresh Grapefruit Salad With
Celery Seed Dressing

Beef Stroganoff

Wild and White Rice Mix

Fresh Pole Beans with Toasted Almonds

Yeast Rolls

Butter Cream Torte

~ Joyce Barber ~

Fresh Grapefruit Salad
with Celery Seed Dressing

Lettuce leaves
4 to 6 grapefruit, peeled
    and sectioned

Celery seed dressing

Place lettuce leaves on individual salad plates. Top with grapefruit sections and celery seed dressing.

Celery seed dressing:
1 cup sugar
1 teaspoon salt
1 teaspoon celery seed
1 teaspoon paprika
1 teaspoon mustard

½ teaspoon onion juice or
    1 teaspoon dried onion
1 cup salad oil
¼ cup vinegar

Combine dry ingredients. Add oil and vinegar, alternately, beating well after each addition. Best results obtained by using an electric mixer. Set at high speed or liquefy. Refrigerate.
Yield: 8 to 10 servings

Beef Stroganoff

1½ pounds sirloin steak
1 pound fresh mushrooms,
    sliced
1 cup butter
1 large onion, chopped
1 can tomato soup

½ (6-ounce) can tomato
    paste
1 teaspoon salt
⅛ teaspoon pepper
1 teaspoon soy sauce
1 cup sour cream
Parsley, minced

Cut meat in very thin strips. Trim off fat. Brown meat and mush-rooms in butter. Add onions. Combine soup, tomato paste and seasonings; add to meat mixture. Cover and simmer until tender. Just before serving, stir in sour cream. Thicken gravy if desired. Serve over wild and white rice. Garnish with parsley. We used this recipe while entertaining former President and Mrs. Jimmy Carter.
Yield: 8 to 10 servings

Similar recipe submitted by Debbie Brown

Butter Cream Torte

2 cups vanilla wafers,
    crushed (divided)
½ pound butter
2 cups powdered sugar
4 eggs

½ cup almonds, finely
    chopped
1 cup whipping cream
½ cup maraschino cherries

Spread 1 cup of vanilla wafers in bottom of 9-inch square pan. Combine butter and powdered sugar, creaming well. Add eggs, one at a time, while beating mixture vigorously. Blend well. Stir in almonds. Spoon mixture evenly over vanilla wafers already in bottom of pan. Sprinkle ¾ cup vanilla wafers on top. Whip cream until thick, and fold in cherries. Spread over wafers. Sprinkle with additional ¼ cup vanilla wafers. Garnish with additional cherries if desired. Refrigerate for 12 or more hours (or freeze for future use). Cut with knife dipped in water to serve.
Yield: 9 to 12 servings

Supper Club on the Bayou

Shrimp Creole

Coconut Fried Shrimp

Chicken and Sausage Jambalaya

Green Salad

French Bread

Bread Pudding with Butterscotch Sauce

~ Sally Tyndall ~

Mama's Shrimp Creole

⅓ cup olive oil
¼ cup flour
3 garlic cloves, peeled and chopped
2 onions, peeled and chopped
1 cup green onions, chopped
1 cup green pepper, chopped
1 cup celery, sliced diagonally
1 pound fresh mushrooms, sliced
1 (8-ounce) can tomato sauce
1 (16-ounce) can chopped tomatoes
1 (6-ounce) can tomato paste
1 cup water
5 teaspoons salt
1 teaspoon pepper
½ teaspoon cayenne pepper, or more to taste
1 dash Tabasco, or more to taste
2 to 3 bay leaves
1 teaspoon sugar
1 teaspoon thyme
1 teaspoon curry powder
3 teaspoons lemon juice
3 pounds shrimp, peeled and cleaned
Rice

Make a roux of flour and olive oil. Add garlic, onions, green onions, green pepper, celery, and mushrooms. Sauté in roux until tender, about 20 to 30 minutes. Add tomato sauce, tomatoes, tomato paste, water and all remaining ingredients, except shrimp. Simmer, covered, for 1 hour. Add shrimp and cook for 5 to 15 minutes. This is best if prepared early in the day or, if possible, the day before so that the flavors will blend. Serve over rice garnished with parsley. *Yield: 8 servings*

Cherie Anne Whiddon
*Similar recipe submitted by Marsha McLean

Coconut Fried Shrimp with Sweet and Tangy Sauce

Seasoning Mix:
1 tablespoon ground red
  pepper (preferably
  cayenne)
2¼ teaspoons salt
1½ teaspoons sweet
  paprika
1½ teaspoons black pepper

1¼ teaspoons garlic powder
¾ teaspoon onion powder
¾ teaspoon dried thyme
  leaves
¾ teaspoon dried oregano
  leaves

Batter:
2 eggs
1¾ cups all-purpose flour
  (divided)
¾ cup fresh beer
1 tablespoon baking
  powder

4 dozen (2 pounds) medium
  shrimp, peeled (with
  tails on) and deveined
3 cups coconut, grated
Vegetable oil for deep
  frying

Thoroughly combine the seasoning mix ingredients in a small bowl. In a separate bowl combine 2 teaspoons of the mix with the eggs, 1¼ cups of flour, beer and baking powder. Mix well, breaking up any lumps. In a small bowl combine the remaining ½ cup flour with 1½ teaspoons of the seasoning mix; set aside. Place the coconut in a separate bowl. Sprinkle both sides of the shrimp with the remaining seasoning mix. Hold shrimp by the tail, and dredge in the flour mixture, shaking off excess. Dip in batter (except for tail), allowing excess to drip off. Coat generously with grated coconut, and place on a baking sheet. Heat oil in a deep fryer to 350 degrees. Drop shrimp, one at a time, into the hot oil and fry until golden brown, about 30 seconds to 1 minute per side. Do not crowd. (You may want to cut the first shrimp in half after frying to best estimate frying time; the batter should be cooked through but the shrimp not overcooked.) Drain on paper towels. Serve immediately with Sweet and Tangy Dipping Sauce. To serve as a main dish, put about ⅓ cup sauce in each of 6 small bowls and place each on a serving plate;

(Continued on next page)

(Coconut Fried Shrimp with Sweet and Tangy Sauce, continued)

surround each bowl with about 8 shrimp. For an appetizer, serve 4 shrimp per person with about 3 tablespoons sauce on the side.
Yield: 6 main dish servings
12 appetizer servings

Sweet and Tangy Dipping Sauce:
1 (18-ounce) jar orange marmalade
5 tablespoons Creole mustard (preferred) or brown mustard
5 tablespoons finely grated fresh horseradish or prepared horseradish

Combine all ingredients and mix well.
Yield: 2½ cups

Mary Campagna

Chicken and Sausage Jambalaya

1 (2½ to 3-pound) broiler-fryer, cooked and cut into bite-sized pieces
¾ pound smoked sausage, cut into ½-inch slices
¼ cup vegetable oil
2½ cups onion, chopped
½ cup green pepper, chopped
2 cloves garlic, minced
2 green onions, chopped
5 cups water
1 pound long-grain rice, uncooked
1 teaspoon salt
¼ to ½ teaspoon black pepper
¼ to ½ teaspoon red pepper

Cook sausage in oil in a Dutch oven until golden brown; remove sausage, drain, and reserve 2 tablespoons of drippings in the Dutch oven. Sauté chopped onion and next 3 ingredients in drippings. Add water, rice, salt, peppers, chicken, and sausage; bring to a boil. Cover, reduce heat, and simmer 20 minutes or until rice is tender and water is absorbed. Let stand 5 minutes before serving.
Yield: 6 to 8 servings

Sally Tyndall

Bread Pudding
With Butterscotch Sauce

1 loaf French bread, cut
   into cubes
6 tablespoons butter,
   melted
6 eggs

6 cups milk
2 teaspoons vanilla
¾ cup sugar
2 teaspoons corn starch
¼ teaspoon salt

Place bread cubes into the bottom of a large pan. Pour melted butter over the bread cubes, and bake at 325 degrees until crispy and brown. Beat 6 eggs and combine with milk, vanilla, sugar, corn starch, and salt. Pour this mixture over the bread cubes. Set pan into another pan of warm water and bake at 325 degrees for 1 hour. Serve with butterscotch sauce.

Butterscotch Sauce:
1 stick of butter
½ pound brown sugar
7 ounces evaporated milk

Pinch of salt
Pinch of baking soda

Melt butter and brown sugar together. Add evaporated milk, salt and baking soda. Cook until hot and serve warm.
Yield: 12 servings

Laura Keith

Summertime Bridge Luncheon

Bloody Marys

Cheese Wafers

Seafood Supreme in Shells

*Grapefruit Aspic on Crisp Lettuce
with Celery Seed Dressing*

Rolled Asparagus Sandwiches

Hershey Bar Pie

Coffee

~ Barbara Hendrick ~

Cheese Wafers

½ cup butter, softened
½ pound sharp cheese, grated
1½ cups all-purpose flour

½ teaspoon salt
Generous pinch of cayenne pepper
Pecan halves

Cream butter and cheese. Add flour, cayenne pepper, and salt. Form into rolls and wrap in wax paper. Put in refrigerator for at least one hour. Slice thin, and place on cookie sheet. Put a pecan half on each slice. Bake in preheated 325 degree oven for 8 to 10 minutes.
Yield: 4 dozen

*Similar recipes submitted by Kathryn McDonald and Cherie Anne Whiddon

Seafood Supreme in Shells

1 cup canned crabmeat
1 cup shrimp, cooked and cut into small pieces
½ cup green pepper, chopped
¼ cup onion, chopped

1 cup celery, finely chopped
1 cup mayonnaise
½ teaspoon salt
1 teaspoon Worcestershire sauce

Topping:
2 cups cornflakes, crushed
2 teaspoons butter, melted

Paprika

Combine first 8 ingredients, and turn into four large baking shells or ramekins. Combine cornflakes and butter, and sprinkle atop seafood. Sprinkle with paprika. Bake in preheated 350 degree oven for 30 minutes.
Yield: 4 to 6 servings

Grapefruit Aspic on Crisp Lettuce with Celery Seed Dressing

Grapefruit Aspic:

1½ tablespoons plain gelatin
1 cup cold water or grapefruit juice
1 cup boiling water
3 tablespoons lemon juice
¾ cup sugar

3 large grapefruit, peeled and sectioned or 2 cans grapefruit sections, drained
¾ cup celery, chopped
½ cup almonds, chopped and toasted (optional)

Soak plain gelatin in cold water or grapefruit juice. Dissolve in boiling water. Add lemon juice, sugar, grapefruit, celery and almonds. Pour into individual molds or 4-cup ring mold and refrigerate.

Celery Seed Dressing:

⅓ cup sugar
1 teaspoon dry mustard
1 teaspoon salt
1 teaspoon paprika
1 teaspoon onion, grated

1 teaspoon celery seed (heaping)
1 cup oil
3 tablespoons plus 1 teaspoon white vinegar

Place dry ingredients in mixing bowl, and mix in one teaspoon vinegar. Add alternately 1 cup Wesson oil and 3 tablespoons white vinegar. Beat until smooth and thick, refrigerate. If all is not used at first serving, refrigerate and beat again before using.
Yield: 8 servings

Rolled Asparagus Sandwiches

Whole wheat or white bread
Butter, softened

Parmesan cheese, grated
1 can asparagus spears
⅓ cup butter, melted

Trim crusts from slices of whole-wheat (or white) bread, and roll bread flat with rolling pin. Spread with soft butter. Sprinkle lightly with Parmesan cheese. Thoroughly drain canned asparagus spears and pat dry with paper towels. Place a spear of asparagus along one edge of bread and roll tightly, as for a jellyroll. Brush with melted butter. Bake in preheated 400 degree oven for about 12 minutes and serve hot. (These sandwiches can be made ahead and frozen after brushing with butter. Place frozen in hot oven and bake until lightly browned.)
Yield: 12 servings

Hershey Bar Pie

1 large Hershey bar with almonds
2 small Hershey bars with almonds

1 carton Cool Whip, (medium-sized)
1 graham cracker crust

Melt candy in double boiler. Fold into the Cool Whip. Pour into the graham cracker crust. Refrigerate. For variation, add 2 dozen marshmallows and melt with candy.
Yield: 6 servings

Similar recipe submitted by Jan Smith

League Fall Luncheon

Semi-Caesar Salad and Dressing

Dried Tomato Pesto

French Bread

Fresh Apple Nut Cake

~ Angela Castellow ~

Semi-Caesar Salad And Dressing

1 head Romaine lettuce
2 heads Bibb lettuce or red-
green leaf lettuce

½ cup croutons
½ cup fresh Parmesan
cheese, grated

Dressing:
1 egg (or egg-beaters)
1 teaspoon garlic salt
3 tablespoons sour cream

½ teaspoon pepper
3 tablespoons oil
½ teaspoon wine vinegar

Tear lettuce and toss. Mix all ingredients for dressing. Just before serving, add croutons and cheese. Pour in dressing and toss well.
Yield: 10 servings

Kim Jarrell

Dried Tomato Pesto

½ cup dried tomatoes
1 cup vegetable broth
(divided)
½ cup fresh basil leaves
1 clove garlic
¼ cup reduced-fat Parmesan
cheese, grated

2 tablespoons pine nuts
1 tablespoon olive oil
¼ teaspoon salt
¼ teaspoon ground white
pepper
1 teaspoon corn starch

Combine tomatoes and ½ cup vegetable broth in a small saucepan, and bring mixture to a boil. Remove from heat; let stand 10 minutes. Position knife blade in food processor bowl. Add tomato mixture, fresh basil, and next 6 ingredients. Process until smooth, stopping twice to scrape down sides. Set tomato mixture aside. Combine remaining ½ cup vegetable broth and corn starch in a small saucepan. Bring to a boil over medium heat, and cook 1 minute, stirring constantly. Stir in tomato mixture. Store in refrigerator up to 3 days or freeze up to 3 months. Use this sauce chilled as a dip for raw vegetables or steamed shrimp, or serve it hot, tossed with pasta.
Yield: 1 cup

Fresh Apple Nut Cake

1½ cups cooking oil
2 cups sugar
4 eggs
3 cups self-rising or all-
purpose flour

1 teaspoon soda
1 teaspoon salt
2 teaspoons vanilla
3 cups apples, diced
1 cup pecans, chopped

Glaze:
1 (3-ounce) package cream
cheese, softened
2 to 2½ teaspoons milk
1 teaspoon vanilla

Dash of salt
1½ cups powdered sugar,
sifted

Mix oil, sugar and eggs until creamy. Sift flour, soda and salt together, and add to mixture. Beat well. Add vanilla, apples and nuts. Pour into well-greased and floured tube pan. Bake at 325 degrees for 1½ hours. Prepare glaze by beating cream cheese at medium speed with an electric mixer until fluffy. Add milk, vanilla and salt; beat until smooth. Add powdered sugar gradually, beating until smooth. Pour over top of cooled cake, allowing to drizzle down the sides.
Yield: 12 to 16 servings

*Similar recipe submitted by Patti Wells

A Morning Celebration

Sunrise Mimosas

Susan's Baked Chicken Soufflé

Marinated Asparagus

Cheese Grits Casserole

Tomatoes Stuffed With Spinach and Artichokes

Country Ham with Pecan Biscuits

Almond Puff Coffee Cake

~ Angela Castellow ~   ~ Maureen Price ~

Sunrise Mimosas

¾ cup vodka
2½ cups cranberry juice

1½ cups orange juice
Orange slices to garnish

Pour first 3 ingredients into a blender and mix. Pour over ice cubes. Garnish with orange slice on rim of glass.
Yield: 5 to 6 servings

Maureen Price

Susan's Baked Chicken Soufflé

8 slices bread, crust
  removed
4 cups (3 whole breasts)
  chicken, cooked and
  diced
½ pound fresh mushrooms,
  sliced
¼ pound butter
1 (8-ounce) can water
  chestnuts, drained
½ cup mayonnaise

8 slices sharp cheese
4 eggs, well beaten
2 cups milk
1 teaspoon salt
1 can mushroom soup
1 can celery soup
1 tablespoon lemon juice
1 (2-ounce) jar pimiento,
  drained and sliced
2 cups coarse breadcrumbs,
  buttered

Butter a large 9 x 13-inch baking pan, and place a layer of bread in the bottom. Spread chicken over bread. Sauté mushrooms in butter and layer on top of chicken. Add water chestnuts, and dot with mayonnaise. Put slices of cheese on top. Combine eggs, milk and salt, and pour over. Stir together soups, lemon juice and pimiento. Pour atop other layers. Cover with foil, and store in refrigerator overnight. Remove foil, and bake at 350 degrees for 1½ hours. Add buttered breadcrumbs.
Yield: 12 to 16 servings

Susan West

Marinated Asparagus

4 pounds fresh asparagus
1 cup olive oil
⅓ cup tarragon vinegar
3 tablespoons parsley, chopped
3 tablespoons sweet pickle relish
1 (2-ounce) jar pimiento, drained and chopped
1½ tablespoons fresh chives, chopped
1 teaspoon salt
⅛ teaspoon pepper
Sieved egg and parsley for garnish

Remove tough ends of asparagus. Remove scales from stalk with knife. Cook asparagus, covered, in boiling salted water for 6 to 8 minutes or until crisp tender. Drain. Combine next 8 ingredients in a jar, and shake well. Place asparagus in shallow container, pour marinade over spears. Cover and chill at least 2 hours. Drain off marinade. Arrange asparagus on serving platter, garnish with sieved egg and parsley if desired.
Yield: 16 servings

Angela Castellow

Cheese Grits Casserole

1½ cups regular grits, uncooked
½ cup butter or margarine
3 cups (12-ounces) medium sharp Cheddar cheese, shredded
1 tablespoon Worcestershire sauce
2 teaspoons paprika (divided)
3 eggs, beaten

Cook grits according to package directions. Add butter and cheese. Stir until melted. Add Worcestershire and 1 teaspoon paprika, mixing well. Add a small amount of hot grits to eggs, stirring well; stir egg mixture into remaining grits. Pour grits into a lightly greased 2-quart baking dish. Sprinkle with remaining paprika. Cover and refrigerate overnight. Remove from refrigerator 15 minutes before baking. Bake, uncovered, at 325 degrees for 1 hour.
Yield: 8 servings

Angela Castellow

Tomatoes Stuffed With Spinach and Artichokes

6 large tomatoes
½ cup green onions, chopped
  with tops included
½ cup butter or margarine
2 (10-ounce) packages frozen
  chopped spinach
1 (14-ounce) can artichoke
  hearts, drained and
  chopped

1 teaspoon Worcestershire
  sauce
3 dashes Tabasco sauce
1 cup sour cream
¾ cup Parmesan cheese,
  grated (divided)
3 tablespoons butter or
  margarine

Wash tomatoes, remove stems, and scoop out seeds. Turn upside down to drain. In a large skillet, sauté onions in butter. Cook spinach, lightly salt and drain. Add spinach, artichoke hearts, Worcestershire, Tabasco, and sour cream to onions. Stir in ½ cup cheese. Stuff tomatoes with spinach mixture and sprinkle with remaining cheese. Dot with butter. Bake in a preheated 350 degree oven for 20 minutes or until thoroughly heated.
Yield: 6 servings

Maureen Price

Country Ham with Pecan Biscuits

2½ cups biscuit baking mix
½ cup pecans, chopped
1 cup whipping cream

2 tablespoons butter or
  margarine, melted

Preheat oven to 450 degrees. In a large bowl, combine baking mix and pecans. Add cream and stir just until a soft dough forms. On a lightly floured surface, use a floured rolling pin to roll out dough to ½-inch thickness. Use a floured 2-inch biscuit cutter to cut out dough. Transfer biscuits to a greased baking sheet and brush tops with melted butter. Bake 7 to 10 minutes or until light brown. Serve with sliced country ham.
Yield: 2 dozen

Maureen Price

Almond Puff Coffee Cake

2 cups all-purpose flour
   (divided)
½ cup butter or margarine,
   softened
1 cup plus 2 tablespoons
   water (divided)
½ cup butter or margarine,
   melted
2½ teaspoons almond
   extract (divided)

3 eggs, beaten
1½ cups powdered sugar,
   sifted
2 tablespoons butter or
   margarine, softened
1½ tablespoons warm
   water
¼ cup sliced almonds

Place 1 cup flour in a medium mixing bowl; cut in ½ cup butter with a pastry blender until mixture resembles coarse meal. Sprinkle 2 tablespoons water evenly over surface; stir with a fork until dry ingredients are moistened. Shape dough into a ball. Divide ball in half, placing halves on an ungreased baking sheet. Pat each half into a 12 x 3-inch strip, leaving 3 inches between strips. Combine 1 cup water and melted butter in a saucepan; bring to a boil. Add 1 teaspoon almond extract and remaining flour, all at once, stirring vigorously over low heat until mixture leaves sides of pan and forms a smooth ball. Remove from heat, and cool slightly. Add eggs; beat until batter is smooth. Spread batter evenly over each pastry strip. Bake at 350 degrees for 1 hour. Remove from oven, and keep warm. Combine powdered sugar, 2 tablespoons butter, remaining almond extract, and warm water in a mixing bowl, beating well. Spread over tops of cakes; sprinkle with almonds. Slice and serve warm.

Yield: 12 servings

Angela Castellow

First Impressions
Appetizers

K. Flowers

First Impressions

Appetizers

Creating the Setting

"Before the Ball," reveals a decorative setting enjoyed by guests in the home of Mr. and Mrs. William G. Fallin of Moultrie. This pen and ink creation was submitted by landscape artist, Kathy Perryman Flowers, a Moultrie native. Kathy attended the Atlanta College of the Arts and taught at Callanwolde Arts Center while in Atlanta. She returned to Moultrie in 1990, joining the staff of the Colquitt County Arts Center. Kathy, mother of four girls, prefers oils on canvas and is known for her impressionistic style. She has paintings distributed from coast to coast and has won many awards.

Combined for your Setting

Selecting an appetizer? Color, texture, and the serving piece are components which enable you to create that right first impression. Whether you are in the mood for a tangy dip or a spicy meatball, entertaining a cozy group or hosting an elaborate affair, let us help you tempt the palette and set the tone from within these pages.

Cheese Ball

1 pound sharp Cheddar
    cheese, grated
4 (8-ounce) packages cream
    cheese
Small amount garlic salt
½ teaspoon baking powder
½ cup evaporated milk

Small amount olives,
    chopped (without
    pimiento)
1 cup pecans, chopped
Chili powder
Paprika

Mix first 5 ingredients in mixer. Add olives and nuts. Roll into 4 balls or loaves. Refrigerate. Before serving, roll in mixture of chili powder and paprika. This recipe can be halved.
Yield: 4 cheese balls

Carol Bannister
*Similar recipe submitted by Katrina McIntosh

Three Cheese Ball

½ pound sharp Cheddar
    cheese, grated
1 (8-ounce) package cream
    cheese
¼ pound Roquefort cheese,
    mashed
1 clove garlic, crushed
2 teaspoons onion, grated

1 tablespoon
    Worcestershire sauce
1 cup black olives, chopped
Lemon juice
Cayenne pepper and garlic
    powder to taste
1 cup parsley, finely
    minced
1 cup pecans, chopped

Thoroughly mix all ingredients except parsley and pecans. Put a dash of parsley and a few of the pecans in the cheese mixture. Spread remaining parsley and pecans on a sheet of wax paper. Form cheese mixture into a ball, and roll in parsley and pecans. Make 2 smaller balls if needed. These freeze beautifully.
Yield: 1 large cheese ball or 2 small

Mary Catherine Turner
*Similar recipe submitted by Peggy Benner

45

Cheese Boxes

½ pound butter
½ pound creamy sharp
   cheese
1 egg white, unbeaten
1 tablespoon cream

½ teaspoon salt
½ teaspoon paprika
Loaf of unsliced bread
   (no crust)

Slice cheese and butter. Allow to stand in warm place until it can be creamed. Then add unbeaten egg white, cream and seasonings. Chill until paste can be easily spread. Cut 1¼-inch cubes from loaf of bread. Spread 5 sides with cheese mixture. Set in cool place until ready to brown in hot oven. Serve at once as canapé on toothpicks. These may be made larger and served with fruit salad.
Yield: 2 dozen

Nadeene Ansley

Oriental Chicken Wings

1 (10-ounce) bottle soy
   sauce
2 teaspoons ginger root,
   peeled and grated
2 cloves garlic, minced

⅓ cup brown sugar
1 teaspoon dark or spiced
   mustard
24 chicken wings
Garlic powder to taste

Mix soy sauce, ginger, garlic, sugar and mustard. Pour over wings and marinate in refrigerator for two hours. Drain and bake at 350 degrees for 1½ hours. Turn and baste frequently. Sprinkle with garlic powder. Put under broiler for 2 minutes.
Yield: 2 dozen wings

Sandy Hooks
*Similar recipe submitted by Barbara Hendrick

Sugared Bacon Curls

1 pound bacon, at room temperature

1¼ cups brown sugar
1 tablespoon cinnamon

Cut each slice of bacon in half. Mix sugar and cinnamon together. Thoroughly coat each side of bacon. Twist bacon to form a curl, and place on a rack inside a baking dish. Bake 15 to 25 minutes at 350 degrees or until crusty and dark brown. Serve at room temperature.
Yield: 3 dozen

Sally Tyndall

Encore Savory Ham Balls

⅓ cup fine dry breadcrumbs
¼ cup milk
¼ cup ketchup
¼ cup onion, minced

1 egg, slightly beaten
¼ teaspoon salt
Dash of pepper
1 pound ham, ground
1 pound pork, ground

Sauce:
1 cup apricot preserves
¼ cup water
1 tablespoon Worcestershire sauce

1 tablespoon prepared mustard
2 tablespoons ketchup
2 tablespoons vinegar

In a large bowl, combine first 7 ingredients. Add meats, and mix thoroughly. Shape into 5 dozen small meat balls. Place in a 13 x 9-inch baking pan, and bake at 350 degrees for 25 to 30 minutes. Cool. Refrigerate or wrap and freeze. To serve, combine sauce ingredients and meatballs in large skillet. Cook, stirring occasionally until meatballs heat through. Serve in chafing dish with crackers and toothpicks.
Yield: 5 dozen

Barbara B. Vereen

Sausage Delight

1 pound hot sausage, cooked

2 cups sharp Cheddar cheese, grated
3 cups biscuit mix

Preheat oven to 350 degrees. Combine all ingredients, and roll tablespoons of dough into balls. Freeze or refrigerate until ready to use. Bake in shallow pan for 15 minutes or until golden.
Yield: 5 dozen

Ann Friedlander

Sweet and Sour Meatballs

4 pounds sausage
4 eggs, slightly beaten
1½ cups soft breadcrumbs
3 cups ketchup

¾ cup brown sugar, firmly packed
½ cup soy sauce
½ cup wine vinegar

Mix sausage, eggs, and breadcrumbs. Shape into balls the size of a small walnut. Sauté in frying pan until brown on all sides. Drain. Combine ketchup, brown sugar, soy sauce, and wine vinegar. Pour over sausage balls. Simmer 30 minutes, stirring occasionally. May be refrigerated or frozen in sauce. To reheat, place in 350 degree oven for approximately 20 minutes.
Yield: 50 servings

Marsha McLean
*Similar recipe submitted by Carol Aguero

Hidden Valley Ranch Pinwheels

2 (8-ounce) packages cream cheese, softened
1 (1-ounce) package Hidden Valley Ranch Dressing mix (original)
2 green onions, minced
4 (12-inch) flour tortillas
1 (4-ounce) jar pimiento, drained and diced
1 (4-ounce) can green chilies, drained and diced
1 (2¼-ounce) can sliced or diced black olives, drained
Salsa

Mix first 3 ingredients. Spread on tortillas. Drain vegetables, and blot dry on paper towels. Sprinkle equal amounts of remaining ingredients on top of cream cheese. Roll tortillas tightly. Chill at least 2 hours. Cut rolls into 1-inch pieces. Discard ends. Serve with spirals facing up, and salsa on the side.
Yield: 3 dozen

Donna Marshall

Party Tarts

1 recipe pie crust mix
2 tablespoons sesame seeds
2 (3-ounce) packages cream cheese, softened
2 tablespoons chives, minced
1 (4½-ounce) can deviled ham spread
Salted pecans, chopped for garnish
Olives, chopped for garnish

Add sesame seeds to prepared pie crust mix. Chill. Roll pastry into large rectangle. Cut into about 3 dozen 2-inch scalloped rounds. Place each in a small muffin tin. Bake at 400 degrees until golden brown, about 12 minutes. Cool. Mix cream cheese and chives together. In pastries, layer cream cheese mixture, then layer of deviled ham. Garnish with pecans and/or chopped olives.
Yield: 3 dozen

Sandra Plant

Marcus' Veggie Bars

2 packages refrigerated
   crescent rolls
2 (8-ounce) packages cream
   cheese
1 (1-ounce) package Hidden
   Valley Ranch Dressing
   mix
1 cup mayonnaise

¾ cup of each, finely
   chopped: tomatoes,
   broccoli, carrots,
   cauliflower, green
   onions
1½ cups Cheddar cheese,
   shredded

Press crescent rolls onto a large cookie sheet and bake at 350 degrees for 10 minutes. Cool. Mix together softened cream cheese, mayonnaise, and dressing mix. Spread over cooked crust. Sprinkle vegetables and cheese over cream cheese mixture. Lightly press vegetables into cream cheese to keep intact. Refrigerate overnight then cut into bars.
Yield: 4 dozen

Patti Wells

Stuffed Mushrooms

12 to 14 mushrooms,
   without stems
½ cup Cheddar cheese,
   shredded

9 pieces cooked bacon,
   crumbled
5 to 6 slices bread, toasted
   and crumbled
⅓ cup butter, melted

Preheat oven to 350 degrees. To butter, add bread, cheese and bacon. Mix well and stuff into mushrooms. Bake for 10 minutes or until done.
Yield: 6 to 8 servings

Roasted Pecans

2 tablespoons oil
2 tablespoons butter
Salt

⅛ teaspoon red pepper
4 cups pecan halves

Melt oil and butter on cookie sheet. Sprinkle with salt. Add red pepper. Spread pecans evenly and stir to coat. Bake for 1 hour at 250 degrees, stirring every 15 minutes.
Yield: 1 pound

Cheryle Reeves

Hot Asparagus Dip

2 (15-ounce) cans
    asparagus (cut spears)
1½ cups mayonnaise

1½ cups Parmesan cheese,
    freshly grated
1 clove garlic, crushed

Drain and mash asparagus, and mix with the remaining ingredients. Pour into round, deep baking dish. Bake at 350 degrees for 20 to 30 minutes or until slightly brown and bubbling. Serve hot with crackers or large corn chips.
Yield: 3 cups

Carol Aguero

Artichoke-Chile Dip

1 (14-ounce) jar artichokes,
    drained and chopped
1 (4-ounce) can green chili
    peppers; rinsed, seeded
    and chopped

1 cup Parmesan cheese
1 cup mayonnaise

Mix ingredients together and place in an 8-inch round pan. Bake at 350 degrees for 20 minutes.
Yield: 3 cups

Peggy Benner
Similar recipes submitted by Sandy Hooks and Marsha McLean

Artichoke Cheese Bread

1 round of pumpernickel
    bread
¼ pound butter, melted
1 bunch of green onions,
    chopped
6 cloves garlic, chopped
1 (8-ounce) package cream
    cheese

1 (16-ounce) carton sour
    cream
1 (12-ounce) package
    Cheddar cheese, grated
1 can artichokes, chopped
1 can black olives, chopped

Cut top off of bread, and hollow out the bottom portion. Save bread, and cube for dipping. Mix remaining ingredients together. Pour mixture into round of bread. Place the top on bread, and wrap in heavy foil. Bake 1½ to 2 hours at 350 degrees. Serve with bread cubes or assorted crackers.
Yield: 3½ cups

Sally Tyndall

Avocado And Lime Dip

2 ripe avocados, peeled and
    seeded
½ cup plain yogurt
¼ cup onion, chopped
2 tablespoons fresh lime
    juice
½ teaspoon salt

⅛ teaspoon hot sauce
4 slices crisp cooked bacon,
    crumbled
1 tablespoon green onion
    tops, chopped (optional)
Chili flavored Fritos

Put first 6 ingredients in a food processor with knife blade. Process until smooth and creamy. Put into dip bowl and top with crumbled bacon and green onion tops. Serve with chili flavored Fritos. This is great for an outdoor party since mayonnaise isn't used.
Yield: 2 cups

Barbara B. Vereen

Audrey Raitt Dip

1 package Good Season's
   Italian dressing mix
2 tablespoons water
1 tablespoon vinegar
2 dashes red pepper

1 cup Hellmann's
   mayonnaise
½ cup sour cream
Raw vegetables

Mix first 6 ingredients together and serve with assortment of your favorite raw vegetables.
Yield: 1½ cups

Kim Jarrell

Caribbean Black Bean
and Shrimp Dip/Salad

1 pound shrimp, boiled and
   peeled
2 (15-ounce) cans black
   beans, rinsed and
   drained
1 cup green bell pepper,
   diced
1 cup celery, chopped
1 small red onion, thinly
   sliced

2 tablespoons parsley,
   chopped
1 teaspoon ground cumin
1 garlic clove, minced
7 tablespoons peanut oil
Juice of 5 limes
Tabasco sauce and salt to
   taste

Clean shrimp and cut into one-thirds. Combine remaining ingredients with shrimp, and refrigerate for several hours. Remove from refrigerator 1 hour before serving. This can be used as a dip with crackers or served on a lettuce leaf for salad.
Yield: 6 to 8 cups

Cooka Hillebrand

Broccoli Cheese Dip

2 (16-ounce) packages
   Velveeta cheese
2 packages chopped frozen
   broccoli

1 can cream of mushroom
   soup
Garlic to taste

Mix all ingredients together in saucepan over medium heat. Heat until melted and hot. Good with vegetables or Fritos.
Yield: 3 cups

Lanelle Rogers

Clam Dip

1 (8-ounce) package cream
   cheese
2 tablespoons mayonnaise
1 teaspoon onion flakes or
   fresh chopped onion

½ lemon, juiced
1 teaspoon Worcestershire
   sauce
1 can minced clams,
   drained slightly

Mix together and serve with your favorite cracker. If doubling this recipe, use 3 cans of clams.
Yield: 2 cups

This recipe was given to me by Lauradeen Vereen.

Cherie Anne Whiddon

Hot Curried Crab Dip

1 (8-ounce) package cream
    cheese
¾ cup mayonnaise
1 tablespoon lemon juice
¼ teaspoon Worcestershire
    sauce

½ pound fresh crabmeat
1¾ ounce slivered almonds
2¼ tablespoons butter,
    melted
¼ teaspoon salt
½ teaspoon curry powder

Mix cream cheese, mayonnaise, lemon juice and Worcestershire sauce in blender. Stir in crabmeat. Brown almonds in butter until golden. Add salt, and stir into crab mixture. Add curry last. Serve in chafing dish. Can be frozen and reheated over low heat, or put in casserole and baked at 350 degrees for 40 minutes. If freezing, do not add curry until ready to serve.
Yield: 2½ cups

Nancy Paine

Crab Dip

1 pound imitation
    crabmeat
1 (8-ounce) carton sour
    cream
4 tablespoons mayonnaise

2 (8-ounce) packages cream
    cheese
1 teaspoon lemon juice
1 teaspoon dry mustard
Dash of garlic
1 cup cheese, grated

Mix first 7 ingredients and top with cheese. Bake at 350 degrees for 45 minutes.
Yield: 4 cups

Hot Virginia Dip

1 cup pecans, chopped
2 teaspoons butter
2 (8-ounce) packages cream
    cheese, softened
4 tablespoons milk

5 ounces dried beef, minced
1 teaspoon garlic salt
1 cup sour cream
4 teaspoons onion, minced

Sauté pecans in butter. Reserve. Mix remaining ingredients thoroughly. Place in 1½-quart baking dish and top with reserved pecans. Chill until serving time. Bake at 350 degrees for 20 minutes. Serve warm with crackers or small bread sticks.
Yield: 3 cups

Barbara Fallin

Jezebelle Dip

1 (12-ounce) jar pineapple
    preserves
1 (12-ounce) jar apple jelly
1 (8-ounce) jar Dijon
    mustard

1 (4-ounce) jar horseradish
Ham, chopped in 1-inch
    cubes

Blend first 4 ingredients together in blender, and mix to taste. Dip ham cubes in with toothpicks. Wonderful!
Yield: 3 cups

Polly Jackson

Jiffy Dip

2 cups small curd cottage
    cheese
¼ cup black olives,
    chopped
¼ cup green pepper, diced

¼ cup Cheddar cheese,
    grated
¼ cup dry Italian dressing
    mix (1 packet)
3 tablespoons mayonnaise

In a small bowl, combine cottage cheese, olives, green pepper and cheese. Blend until thoroughly mixed. Add Italian dressing mix and mayonnaise. Serve at room temperature with crackers or corn chips.
Yield: 3 cups

Mary Campagna

Kahlúa Pecan Brie

1 (15-ounce) package brie
½ cup pecans, finely
    chopped and toasted
1½ tablespoons brown
    sugar

2 tablespoons Kahlúa
Apple slices or ginger
    snaps

Remove rind from top of brie. Place on microwave safe dish. Combine pecans, sugar and Kahlúa. Spread mixture over top of cheese. Microwave on high until melted. Serve with apple slices or ginger snaps.
Yield: 12 to 15 servings

Joan V. Stallings

Margie's Hot Dip

1 large onion, chopped	½ pound Monterey Jack
2 tablespoons butter	cheese with jalapeño
1 (16-ounce) can whole	peppers
tomatoes, drained and	½ teaspoon marjoram
diced	½ teaspoon salt

Sauté onion in butter in skillet. Add tomatoes, cheese, marjoram, and salt. Cook over low heat until cheese has melted. Serve in chafing dish with French bread or Fritos.
Yield: 2 cups

Marie Saunders

Mexican Caviar

2 to 3 (4¼-ounce) cans	3 teaspoons extra virgin
black olives, chopped	olive oil
2 (4-ounce) cans green	2 teaspoons red wine
chilies, chopped	vinegar
2 tomatoes, peeled and	1 teaspoon black pepper
chopped	Dash of seasoning salt
3 green onions, chopped	1 ripe avocado, peeled and
½ to 1 teaspoon garlic,	chopped
chopped	Lemon juice

Combine first nine ingredients, mix well and chill for several hours. Just before serving, sprinkle lemon juice on avocado, and add to dip. Enjoy with Fritos or tortilla chips.
Yield: 3 cups

Mary Campagna

Mexican Corn Relish

¾ pound sharp Cheddar
   cheese, shredded
½ cup sour cream
½ cup mayonnaise
¼ cup green onions, finely
   chopped
½ teaspoon salt

2 (12-ounce) cans Green
   Giant Mexi-Corn,
   drained
1 (4-ounce) can green
   chilies, drained and
   chopped
1 jalapeño, finely chopped
1 small jar of pimiento,
   drained and chopped

Mix all ingredients together and chill overnight. Delicious with tortilla chips or blue corn chips.
Yield: 4 cups

Sally Tyndall

Pineapple Cracker Spread

2 (8-ounce) packages cream
   cheese
1 small can crushed
   pineapple, drained
1 cup nuts, chopped

¼ cup green pepper,
   chopped
2 tablespoons onion,
   minced
1 tablespoon seasoned salt

Mix well and form into ball or log. Serve with your favorite crackers.
Yield: 1 ball or log

Kristy Allen

Ranchero Dip

⅔ cup mayonnaise
⅔ cup sour cream
2 teaspoons parsley,
   chopped
1 teaspoon Beau Monde

1 teaspoon dill weed
1 (1-ounce) package Hidden
   Valley Ranch Salad
   Dressing mix (original)

Combine all ingredients and chill. This quick, easy dip is good as an hors d'oeuvre with vegetables or chips. It is also good served on baked potatoes.
Yield: 1½ cups

Ann Friedlander

Reuben Melt

1 (4-ounce) package mild
   Cheddar cheese,
   shredded
1 (4-ounce) package Swiss
   cheese, shredded
1 (8-ounce) can sauerkraut,
   drained

2 (2½-ounce) cans corned
   beef, shredded
¼ cup Hellmann's
   mayonnaise
Rye party rounds
Dijon mustard

Mix cheeses, sauerkraut, corned beef and mayonnaise until moist. Put into baking dish. Bake at 350 degrees for 30 minutes or until bubbly. Serve in a chafing dish with rye party rounds and Dijon mustard alongside.
Yield: 2 cups

Kim Jarrell

Shrimp Dip

1 (8-ounce) package cream
   cheese
⅔ cup sour cream
2 tablespoons mayonnaise
1 tablespoon onion juice
3 teaspoons lemon juice

2 teaspoons Worcestershire
   sauce
Pinch of salt to taste
2 cups cooked shrimp,
   finely chopped

Mix all ingredients except shrimp in the blender. Add shrimp and mix thoroughly. Serve with crackers.
Yield: 4 cups

Donna Marshall

Spinach Dipping Sauce

1 (4-ounce) can green
   chilies, finely chopped
1 medium onion, chopped
2 tablespoons vegetable oil
2 tomatoes, peeled, seeded
   and chopped
1 (10-ounce) package frozen
   chopped spinach,
   thawed and squeezed
   dry

1½ tablespoons red wine
   vinegar
1 (8-ounce) package cream
   cheese, softened
1 (8-ounce) package
   Monterey Jack cheese,
   grated
1 cup half and half
Salt, pepper and paprika to
   taste

In a small skillet, sauté chilies and onions in oil for 4 minutes or until soft. Add chopped tomatoes and cook, stirring constantly for 5 minutes. Remove from heat and transfer to mixing bowl. Stir in spinach, vinegar, cream cheese, Monterey Jack cheese, half and half, salt and pepper. Pour into a buttered 10-inch round baking dish. Sprinkle with paprika. Bake at 400 degrees for 20 to 25 minutes, or until hot and bubbly. Serve with tortilla chips.
Yield: 4 cups

Gail Qurnell

Hot Spinach and Artichoke Dip

2 (10-ounce) packages
  frozen spinach
1 (8-ounce) package light
  cream cheese

3 tablespoons butter or
  margarine
Juice of 2 lemons
1 can artichoke hearts
2 cloves of garlic, minced

Cook spinach until thawed. Drain well. In double boiler, heat cream cheese, butter and lemon juice. Process artichoke hearts in processor, and add to cream cheese mixture. Do the same with spinach and add the garlic. Pour into greased baking dish and bake at 350 degrees for 30 minutes. (This can also be used as a vegetable.)
Yield: 3 to 4 cups

Cooka Hillebrand

Hidden Valley Ranch Spinach Dip

1 package Hidden Valley
  Original Salad Dressing
  mix
2 cups sour cream
1 (10-ounce) package frozen
  chopped spinach,
  cooked and drained

¼ cup onion, minced
¾ teaspoon basil
½ teaspoon oregano
Round loaf of French bread

Combine ingredients. Stir to blend. Chill for at least 1 hour. Serve in hollowed-out round loaf of French bread. Use hollowed out section to make bread cubes for dipping.
Yield: 3 cups

Jan Smith

Fresh Palettes
Salads

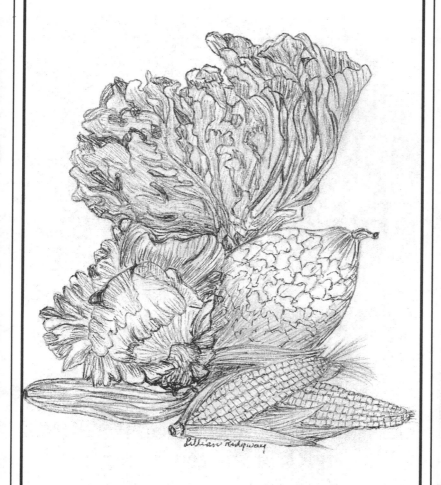

Lillian Ridgway

Fresh Palettes

Salads

Creating the Setting

"Array of Fresh Vegetables" was done by Lillian Ridgeway, now of Moultrie. She and her husband moved to Georgia from Falls Church, Virginia. Ridgeway remains active with art groups both in Moultrie and Valdosta. She paints daily in her home studio, where she enjoys working with pastels and oils. Presently, she is experimenting with oil palette knife painting. She loves the challenge of new subjects and techniques.

Combined for your Setting

The ambiguity of a salad adds mystery to your setting. One is never quite sure how a leafy composition will lay on a chilled plate, or how the color will react with the other mediums. Will a fruit mold set the tone or perhaps a chicken salad mousse is in order? Whatever your choice, your guests will enjoy that fresh flair.

Almond - Orange Salad

½ large head lettuce
1 cup celery, chopped
1 tablespoon parsley,
  chopped
2 green onions, chopped
1 (11-ounce) can mandarin
  oranges, drained
½ teaspoon salt

2 tablespoons sugar
¼ cup salad oil
Dash of pepper and
  Tabasco
2 tablespoons vinegar
2 tablespoons sugar
½ cup almonds, chopped

Toss first five ingredients. Mix salt, sugar, oil, pepper, Tabasco and vinegar to make dressing. Shake well. Caramelize almonds by placing sugar and almonds in heavy skillet. Heat until sugar melts to coat almonds. Cool and break apart. Sprinkle caramelized almonds over tossed vegetables. Add dressing. Toss salad.
Yield: 4 servings

Anna Pritchett

Artichoke Rice Salad

1 package chicken flavored
  Rice a Roni
4 green onions, thinly
  sliced
½ green pepper, chopped
12 pimiento olives, sliced

2 (6-ounce) jars marinated
  artichoke hearts
½ to ¾ teaspoon curry
  powder
⅓ cup mayonnaise

Cook rice according to directions, omitting the first step using butter. Cool rice in a large bowl. Add onions, green peppers and olives to rice. Drain artichokes, reserving the marinade, and discard any tough outer portions. Slice artichokes, and add to rice. Combine marinade with curry powder and mayonnaise. Pour over rice mixture and toss thoroughly. Chill until served. This may be made a day ahead.
Yield: 4 to 6 servings

Ellen Dekle Alderman

Broccoli Salad

¾ cup mayonnaise
¼ cup sugar
2 tablespoons cider vinegar
4 cups broccoli flowerets
¼ cup purple onion,
    chopped

¼ cup nuts, chopped
¼ cup raisins, soaked in
    water and drained
¼ cup bacon bits

Mix mayonnaise, sugar, and vinegar. Toss with remaining ingredients. Cover and chill.
Yield: 6 servings

Kristy Allen

Cabbage Slaw

1 cabbage, shredded finely
1 large onion, thinly sliced
1 bell pepper, thinly sliced
1 cup sugar

1 cup vinegar
¾ cup salad oil
2 teaspoons celery seed
2 teaspoons salt

Toss first three ingredients together. Sprinkle sugar over mixture. In saucepan, boil remaining ingredients. Pour over vegetable mixture while hot. Mix well. Refrigerate 24 hours. Recipe will keep 10 to 12 days.
Yield: 12 to 15 servings

Cherie Anne Whiddon

Copper Penny Carrots

2 pounds carrots, sliced
1 medium onion, sliced
1 green bell pepper, sliced
¼ cup vinegar
½ cup salad oil
1 can tomato soup

1 cup sugar
1 teaspoon Worcestershire
  sauce
1 teaspoon prepared
  mustard
Salt and pepper to taste

Cook carrots until tender and drain. Layer carrots, onion and pepper in a casserole. Heat remaining ingredients for about 5 minutes. Pour over vegetables. Cover and let stand overnight in refrigerator. These will keep for several days.
Yield: 10 to 12 servings

Sandy Hooks

Corn Salad Caliente

2 (10-ounce) packages
  frozen yellow corn,
  cooked and drained
1 (15½-ounce) can dark red
  kidney beans, drained
¾ cup commercial oil and
  vinegar salad dressing
1 small purple onion,
  chopped
1 small green pepper,
  chopped

½ cup Monterey Jack
  cheese with jalapeño
  pepper, diced
½ cup celery, sliced
½ cup ripe black olives,
  sliced
1 (2-ounce) jar pimiento,
  diced and undrained
½ teaspoon salt
¼ teaspoon ground cumin
⅛ teaspoon ground red
  pepper

Combine all ingredients in a large bowl; toss gently. Cover and refrigerate up to 24 hours. Serve with a slotted spoon.
Yield: 10 to 12 servings

Jessica Jordan

Crunchy Pea Salad

1¼ cups long grain and
    wild rice mix, cooked
1 (17-ounce) can sweet
    peas, drained
½ cup walnuts, chopped
½ cup sweet red pepper,
    chopped

¼ cup green onions, sliced
⅓ cup buttermilk dressing
    or creamy Italian salad
    dressing
Cherry tomatoes and green
    onions for garnish

In a bowl, combine rice with peas, walnuts, red pepper, and onions.
Add salad dressing and gently toss to coat. Chill. Toss just before
serving. Serve on lettuce-lined plates. Garnish with tomato roses
and green onion fans.
Yield: 6 servings

JoAnn M. Caldwell

Creamy English Pea Salad

1 large can LeSueur
    English peas, drained
1 cup celery, chopped
1 cup carrots, shredded
3 tablespoons bell pepper,
    diced
1 tablespoon onion, grated

1 envelope plain gelatin
1 teaspoon salt
1 teaspoon dry mustard
3 tablespoons vinegar
1 (8-ounce) jar salad
    dressing (not
    mayonnaise)

Mix together first 5 ingredients and set aside. Add salt, dry mustard and vinegar to gelatin. Dissolve over low heat. Let cool. Add
salad dressing. Pour over vegetables and let chill for 24 hours.
Yield: 6 servings

Karen Willis

Gingered Rice Salad

2½ cups water
1 teaspoon salt
2 tablespoons salad oil
2 tablespoons green onions,
    chopped
1 cup white rice, uncooked
3 tablespoons lemon juice
1 tablespoon sugar
¼ cup mayonnaise

½ cup cashews, chopped
¼ cup golden seedless
    raisins
1 cup seedless green
    grapes, halved
¼ cup crystallized ginger,
    finely chopped (or ½
    teaspoon sugar and ½
    teaspoon ground ginger)

Combine water, salt, onion, and oil in saucepan. Bring to a boil. Add rice and cook over low heat 20 to 25 minutes until rice is tender and liquid is absorbed. Remove from heat. Add remaining ingredients and refrigerate.
Yield: 6 servings

Mary Stapleton

Greek Salad

2 small zucchini, sliced
1 purple onion, ringed
2 medium tomatoes, peeled
    and cut into 8 sections
    and seeded
Black olives, sliced

Feta cheese, crumbled
Marinated artichokes,
    drained with liquid
    reserved
Black pepper
¼ cup red wine vinegar

Toss first 7 ingredients together. To the artichoke liquid, add vinegar and shake well. Pour over vegetables.
Yield: 8 servings

Harriett Whelchel

Papa's Greek Salad

1 head lettuce, broken into
    bite-sized pieces
1 onion, thinly sliced, or ½
    onion and 1 bunch of
    green onions, sliced
    with green tops
1 large tomato, peeled
    partially and cut in
    chunks
Green pepper, thinly sliced
Cucumber, thinly sliced
    (optional)
1 to 2 tablespoons oregano

1 to 2 teaspoons onion or
    garlic salt
1 teaspoon black pepper
¾ block feta cheese,
    crumbled
1 to 2 tablespoons red wine
    vinegar or 1 to 2
    tablespoons lemon juice
2 to 3 tablespoons olive oil
    (no substitution)
Black or green olives,
    sliced
Mild peppers

Toss first five ingredients. Sprinkle with seasonings. Crumble feta cheese over salad. Just before serving, add wine vinegar or lemon juice and olive oil. Garnish with olives and peppers, if desired. We watched this being made at Papa's Pizza Restaurant many years ago.
Yield: 4 to 6 servings

Cherie Anne Whiddon

Layered Mexican Salad

1 head lettuce, torn into
    bite-sized pieces
2 tomatoes, chopped
2 avocados, peeled and
    chopped (season with
    salt and add lemon to
    retain color)

Green onions, sliced
½ cup cheese, grated
Tortilla chips, crushed
1 (8-ounce) bottle Italian
    dressing

Layer salad ingredients in order listed. Top with bottle of Italian dressing just before serving.
Yield: 8 servings

Cheryle Reeves

Susie's Luncheon Potato Salad

4 potatoes, peeled and
   sliced ¼-inch thick
2 medium onions, peeled
   and sliced into rings
1 cup mayonnaise
¼ cup vinegar
Salt, pepper, garlic salt,
   and oregano leaves to
   taste
Lettuce, torn
Tomatoes, quartered

Cucumbers, sliced
Bell pepper, sliced into
   rings
Green and black olives,
   sliced
Boiled egg, sliced
Meats: shrimp, turkey
   strips, ham strips, etc.
Greek peppers
Bleu cheese, crumbled

Dressing:
1 cup olive or vegetable oil
¼ cup vinegar

Salt, pepper, garlic salt and
   oregano to taste

Cook potatoes in boiling water until tender. Do not overcook. Drain. Place in 3-quart Pyrex casserole dish. Place onion rings over potatoes. Mix mayonnaise, vinegar and seasonings. Pour over potatoes and onions. Refrigerate overnight. Just before serving, put torn lettuce and any of the next toppings desired on top of potato mixture. Pour dressing over salad when ready to serve.
Yield: 8 servings

Susie Mobley Cross

Oriental Cabbage Slaw

1 head cabbage, shredded
4 green onions, chopped
1 package chicken flavored
    Ramen noodles, crushed
    (reserve flavoring
    packet for dressing)

½ cup sliced almonds
2 tablespoons sesame seeds
3 tablespoons sunflower
    seeds

Dressing:
1 packet Ramen chicken
    flavoring
1 tablespoon sugar
½ cup oil

3 tablespoons vinegar
½ teaspoon salt
½ teaspoon pepper

Toss cabbage and green onions. Combine crushed Ramen noodles, almonds and seeds. Mix dressing ingredients and shake well. Pour dressing over slaw just before time to serve.
Yield: 6 to 8 servings

Mary Campagna
*Similar recipe submitted by Marilyn Huber

Taco Salad

1 head lettuce, torn
1 large tomato, chopped
1 bell pepper, cut small
1 large onion, cut small
1 can kidney beans,
    drained

4 to 6 ounces Cheddar
    cheese, grated
¾ cup Doritos, crushed
2 tablespoons Catalina
    dressing

Mix. Toss. Enjoy.
Yield: 6 servings

Ellen Dekle Alderman

Oriental Salad

1 (17-ounce) can tiny peas, drained
1 (16-ounce) can bean sprouts, drained
1 (12-ounce) can whole kernel white corn, drained
2 (5-ounce) cans sliced water chestnuts, drained and chopped
1 (6-ounce) can sliced mushrooms, drained
1 (4-ounce) jar sliced pimiento, drained
1 large green pepper, thinly sliced
1 large onion, thinly sliced
1 cup celery, sliced
1 cup salad oil
1 cup water
1 cup sugar
½ cup vinegar
Salt and pepper to taste

Mix together vegetables in a large bowl, stirring gently. Combine remaining ingredients and pour over vegetables. Cover and chill overnight. Drain before serving.
Yield: 10 to 12 servings

Edna Reeves
*Similar recipe submitted by Marsha McLean

Spinach Salad

12 cups fresh spinach, torn
1 tomato, cut in wedges
2 eggs, hard-cooked and cut in wedges
1 small red onion, thinly sliced and separated into rings
½ cup feta cheese, crumbled
⅓ cup olive oil
2 tablespoons wine vinegar
½ teaspoon dried oregano, crushed
½ teaspoon pepper

Place spinach and tomato in salad bowl. Arrange eggs, onion, and cheese on top. In screw-top jar combine oil, vinegar, oregano, and pepper. Cover and shake. Pour over salad and toss slightly.
Yield: 10 servings

Lisa Horkan

Spinach Salad With Hearts of Palm

3 tablespoons red wine
vinegar
2 teaspoons Dijon mustard
1 teaspoon sugar
⅓ cup olive oil
Salt and pepper to taste

2 pounds fresh spinach,
stems trimmed
1 (14-ounce) can hearts of
palm, drained and sliced
1½ teaspoons lemon peel,
grated

Mix first 3 ingredients in small bowl. Gradually whisk in oil. Season to taste with salt and pepper. (Dressing can be prepared 1 day ahead. Cover and let stand at room temperature.) Combine spinach, hearts of palm and lemon peel in bowl. Add enough dressing to season to taste and toss gently. Divide among plates and serve.
Yield: 10 servings

Harriett Whelchel

Cranberry Congealed Salad

1 cup hot water
1 (3-ounce) package lemon
Jello
1 cup sugar
1 cup fresh cranberries,
crushed fine with food
processor

1 cup crushed pineapple,
drained well
1 cup pecans, finely
chopped
1 cup celery, finely
chopped

Mix hot water and Jello together until all Jello has dissolved. Slowly add sugar to Jello mixture. Stir until sugar has dissolved. Add remaining ingredients. Stir well. Pour gelatin mixture into glass dish. Store in refrigerator until congealed. Cut in squares and serve on lettuce leaf. Keep refrigerated.
Yield: 10 servings

Gail Qurnell

Yellow Rice And Avocado Salad

½ cup long grain rice with
    saffron
3 cups Romaine lettuce, torn
3 cups red leaf lettuce, torn
4 slices Swiss cheese, cut
    into thin strips

1 large avocado, halved,
    seeded, peeled and
    sliced
1 medium tomato, sliced
2 hard-boiled eggs, sliced

Lemon Dressing:
¼ cup olive oil
¼ cup water
3 tablespoons lemon juice
1 tablespoon Dijon-style
    mustard

1 teaspoon sugar
½ teaspoon salt
⅛ teaspoon pepper

Cook rice as directed with saffron and salt. Cool slightly. Prepare lemon dressing by combining ingredients and shaking well. Pour 2 tablespoons of lemon dressing over rice. Cover and chill. In a large salad bowl, arrange lettuces and mound rice in center. Place cheese, avocado, tomato, and eggs around rice. Pour remaining dressing over salad and toss.
Yield: 6 to 8 servings

Polly Boetcher

Congealed Cranberry Salad

1 (6-ounce) package
    raspberry Jello
1 can cranberry sauce
2 cups boiling water

1 cup grapes (or Royal
    Anne cherries)
1 cup grapefruit, finely cut
    (or canned)

Dissolve Jello and cranberry sauce in boiling water. Cool. Add grapes (or cherries) and grapefruit. Chill until congealed.
Yield: 10 servings

Mrs. William E. Smith, Sr.

Frozen Cranberry Salad

1 (14-ounce) can sweetened
   condensed milk
¼ cup lemon juice
1 can cranberries or
   cranberry sauce with
   whole berries

1 large can crushed
   pineapple, drained
½ cup nuts, chopped
1 (8-ounce) carton Cool
   Whip

Mix all ingredients. Pour into 9 x 12-inch pan. Freeze. Cut in squares and serve on a bed of lettuce.
Yield: 12 servings

Debbie Brown

Frozen Banana Salad

2 cups sour cream
1 (20-ounce) can crushed
   pineapple, small amount
   of juice reserved
2 bananas, mashed
¾ cup sugar

½ cup pecans or walnuts,
   chopped
2 tablespoons maraschino
   cherries, chopped
¼ teaspoon salt

Combine all ingredients. Stir until well blended. Freeze overnight in greased mold. Unmold and let stand 15 minutes before serving. Can be frozen in muffin tin or baking cups for individual salads.
Yield: 6 to 8 servings

Patti Wells

Honeyed Citrus Nut Salad

1 bunch red leaf lettuce
1 (11-ounce) can mandarin
   orange sections, drained
3 green onions, finely
   chopped

1 teaspoon fresh parsley,
   chopped
2 tablespoons honey
1 (4-ounce) package
   slivered almonds or
   chopped pecans

Sweet and Sour Dressing:
¼ cup salad oil
2 tablespoons vinegar

2 tablespoons sugar
½ teaspoon salt

Gently toss lettuce, oranges, onions and parsley. Heat honey in skillet. Add almonds to honey and stir until browned. Sprinkle almonds over salad. Combine Sweet and Sour Dressing ingredients well, pour over salad and toss.
Yield: 8 to 10 servings

Carol Ann Cannon

Nancy's Bing Cherry Salad

1 can black pitted cherries,
   liquid reserved
¾ cup sugar
1 (3-ounce) package cherry
   Jello

1 small can crushed
   pineapple
1 cup pecans, chopped
3 tablespoons lemon juice
Pinch of salt

Pour the juice from the cherries into a saucepan. Add sugar and bring to a boil. Remove from heat. Add Jello and 1 heaping teaspoon of gelatin, dissolved in 2 tablespoons of water, to the hot juice. Add the reserved cherries, pineapple, pecans, lemon juice and salt. Mix well and pour into gelatin mold. Refrigerate until firm. This is a wonderful holiday salad.
Yield: 12 servings

Jessica Jordan

Mandarin Orange Salad

1 cup water
1 (3-ounce) package lemon
   Jello
1 (3-ounce) package orange
   Jello
1 large can crushed
   pineapple, liquid
   reserved

2 cans mandarin oranges
2 cups miniature
   marshmallows
4 ounces sour cream
½ cup mayonnaise
¾ cup Cheddar cheese,
   grated

Boil 1 cup water, and dissolve both packages of Jello. Add pine-apple with juice, 1 can mandarin oranges with juice and 1 can mandarin oranges, drained. Add marshmallows. Pour into a 9 x 13-inch pan. Chill for 2 hours. Combine sour cream and mayonnaise. Spread over Jello. Add grated cheese. Refrigerate.
Yield: 10 to 12 servings

Carolyn Lodge

Orange Jello Salad

1 (6-ounce) package orange
   Jello
1 cup boiling water
1 cup orange juice

1 (20-ounce) can crushed
   pineapple
1 (20-ounce) can mandarin
   oranges, drained

Dissolve Jello in boiling water. Add remaining ingredients. Pour into 9 x 12-inch dish. Refrigerate and let congeal. Cut into 12 squares.
Yield: 12 servings

Anne Norman
(Founding Member of Moultrie Service League)

Pimiento Cheese

1 stick medium Cracker
  Barrel cheese (silver
  wrapper)
1 small jar pimientos,
  chopped

¼ teaspoon salt
¾ cup Hellmann's
  mayonnaise
1 teaspoon onion, grated

Grate cheese by hand on small openings on grater. Add other
ingredients and mix well. Store in refrigerator.
Yield: 4 to 6 servings

Koala Fokes

Pineapple Cheddar Cheese Salad

1 (3-ounce) package lemon
  gelatin
1 cup boiling water
¾ cup sugar
1 (8-ounce) can of crushed
  pineapple, undrained

½ pint whipped cream
1 cup mild Cheddar cheese,
  grated in food processor
½ cup pecans, chopped

Dissolve gelatin in boiling water. Stir in sugar and pineapple. Cool.
Fold in remaining ingredients. Chill.
Yield: 8 to 10 servings

My Original Spiced Peach Salad

1 large can peaches, liquid
   reserved
2 tablespoons vinegar
¼ cup sugar
½ teaspoon cloves

½ teaspoon cinnamon
1 tablespoon lemon juice
1 (3-ounce) package peach
   Jello
Small container Cool Whip

Drain juice from peaches and reserve. Add water to juice if needed to make one cup. Combine juice with vinegar, sugar, cloves, cinnamon and lemon juice. Bring to a boil. Stir in peach Jello until dissolved. Mash peaches and add to gelatin mixture. Refrigerate until thick but not completely jelled in 8-inch square pan. Stir in Cool Whip. Refrigerate until firm.
Yield: 8 to 10 servings

Carolyn Lodge

Strawberry - Pretzel Salad

2 cups pretzels, crushed
1½ sticks margarine
¼ cup sugar
1 (8-ounce) package cream
   cheese, softened
2 cups Cool Whip

1 cup sugar
2 cups pineapple juice
1 (6-ounce) package
   strawberry Jello
2 (10-ounce) cartons
   strawberries, thawed

Mix first 3 ingredients and put in a greased 9 x 13-inch pan. Cook in a 350 degree oven for 8 minutes and cool. Beat cream cheese, Cool Whip and cup of sugar, and spread over pretzel layer. Heat pineapple juice and dissolve Jello. Cool and then add strawberries. Refrigerate until thickened. Spread over cream cheese mixture. Return to refrigerator until ready to serve. Slice in squares and arrange on lettuce leaves. Men love this congealed salad!
Yield: 12 to 15 servings

Edna Reeves

Sug's Bing Cherry Mold

1 can Bing cherries, liquid
   reserved
1 small can crushed
   pineapple, liquid
   reserved

1 (3-ounce) package black
   cherry Jello
½ to 1 cup Port Wine
Pecans, chopped (optional)

Drain cherries and pineapple, saving juices. Heat the juices to boiling and dissolve Jello. Add Port Wine to dissolved gelatin. Stir in cherries and pineapple. Pour into mold and place in refrigerator. Chopped nuts may also be included. Double recipe for a large mold.
Yield: 8 servings

Cooka Hillebrand

Under the Sea Salad

3 (3-ounce) packages lime
   Jello
4½ cups boiling water
1½ cups pear juice
¾ teaspoon salt

1 tablespoon vinegar
2 (8-ounce) packages cream
   cheese
¾ teaspoon ginger
6 cups canned pears, diced

Dissolve Jello in boiling water. Add pear juice, salt and vinegar. Pour ½-inch layer in 13 x 9-inch pan. Chill in refrigerator until firm. Chill remaining Jello mixture until cold and syrupy. Cream cheese with ginger. Place cheese and cold thickened Jello in blender and whip until thick. This will need to be done in two parts. Add diced pears. Pour gently over first layer. Chill until firm. Turn over when serving so that clear green layer is on top.
Yield: 12 servings

Mrs. William E. Smith, Sr.

Tomato Aspic

3 envelopes plain gelatin
½ cup cold water
3 cups boiling tomato juice
½ cup ketchup
¼ cup lemon juice

2 tablespoons onion, grated
1 tablespoon prepared
 horseradish
¾ teaspoon salt

Soak gelatin in cold water. Add to tomato juice. Add other ingredients. Stir well. Pour into mold and chill.
Yield: 8 to 10 servings

Koala Fokes

Chicken Salad Mousse

2 cans chicken rice soup
 (undiluted)
2 envelopes plain Knox
 gelatin
6 ounces of cream cheese,
 softened and cut in
 small pieces
6 tablespoons Hellmann's
 mayonnaise
8 boneless chicken breasts,
 steamed and diced

1 (16-ounce) can LeSueur
 English peas
1 cup celery, finely diced
½ cup salad olives with
 pimiento, chopped
10 spring onions, diced
 with tops
1 medium bell pepper,
 finely diced
1 teaspoon salt
Mayonnaise
Paprika

Heat soup and dissolve gelatin. Mix remaining ingredients well. Pour into a greased 3-quart, rectangular Pyrex dish. Refrigerate overnight. When serving, cut into 15 squares. Garnish with a dollop of mayonnaise sprinkled with paprika.
Yield: 15 servings

Note: We prepared 24 recipes to serve 360 people for one of the League luncheons, and everyone seemed to enjoy.

Barbara Hendrick

Watergate Salad

1 package Pistachio instant
    pudding
1 (12-ounce) carton Cool
    Whip
1 can crushed pineapple,
    drained

1 cup pecans, chopped
1 cup miniature
    marshmallows
½ or 1 envelope gelatin

Mix all ingredients together. Refrigerate until ready to serve.
Yield: 6 to 8 servings

Marsha McLean

Chicken Waldorf Salad Pitas

2 cups chicken, cooked and
    chopped
1 cup apple, chopped and
    sprinkled with lemon
    juice
⅓ cup celery, chopped
¼ cup pecans or walnuts,
    chopped

¼ cup (or more) raisins
1 tablespoon onion, minced
¼ teaspoon dill weed
½ cup or more mayonnaise
Pita pouches
Shredded lettuce

Combine first five ingredients. Mix onion, dill weed and mayonnaise. Add to chicken mixture. Put a little shredded lettuce in pita pouch, then the salad, then more lettuce. Eat and enjoy. (Extra salt is not needed as the lemon juice on the apples lends flavor.)
Yield: 12 servings

Barbara B. Vereen

Chicken And Wild Rice Salad

1 (16-ounce) package long
   grain and wild rice
2 cups chicken breast,
   cooked and cubed

2 cups seedless green
   grapes, halved
½ cup pecans, chopped

Dressing:
½ teaspoon salt
½ teaspoon prepared
   mustard

¼ cup wine vinegar
1 tablespoon mayonnaise

Prepare rice mixture, omitting margarine. Cool and add chicken, grapes and pecans. Combine dressing ingredients, and pour over chicken mixture. Stir well. Chill.
Yield: 4 to 6 servings

Anna Pritchett

Mandarin Chicken Salad

½ cup mayonnaise
½ cup marshmallow cream
½ teaspoon orange rind,
   grated
½ teaspoon crystallized
   ginger, chopped
3 cups chicken, chopped
   and cooked

1 cup celery, chopped
1 cup seedless grapes,
   halved
1 (11-ounce) can mandarin
   oranges, drained
1 cup pineapple tidbits,
   drained

Stir together mayonnaise, marshmallow cream, orange rind, and ginger. Mix until well blended. Combine chicken, celery, grapes, oranges, and pineapple. Pour mayonnaise mixture over chicken mixture. Toss lightly. Serve on bed of leafy lettuce.
Yield: 6 servings

Mary Stapleton

Corned Beef Salad

1 envelope unflavored
  gelatin
2 tablespoons fresh lemon
  juice
1 can consommé
½ teaspoon water
1 (12-ounce) can corned
  beef
1 (4-ounce) can sliced
  mushrooms, drained
2 cups celery, chopped

4 hard-cooked eggs,
  chopped or sliced
2 tablespoons onion, finely
  chopped
2 tablespoons green
  pepper, finely chopped
1 cup Hellmann's
  mayonnaise
Season All, garlic powder
  and celery leaves to
  taste (optional)

Dissolve gelatin in hot water, and add lemon juice. Heat the consommé and ½ teaspoon water. Pour this into mixture, and allow to cool. Combine corned beef, mushrooms, celery, eggs, onion, and green pepper. Stir the corned beef mixture into gelatin. Pour into mold. Chill until firm. Serve on lettuce topped with mayonnaise, if desired.
Yield: 10 to 12 servings

Kathryn H. McDonald

Hot Chicken Salad

2 cups chicken, cooked and
  diced
2 cups celery, finely
  chopped
2 tablespoons lemon juice

½ cup sharp cheese, grated
¾ cup mayonnaise
Pimiento, diced
Salt and pepper to taste
Potato chips, crumbled

Mix all ingredients, except chips. Put in a greased casserole dish. Top with crumbled potato chips. Cook at 350 degrees until bubbly. Do not overcook. Celery should remain crisp.
Yield: 4 servings

Jane H. Brown
Similar recipe submitted by Ellen Dekle Alderman

85

Curried Chicken Salad

2 cups chicken breasts,
   cooked and chopped
½ cup almonds, toasted
½ cup raisins
½ cup coconut, shredded
1 (8-ounce) carton sour
   cream

1 tablespoon lime juice
1 teaspoon curry powder,
   or to taste
Dash of ground ginger
4 kiwi fruit, peeled and
   sliced

Toss together chicken, almonds, raisins and coconut. Set aside. Combine sour cream, lime juice, curry and ginger. Add chicken mixture, and toss well until all ingredients are coated. Arrange chicken salad on lettuce leaves. Place kiwi slices around the outer edge. Serve chilled. Best if prepared the day before.
Yield: 4 servings

Gail Qurnell

Curried Turkey Salad

2 cups turkey, cooked and
   cubed
1½ cups rice, cooked
⅔ cup celery, finely
   chopped

⅔ cup sliced water
   chestnuts, drained and
   chopped
16 green olives, sliced
⅔ cup mayonnaise
2 teaspoons lemon juice
1 teaspoon curry powder

Toss together turkey, rice, celery, water chestnuts and olives. Combine mayonnaise, lemon juice, and curry powder, mixing well. Stir into turkey mixture. Chill until ready to serve.
Yield: 4 to 6 servings

Seafood Salad

2 envelopes plain gelatin
½ cup cold water
1 can tomato soup
2 (3-ounce) packages cream
   cheese
1 cup celery, chopped
½ cup green pepper,
   chopped

2 or 3 spring onions,
   chopped
1 cup mayonnaise
¾ teaspoon salt
½ cup lemon juice
2 cans white crabmeat
Olives - Eyes
Lemon Peel - Mouth

Soak gelatin in cold water. Heat soup and add cream cheese. Stir until smooth. Add gelatin and stir to dissolve. Add chopped vegetables, mayonnaise, salt, lemon juice and crabmeat. Pour in fish mold and chill.
Yield: 10 to 12 servings

Exotic Shrimp Salad

3 pounds shrimp, cooked
   and cleaned
2 cups water chestnuts,
   sliced
½ cup green onions, minced

½ cup celery, diced
3 cups seashell pasta,
   cooked al dente
1 cup slivered almonds,
   toasted

Dressing:
1½ cups mayonnaise
4 teaspoons curry powder

4 tablespoons soy sauce

Mix dressing ingredients thoroughly, using wooden spoon. Cut shrimp in large pieces. Add water chestnuts, onion, celery, and pasta. Mix gently. Add dressing and toss. Refrigerate overnight, if possible, for flavors to blend. Arrange salad portions on crisp lettuce. Garnish with almonds just before serving.
Yield: 12 servings

Laura Keith

Festive Shrimp and Pasta Salad

3¾ cups corkscrew tri-
   colored pasta, uncooked
1 (6-ounce) package frozen
   Chinese pea pods
1½ pounds shrimp, cooked,
   peeled, and deveined
½ cup sliced water
   chestnuts

½ to 1 cup mayonnaise
2 tablespoons parsley,
   chopped
1½ tablespoons pimiento
⅛ teaspoon salt
⅛ teaspoon pepper

Cook pasta and drain. Rinse with cold water and drain. Cook pea pods and drain. Peas should still be crisp. Combine pasta and pea pods with remaining ingredients. Toss gently. Chill for 6 hours before serving.
Yield: 6 to 8 servings

Sally Tyndall

Shrimp Salad

1½ cups rice, cooked
¼ cup oil and vinegar salad
   dressing
¾ cup mayonnaise
1 tablespoon onion or
   scallions, chopped
¾ teaspoon curry powder

½ teaspoon dry mustard
½ teaspoon salt
½ teaspoon pepper
1½ cups celery, chopped
1½ pounds shrimp, cooked
   and chopped

Toss rice and salad dressing. Put in refrigerator and cool. Mix mayonnaise, onions, and remaining ingredients together. Add to rice mixture.
Yield: 6 servings

Carol Aguero

Brilliant
Watercolors
Soups

Brilliant Watercolors

Soups

Creating the Setting

Moultrie artist Cornelia Pattillo Hardy (for biographical sketch, see page 10) invites you into this quaint setting in the home of Mr. and Mrs. Warren B. Taylor, Sr., of Moultrie, with her pen and ink drawing, "Anna Elizabeth's Dining Room."

Combined for your Setting

The indiscreet nature of soup allows you, the artist, to create a medium that has no defined boundaries and many possibilities. Colors travel within each other, overlapping and drawing one into the serving dish. You may be searching for a hearty meal on a wintry day, or a light addition to an afternoon luncheon. Spoons will be ready when you finalize your brilliant watercolor.

Black-eyed Pea Chowder

½ pound bacon, diced
2 cups celery, chopped
2 cups green pepper,
    chopped
2 cups onion, chopped

1 (10½-ounce) can beef
    consommé
2 (16-ounce) cans tomatoes
2 (16-ounce) cans black-
    eyed peas

In a soup pot or Dutch oven, sauté bacon with celery, green pepper and onion. Add consommé, tomatoes and black-eyed peas. Simmer 30 to 40 minutes.
Yield: 6 to 8 servings

Mary Beard
(Founding Member of Moultrie Service League)

Creamy Broccoli Soup

1 (10-ounce) package frozen
    chopped broccoli
1 stick margarine
1 (8-ounce) package cream
    cheese

2 cans cream of chicken
    soup
½ gallon milk
Salt and pepper to taste

Cook broccoli until tender and drain. Add margarine, cream cheese and soups. Let come to a boil. Add milk. Stir well. Heat to scalding point. Season to taste. For variation, use cream of celery soup.
Yield: 16 (8-ounce) servings

Paula Neely
*Similar recipe submitted by Marilyn Huber

91

Cream Of Broccoli Soup

1 (20-ounce) package frozen
  chopped broccoli
2 cans chicken broth
2 bay leaves

Salt to taste
¼ cup margarine
¼ cup flour
2 cups milk

Cook broccoli in broth with bay leaves. Salt to taste. Cool. Process in blender by portions and return to saucepan. Melt margarine in small saucepan, and stir in flour. Simmer 2 to 3 minutes. Slowly add milk while stirring. When thickened, gradually add to broccoli. Heat thoroughly.
Yield: 8 servings

Frank's Brunswick Stew

5 pounds ground Boston
  Butt, browned
5 pounds ground beef,
  browned
1 (6-pound) hen, cooked
  and boned
2 cans whole kernel corn
2 cans LeSueur Peas

2 medium onions, chopped
  and sautéed
3 pounds Irish potatoes,
  diced and cooked
4 small bottles ketchup
1 bottle barbecue sauce
Salt
Red pepper
Black pepper

Shred meats and hen. Combine with corn, peas, onions, potatoes, ketchup, and barbecue sauce. Add salt, red and black pepper to taste. Cook slowly, being careful not to scorch.
Yield: 3 gallons

Betty Hendrick

Congressional Bean Soup

By tradition, bean soup is served daily in the House and Senate restaurants. The House restaurant dates its practice back to 1904 when Speaker Joseph G. Cannon found the soup missing from the menu. "Thunderation," roared the Speaker, "I had my mouth set for bean soup. From now on, hot or cold, rain, snow or shine, I want it on the menu every day." The House and Senate recipes are similar, except that the House version omits the onions:

2 pounds small navy beans	**1 onion, chopped**
4 quarts hot water	**2 tablespoons butter**
1½ pounds smoked ham hocks	**Salt and pepper to taste**

Wash navy beans, and run hot water through them until slightly whitened. Place beans in pot with hot water. Add ham hocks and simmer approximately 3 hours in a covered pot, stirring occasionally. Remove ham hocks and set aside to cool. Dice meat and return to soup. Lightly brown onion in butter and add to the soup. Before serving, bring to a boil, and then season with salt and pepper. *Yield: 8 servings*

(If you visit our Congressman, Saxby Chambliss, be sure to have lunch in the House restaurant and order Congressional Bean Soup!)
LaDonna Funderburk

Homemade Brunswick Stew

1½ pounds ground beef
1½ pounds ground pork
3 cans white whole kernel
   corn, undrained
3 large cans tomatoes
2 medium onions

⅓ cup ketchup
Juice of 1 lime
3 tablespoons vinegar
Salt to taste
1 teaspoon Tabasco sauce
2 cups breadcrumbs

Brown meat. Add undrained corn, tomatoes and onions. Combine ketchup, lime juice, vinegar, salt and Tabasco. Stir into stew. Add breadcrumbs and bring to a boil. Reduce heat, cover and simmer for 1 hour. This freezes very well. To make enough for one meal, use a third of ingredients.
Yield: 12 servings

Polly Boetcher

Chili

1 pound ground beef,
   browned
1 can tomato soup
1 teaspoon Tabasco sauce
2 tablespoons
   Worcestershire sauce

1 tablespoon chili powder
1½ cups water
1 can red kidney beans,
   drained
½ teaspoon celery salt
Salt and pepper to taste

Combine all ingredients. Simmer on low heat for about 1 hour.
Yield: 4 servings

Lee Willis

Chili Con Carne

1½ pounds ground beef
2 medium onions, sliced
1 (28-ounce) can whole
 tomatoes
1 (6-ounce) can tomato
 paste
1 cup water
1 beef bouillon cube
1 (16-ounce) can red kidney
 beans

2 tablespoons green
 pepper, diced
2 cloves garlic, minced
2 teaspoons salt
2 teaspoons oregano
2 teaspoons chili powder
½ teaspoon crushed red
 pepper (or to taste)
1 bay leaf

Brown ground beef and onions in a large saucepan, and drain off
fat. Add remaining ingredients; stir to blend. Cover and simmer
1½ hours. Stir occasionally. Remove bay leaf and serve.
Yield: 6 servings

Marie Saunders

Wilma's Clam Chowder

¼ pound bacon
4 medium potatoes, cubed
2 cups water
1 small onion, chopped
1 can evaporated milk
2 cans minced clams

1 small can sliced
 mushrooms (optional)
1 can New England clam
 chowder
Salt and pepper to taste

Fry bacon until crisp. Cook potatoes and onions in 2 cups of water
until tender. Add all other ingredients, and simmer until ready to
serve. Do not boil.
Yield: 4 to 6 servings

Kathy Heard

Florida Cioppino

1 large onion, chopped
1 cup celery, finely
   chopped
2 small zucchini squash,
   shredded
4 tablespoons olive oil
   (divided)
2 cloves garlic, minced
2 tablespoons flour
1 can crushed tomatoes or
   2 cans peeled tomatoes,
   crushed
2 cans whole mushrooms,
   plus liquid

2 tablespoons granulated
   chicken broth
2 cans chicken broth
1 quart water
1 cup white wine (divided)
2 bay leaves
2 teaspoons seasoned salt
½ teaspoon pepper
Pinch of sage
¼ teaspoon summer savory
2 pounds shrimp, cleaned
   and deveined
1½ pounds scallops
1½ pounds mild, firm fish,
   cut in 1-inch pieces

Sauté onions, celery and shredded zucchini in 2 tablespoons olive oil in frying pan for about 3 minutes. Add garlic, and cook for 1 more minute. Put mixture in large saucepan. Add remainder of olive oil and the flour to the frying pan. Cook until light brown. Add this roux, plus the tomatoes, mushrooms, broth, water and ½ cup wine to saucepan. Mix well, and add all the seasonings. Cook on low heat for 2 hours or more. Just before serving, bring to a boil and add the remaining wine and the seafood. Cook just until shrimp looks almost done, no more than 5 minutes. Do not overcook. Pour into a large tureen or ladle into large bowls. Wonderful with a vegetable salad and garlic bread. Note: I sometimes add a few drops of hot sauce, if I think the crowd would like it.

Yield: 8 to 10 servings

Barbara B. Vereen

Crab Bisque

1 (10¾-ounce) can
   condensed cream of
   asparagus soup
1 (10½-ounce) can
   condensed cream of
   mushroom soup

1½ soup cans of milk
1 cup half and half
1 cup crabmeat, flaked
¾ cup dry white wine or
   dry sherry

Blend soups. Stir in milk and cream. Heat just to boiling. Add crabmeat. Heat thoroughly. Stir in wine just before serving.
Yield: 6 to 8 servings

Carol Ann Cannon

Crab Soup

1 pound fresh crabmeat (if
   using canned, squeeze
   out excess water)
½ cup, plus 1 tablespoon
   sherry
1 tablespoon onion, grated
6 tablespoons butter or
   margarine

4 tablespoons flour
3 cups milk
2 chicken bouillon cubes
1 teaspoon salt (or to taste)
2 cups half and half
2 tablespoons parsley,
   chopped
Dash of hot sauce

Soak crabmeat in 6 tablespoons sherry while preparing the soup. Briefly cook the onion in butter, then add flour. Cook until well blended and golden color. Slowly add milk. When all is mixed and hot, add bouillon cubes and a little salt. Cook until slightly thickened and smooth. Add crabmeat, and cook covered 5 minutes. Add half and half, plus remaining sherry. Lastly, add hot sauce and parsley. Do not let this boil. Serve at once. (Be sure you pick the crabmeat well to eliminate little shells.)
Yield: 6 servings

Bunnie Vereen
(Founding Member of Moultrie Service League)

Mexican Stew

1 pound ground beef
1 pound smoked beef
    sausage, cut in chunks
1 package taco seasoning
    mix
1 (46-ounce) can tomato
    juice

1 (16-ounce) package frozen
    mixed vegetables
1 (15-ounce) can chili hot
    beans
1 (12-ounce) can tomato
    paste
2 cups corn chips, crushed
Cheese, grated

In large Dutch oven, brown ground beef and sausage. Drain. Add taco seasoning mix, tomato juice, vegetables, chili beans and tomato paste. Mix well. Bring to a boil. Reduce heat and simmer uncovered for 20 to 25 minutes, stirring occasionally. Top each serving with corn chips and cheese.
Yield: 10 servings

Carolyn Lodge

Mushroom Soup

2 pounds fresh mushrooms,
    ground
2 cans bouillon or
    consommé
2 cans water
1 to 2 onions, chopped
Salt and pepper to taste

Worcestershire sauce to
    taste
4 tablespoons margarine
2 tablespoons flour
¾ cup whipping cream
½ cup sherry

Boil mushrooms together with bouillon, water, onions and seasonings for 15 minutes. Add margarine and flour to thicken. Cook 5 minutes more. Stir in cream and sherry. Best if made 24 hours ahead.
Yield: 6 to 8 servings

Carol Ann Cannon

Okra Chowder

1 medium onion, chopped
1 green pepper, chopped
2 tablespoons olive oil
4 cups okra, sliced
4 medium tomatoes, peeled
   and chopped
1 cup butter beans
1 cup corn

½ cup ham, cooked and
   diced
½ teaspoon salt
¼ teaspoon pepper
2 cups water
Dash of Worcestershire
   sauce

Sauté onion and green pepper in olive oil until tender. In a large pot, cook all ingredients at least 2 hours. You can may use fresh or frozen vegetables.
Yield: 8 to 10 servings

Jane Holman

Onion Soup

2 cups sweet onion, thinly
   sliced
½ cup butter
¼ cup flour
1½ teaspoons salt

¼ teaspoon pepper
4 cups milk
Parmesan cheese
French bread
Swiss cheese

Sauté onions in butter over low heat for 20 minutes. Mix in flour and seasonings. Add milk, stirring constantly and bring to boil. Sprinkle in Parmesan cheese. Pour in individual bowls. Top with French bread and Swiss cheese. Cover with foil. Place in 350 degree oven for 10 minutes until cheese melts.
Yield: 4 to 6 servings

Kristy Allen

Oyster Stew

3 tablespoons butter or
    margarine
1 pint raw oysters, with
    juice

3 cups milk
Dash of Tabasco sauce
Salt to taste

In a heavy saucepan, melt butter. Add oysters and juice to butter.
Cook until oysters' edges curl. Add milk, Tabasco sauce and salt.
Heat thoroughly.
Yield: 4 servings

Cooka Hillebrand
*Similar recipe submitted by Marie Saunders

Ann's Sweet And Sour Cabbage Soup

1½ to 2 pounds stew beef
    (or cubed shoulder or
    chuck roast)
Water
Salt and pepper to taste
2 stalks celery, chopped
2 onions, quartered
1 large can crushed
    tomatoes with puree
    (Progresso)

1 can tomatoes, drained
    and chopped
1 small can tomato paste
Juice of 1 or 2 lemons
¼ cup white sugar
½ to ¾ cup brown sugar to
    taste
½ to ¾ head of cabbage,
    chopped

Cover beef with water. Add salt, pepper, celery and onions. Cook
over medium to low heat for 2 to 3 hours, adding water as needed.
Skim broth. Add crushed tomatoes, chopped tomatoes, and tomato
paste. Cook for about 1 hour. For the sweet and sour taste, add
lemon juice and sugars. Then add cabbage, and simmer for about 1
hour or until cabbage is cooked. Serve with cornbread or rolls for a
hearty meal.
Yield: 10 servings

Ann Friedlander

Laura Keith's Fresh Pimiento Bisque

½ cup long grain white rice
4 cups water (divided)
4 large red bell peppers,
   coarsely chopped
1 small onion, chopped
2 cups chicken stock
   (divided)
2 cups milk

½ cup heavy cream
¼ teaspoon cayenne pepper
¼ teaspoon imported sweet
   paprika
⅛ teaspoon white pepper,
   freshly ground
Salt to taste

Place the rice in a saucepan with 2 cups water. Bring to a boil. Reduce heat to low. Simmer uncovered until the rice is overcooked and mushy, and the water has almost boiled away (about 40 minutes). In a medium saucepan, combine red peppers, onion and 2 cups of water. Boil over moderate heat until the peppers are tender but still bright red (about 10 minutes). Drain at once. Put the rice, red peppers, onion and 1 cup of the chicken stock into a blender or food processor. Puree until smooth. Strain the puree into a medium saucepan, add milk and the remaining 1 cup of stock. Simmer over low heat for 5 minutes to thicken slightly. Stir in cream, cayenne, paprika, and white pepper. Season with salt to taste. Cover the bisque and set aside for 1 hour to blend the flavors. Rewarm over low heat before serving.

Yield: 6 to 8 servings

Laura Keith

Potato Soup

1 onion, chopped
4 tablespoons margarine
6 or 7 medium potatoes
Water
Salt, pepper and garlic salt
    to taste

1 can cream of chicken
    soup
2 soup cans of milk
1 medium package Velveeta
    cheese

Sauté onion in margarine. Peel and cube potatoes. Add to onion and margarine. Put in saucepan and barely cover with water. Season with salt, pepper and garlic salt. Cook until potatoes are mushy. Add soup, milk, and cheese. Heat on low until cheese melts.
Yield: 8 servings

Jan Smith

Rootin' Tootin' Soup

1 large onion, chopped
2 tablespoons olive oil
2 medium potatoes, peeled
    and chopped
2 small carrots, thinly
    sliced
2 medium turnips, chopped
    (roots only)

2 cloves garlic
3 cups chicken broth
⅛ cup vodka
Salt and pepper to taste
Yogurt
Green onions, chopped

Sauté the onion in olive oil until soft. Add the other vegetables and garlic. Cook over low heat for about 5 minutes. Add chicken stock, and cook for about 30 minutes over low heat. Remove from heat, and add the vodka. Divide and puree in a food processor, according to amount the processor will hold. Salt and pepper to taste. Ladle into bowls. Add a dollop of yogurt. Sprinkle with chopped green onions and serve.
Yield: 6 servings

Barbara B. Vereen

Sausage Bean Chowder

1 pound bulk pork sausage	1½ teaspoons seasoned salt
2 cans kidney beans	½ teaspoon garlic salt
1 can tomatoes, chopped	½ teaspoon thyme
1 quart water	¼ teaspoon pepper
1 large onion, chopped	1 cup potatoes, diced
1 bay leaf	½ cup bell pepper, chopped

In skillet, cook sausage until brown. Drain. In large pot, combine beans, tomatoes, water, onions and seasonings. Add sausage, and cook covered for 1 hour. Add potatoes and bell pepper. Cook an additional 15 to 20 minutes until potatoes are tender. Remove bay leaf. This makes a great winter dish, served with cornbread. You may add another pound of sausage if desired.
Yield: 8 servings

Nanci Lewis
Similar recipe submitted by JoAnn Caldwell

Taco Soup

1½ pounds ground beef	1 (10½-ounce) can beef broth
2 cups celery, chopped	1 (8-ounce) can tomato sauce
2 cups carrots, chopped	1 package taco seasoning
2 cans potato soup	2 cans kidney beans, drained
2 (16½-ounce) cans tomatoes	Tortilla chips (optional)
1 medium onion, chopped	

Brown ground beef and drain well. Add remaining ingredients, and simmer for 1½ hours. Serve with tortilla chips.
Yield: 8 servings

Barbara Hendrick
Similar recipe submitted by Ann Friedlander

Taco Chili

½ package taco seasoning
    mix
1 (4-ounce) package Hidden
    Valley Ranch Salad
    Dressing mix
2 pounds ground beef,
    browned and drained
½ (12-ounce) jar mild
    jalapeño peppers,
    drained and chopped

2 (15-ounce) cans kidney
    beans, undrained
2 (15-ounce) cans pinto
    beans, undrained
1 (18-ounce) can tomato
    juice
Cheddar cheese (optional)
Sour cream (optional)
Tortilla chips (optional)

Mix dry ingredients with browned ground beef in large soup pot and stir well. Add jalapeño peppers, kidney beans and pinto beans. Add tomato juice and mix well. Cook over low heat about 1 hour or simmer 3 hours. (The longer it simmers, the better.) Serve with grated Cheddar cheese, sour cream and tortilla chips if desired.
Yield: 8 servings

Carol Bannister

Vegetable Soup

1 pound hamburger
Water or chicken stock
1 or 2 cans tomatoes
1 or 2 cans tomato soup
Large onion, diced
Salt to taste

1 can creamed corn
Okra, peas, carrots, rice,
    beans, celery, potatoes,
    butter beans
V-8

Brown meat in soup pot. Add water or chicken stock, tomatoes and tomato soup, onion and salt. Simmer. Add creamed corn and other vegetables and enough liquid to cook the quantity of vegetables. Cook until vegetables are done. Add V-8 to thin. I make enough to freeze and add V-8 when heating to serve.
Yield: 8 to 10 servings

Becky Duggan
Similar recipes submitted by Mary Jo Stone and Terrie Moody

Spicy Vegetable Soup

1 pound ground beef
1 cup onion, chopped
2 cloves garlic, pressed
1 (30-ounce) jar chunky
    garden-style spaghetti
    sauce with mushrooms
    and peppers
1 (10½-ounce) can beef
    broth
2 cups water
1 cup celery, sliced

1 teaspoon sugar
1 teaspoon salt
½ teaspoon pepper, freshly
    ground
1 (10-ounce) can diced
    tomatoes and green
    chilies
1 (16-ounce) package frozen
    mixed vegetables
2 cups potatoes, diced
    (optional)

Cook first 3 ingredients in a large Dutch oven over medium heat until meat is browned, stirring to crumble. Drain and return meat to Dutch oven. Add spaghetti sauce and next 6 ingredients. Cover, reduce heat and simmer 20 minutes, stirring occasionally. Stir in tomatoes, vegetables and potatoes. Return to a boil. Cover and simmer 10 to 12 minutes or until vegetables are tender.
Yield: 8 to 10 servings

Carol Bannister

Williamsburg Turkey Soup

1 turkey carcass
4 quarts water
2 tablespoons butter
3 onions, chopped
2 large carrots, diced
2 stalks celery, diced

1 cup long grain rice,
 uncooked
2 teaspoons salt
¾ teaspoon pepper
1 to 2 chicken bouillon
 cubes (optional)

Place turkey carcass and water in a large Dutch oven; bring to a boil. Cover, reduce heat and simmer for one hour. Remove carcass from broth, and pick meat from bones. Set broth and meat aside. Measure broth, adding water if necessary, to measure 3 quarts. Heat butter. Sauté onions, carrots, and celery. Combine broth, turkey, sautéed vegetables, rice, salt and pepper; bring to a boil. Cover, reduce heat, and simmer 20 minutes or until rice is tender. You may wish to add 1 or 2 chicken bouillon cubes. This freezes beautifully.
Yield: 4½ quarts

LaDonna Funderburk

Masterpieces
Beef, Lamb, Pork, Poultry, Seafood & Game

Masterpieces

Beef, Lamb and Pork; Poultry; Seafood and Game

Creating the Setting

Though born in Indiana, John A. Zuck captures the serenity of a southern setting in his pen and ink drawing "Piney Woods Connection." His flying experience with the U. S. Army Air Corp during World War II eventually lead him to Moultrie, where he met and married the former Miss Dorothy Dean. He later continued his education in clinical lab science at the University of Alabama, which lead him to work with the Moultrie hospital. Now retired from his profession and from the Air Force as Lieutenant Colonel, Zuck pursues his hobby of painting and drawing. "I have driven, flown, fished, sailed, canoed, skied, hiked, biked, gardened, become a father, grandfather and great-grandfather, and loved every minute of it," says Zuck.

Combined for your Setting

The main course tells the story of your meal, allowing many possibilities for expression. The accompanying mediums draw out the savor and must be carefully selected to avoid distraction. Stimulate that creative genius as you mark your preference in the entrée section, and delight yourself in designing yet another masterpiece.

Boneless Ribeye Loin with Garlic

1 boneless ribeye loin
   (not more than 10 to 11
   pounds)

Garlic cloves
Salt
Lemon-pepper seasoning

Preheat oven to 500 degrees. Cut small slits in loin and stuff generously with garlic cloves. Season. Cook in oven for 5 minutes per pound, then turn oven off. Continue cooking 20 to 25 minutes per pound, but do not open oven door! Meat will be rare to medium rare. You may use meat thermometer if desired. Insert thermometer in thickest part of loin. Take out when thermometer reaches 130 to 135 degrees. Let stand 5 to 10 minutes to finish cooking.
Yield: Dependent on size of loin

Mary Ann Blank

Marinated Fillet of Beef

Fillet of beef or tenderloin
   (7 to 8 pounds)
Salt
Pepper
Celery salt
Onion salt

2 lemons
⅔ cup A-1 sauce
¼ cup Worcestershire
   sauce
1 bottle paprika

Rub seasonings, except paprika, into roast separately. Use more seasoning than you think necessary. Mix the juice of 2 lemons, A-1 sauce, Worcestershire sauce together. Rub this mixture into the entire roast. If you have any sauce left, save it. Put meat into shallow pan. Coat top, sides and ends heavily with paprika. Marinate in refrigerator 8 to 10 hours. Allow roast to come to room temperature. It will draw its own juice. Baste with this and any leftover sauce. To cook, pour off sauce. Bake in preheated oven at 550 degrees for 10 minutes. Turn oven to 450 degrees, and bake uncovered 8 to 10 minutes per pound.
Yield: Dependent on size of the roast

Barbara B. Vereen

Chuck's Favorite Country Fried Steak

6 cube steaks (or sirloin, cubed)
All-purpose flour
1 can water
4 tablespoons vegetable shortening
1 large onion, sliced
1 can beef stock
Salt and pepper to taste
¼ cup flour, mixed with water

Coat steaks in flour, heavily seasoned with salt and pepper. Melt shortening in large skillet. Add steaks and fry over medium-high heat until they are brown on both sides. When steaks are brown, add onion. Sauté for just a moment. Add beef stock and water. Stir to break up any scrapings that are on bottom of pan. Cover, and allow meat to simmer on low heat for about 1½ hours. When ready to serve, combine ¼ cup flour with a little water and add to meat and gravy. Stir and heat until thickened.
Yield: 4 to 6 servings

Carol Bannister

Busy Day Oven Stew

2 to 3 pounds stew beef
3 potatoes, quartered
4 stalks celery, chopped
3 small onions, quartered
½ to 1 pound carrots, sliced
3 tablespoons soy sauce
4 tablespoons corn starch
2 (16-ounce) cans tomatoes
1 can of water
Salt and pepper to taste

Place uncooked meat, potatoes, celery, onions, carrots in large pot. Mix tomatoes and all other ingredients together. Pour this mixture over meat and vegetables. Cover and cook at 350 degrees for 2½ hours. You may stir once during cooking. Serve over rice.
Yield: 4 to 6 servings

Barbara Hendrick

Lobster-Stuffed Beef Tenderloin

3 (4-ounce) frozen lobster
  tails
1 (4 to 6 pound) beef
  tenderloin, trimmed
½ cup plus 1 tablespoon
  butter or margarine,
  melted (divided)
1½ teaspoons lemon juice
Garlic salt

Freshly ground pepper
6 slices bacon
½ cup green onions, sliced
½ cup dry white wine
⅛ teaspoon garlic salt
Lemon wedges, onion curl,
  and radicchio for
  garnish

Place frozen lobster tails in boiling salted water to cover. Simmer 5 minutes. Drain. Remove lobster in one piece from shells. Trim excess fat from beef tenderloin. Remove 3 inches of small end; reserve for other uses. Cut tenderloin lengthwise to within ½-inch of other edge. Leave one long side connected. Place lobster tails, end to end, inside tenderloin. Slice lobster tails lengthwise, if necessary, to extend entire length of tenderloin. Combine 1 tablespoon butter and lemon juice. Drizzle over lobster. Fold top side of beef tenderloin over lobster. Tie tenderloin securely with heavy string at 2 to 3 inch intervals. Sprinkle outside of meat evenly with garlic salt and freshly ground pepper. Place on a rack in a shallow roasting pan. Bake at 425 degrees for 35 to 40 minutes or until a meat thermometer registers 140 degrees (rare) or 160 degrees (medium). Cook bacon until transparent. Drain and arrange crosswise on top of tenderloin. Bake 4 minutes or until bacon is crisp. Remove to platter. Slice to serve. Garnish, if desired. Sauté green onions in butter in a small saucepan until crisp-tender. Add wine and garlic salt. Heat thoroughly. Serve with the sliced beef tenderloin.

Yield: 10 to 12 servings

Barbara B. Vereen

Marinated Steak and Vegetable Kabobs

½ cup Chablis
1 clove garlic
½ teaspoon salt
½ cup vegetable oil
1 teaspoon Worcestershire sauce
2 tablespoons chili sauce
1 tablespoon vinegar
½ teaspoon dried whole oregano
½ teaspoon dried whole thyme
2 pounds sirloin (or beef of choice), cut into large cubes
½ pound fresh mushrooms
2 large green peppers, cut in large chunks
1 pint cherry tomatoes
4 small yellow squash, sliced thick

Combine first nine ingredients. Add meat, cover and marinate 2 hours. Remove meat marinade and reserve. Alternate meat and vegetables on skewers. Brush with marinade as it grills over medium coals.
Yield: 4 servings

Lynne Stone

Sauterne Beef

3 pounds beef chuck, cut in bite size cubes
2 cans golden mushroom soup
1 envelope Lipton onion soup mix
1 cup Sauterne (a dry white wine)

Place beef in 10 x 14-inch casserole. Mix soups and sauterne. Pour over beef. May marinate 1 to 2 hours. Cook covered at 300 degrees for 3 hours. Serve over rice.
Yield: 10 servings

Gloria Rogers
*Similar recipe submitted by Christy Hendrick

Roast Peppered Rib Eye of Beef

½ cup coarsely cracked
   pepper
½ teaspoon ground
   cardamom seed
Rib eye roast (5 pounds),
   fat trimmed
1 tablespoon tomato paste

½ teaspoon garlic powder
1 teaspoon paprika
1 cup soy sauce
¾ cup vinegar
1 cup water
1½ tablespoons corn starch
¼ cup cold water

Combine pepper and cardamom seed. Rub into beef and press in with the heel of your palm. Combine tomato paste, garlic powder and paprika. Gradually add soy sauce and vinegar to tomato paste mixture. Pour marinade over beef and marinate overnight. Remove meat from marinade and let stand at room temperature 1 hour. Wrap meat in foil, and place in shallow pan. Roast at 300 degrees for 2 hours for medium rare. Open foil. Ladle out and reserve pan drippings. Brown roast, uncovered, at 350 degrees while making gravy.

For gravy, strain pan drippings and skim excess fat. To 1 cup meat juice, add 1 cup water. Bring to a boil and taste. If desired, add a little marinade for flavor. Combine corn starch and water, stirring until smooth. Add to gravy. Cook, stirring constantly, until thickened.
Yield: 8 to 10 servings

Peggy Benner

113

Steak Diane

1 tablespoon butter
2 tablespoons onion or
   shallots, finely chopped
2 cloves garlic, crushed
1 cup fresh mushrooms,
   sliced
4 boneless beef top loin
   or rib eye steaks, cut
   ¾-inch thick

¼ cup beef broth
2 tablespoons brandy
2 teaspoons Dijon-style
   mustard
1 teaspoon Worcestershire
   sauce
2 teaspoons parsley, finely
   chopped

Melt butter in a large non-stick skillet over medium heat. Add shallots and garlic. Cook 2 minutes. Stir in mushrooms. Cook and stir 3 to 4 minutes. Remove and set aside. Increase heat to medium high. Add steaks to skillet. Cook 6 to 7 minutes for medium rare, turning once. Remove to warm platter. Decrease heat to medium. Add broth, brandy, mustard, Worcestershire sauce and reserved mushroom mixture. Bring to a boil. Cook and stir until liquid is slightly reduced, about one minute. Spoon sauce over steaks and sprinkle with parsley.

Yield: 4 servings

Farolyn Mobley

Italian Meat Loaf

2 slices rye bread
2 slices firm white bread
1 cup water
1 pound lean ground beef
1 medium onion, finely
  chopped
1 egg, slightly beaten
3 tablespoons Parmesan
  cheese, freshly grated

2 tablespoons fresh parsley,
  minced
1 teaspoon salt
¼ teaspoon pepper
1 (8-ounce) can tomato
  soup
1 teaspoon dried oregano,
  crumbled

Grease 9 x 5-inch loaf pan. Place rye and white breads in large bowl. Pour water over. Let soak 5 minutes. Drain off any excess water. Mash bread finely with fork. Add ground beef, onion, egg, Parmesan, parsley, salt and pepper. Mix well. Transfer to prepared dish. (Can be prepared 6 hours ahead. Chill.) Bake meat loaf at 375 degrees for 30 minutes. Pour tomato sauce over. Sprinkle with oregano. Bake 20 more minutes. Let stand 5 minutes.
Yield: 4 to 6 servings

Harriett Whelchel

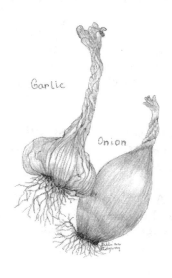

Garlic

Onion

Marzetti

2 pounds ground beef	1 cup stuffed green olives,
1 onion, chopped	chopped
1 green pepper, chopped	1 teaspoon garlic salt
1 (6-ounce) can tomato	1 teaspoon pepper
paste	1 (12-ounce) box thin
2 (15-ounce) cans tomato	spaghetti
sauce	1 cup sharp cheese,
½ cup dry red wine	shredded

Brown beef and onion. Drain fat. Add green pepper, then next 6 ingredients. Simmer 30 minutes, uncovered. Cook spaghetti while simmering sauce. Drain spaghetti, and combine with meat mixture. Place in a 9 x 13-inch casserole dish, and top with cheese. Bake at 325 degrees for 1 hour. I use two 8-inch square dishes to make two casseroles.

Yield: 8 to 12 servings

Lynn Acuff

Pam Yocom's Enchilada Pie

1 pound ground beef	6 to 9 tortillas, cut in strips
1 onion, chopped	2 cups sharp Cheddar
1 clove garlic, minced (or ¼	cheese, shredded
teaspoon garlic powder)	2 cups mozzarella or
1 teaspoon salt	Monterey Jack cheese,
Dash of pepper	shredded
1 tablespoon chili powder	1 small can black olives,
1 small can tomato sauce	sliced
1 can enchilada sauce	

Sauté beef and onion. Add seasonings, tomato sauce and enchilada sauce. Grease a 10 x 14-inch baking dish. Layer tortilla strips, meat, cheeses and olives, ending with cheese and olives. Sprinkle water around edges. Bake for 30 minutes at 400 degrees.

Yield: 8 to 10 servings

Ellen Dekle Alderman

Mexican Casserole

1 tablespoon oil
½ cup onion, chopped
2 garlic cloves, minced
1 pound lean ground beef
1 (28-ounce) can stewed
   tomatoes
1 package taco seasoning
   mix
1 (4-ounce) can diced green
   chilies
1 (2½-ounce) can black
   olives, chopped

2 (7 to 8-ounce) packages
   cheese-flavored tortilla
   chips, lightly crushed
1 (8-ounce) package
   mozzarella cheese,
   shredded
2 cups sour cream or plain
   yogurt
½ cup Cheddar cheese,
   shredded

Heat oil in large skillet over medium heat. Add onion and garlic. Sauté until translucent. Add meat and cook until browned, stirring frequently. Blend in tomatoes, taco seasoning, chilies and olives. Simmer about 10 minutes. Grease 9 x 13-inch baking dish. Layer half of chips over bottom. Add all of meat mixture, then mozzarella and sour cream or yogurt. Top with remaining chips. Bake at 350 degrees until heated through, about 30 minutes. Sprinkle with Cheddar cheese, and continue baking until cheese melts. Let stand 5 minutes before serving.

Yield: 6 to 8 servings

Carol Bannister
*Similar recipe submitted by Harriett Whelchel

Spaghetti Meat Sauce

3 cans tomato sauce
2 bay leaves
1 teaspoon oregano
2 garlic cloves
Salt and pepper to taste
2 medium onions, diced

2 (4½-ounce) jars
   mushrooms, sliced
1 bell pepper, diced
Olive oil
3 pounds lean ground beef

In a large saucepan, put tomato sauce, bay leaves, oregano, salt, pepper and garlic cloves. Cook on a medium heat while sautéing other ingredients. Sauté onions, mushrooms and bell pepper in olive oil over low heat until translucent. Add to tomato sauce. Brown ground beef. Drain off fat and add meat to tomato sauce mixture. Cover and simmer for several hours. Remove garlic cloves and bay leaves before serving. I usually allow it to cook all day. This is a great base sauce for lasagna too.
Yield: 10 servings

Cooka Hillebrand

Taco Pie

1 pound ground beef
1 medium onion, chopped
1 (1¼-ounce) package taco
 seasoning mix
¾ cup water
1 (16-ounce) can refried
 beans
1 (8-ounce) jar taco sauce
 (divided)

1 (9-inch) deep dish pie
 shell, baked
2 cups Cheddar cheese,
 shredded (divided)
¾ cup Fritos, crushed
Lettuce, shredded
Tomato, chopped

Brown beef and onion in skillet, stirring to crumble meat. Drain. Add taco seasoning mix and water. Bring to a boil, reduce heat, and simmer 20 minutes, stirring occasionally. Combine refried beans and ⅓ cup of taco sauce. Spoon half of bean mixture in bottom of pastry shell. Top with half of meat mixture, half of cheese and all of corn chips. Repeat layers with remaining bean mixture, meat mixture and cheese. Bake at 400 degrees for 20 to 25 minutes. Top with lettuce and tomato. Serve with remaining taco sauce.
Yield: 6 servings

Ava English

Tijuana Torte

2 pounds ground beef or
turkey
1 medium onion, chopped
1 (16-ounce) can stewed
tomatoes
1 (8-ounce) can tomato
sauce
1 (4-ounce) can green chili
pepper, diced

1 package taco seasoning
mix
4 large tortillas
1 pound Cheddar cheese,
grated
1½ cups sour cream
½ cup cheese, grated (for
topping)

Brown ground beef and onion. Drain. Add stewed tomatoes, tomato sauce, chili peppers and taco seasoning mix. Simmer for 10 to 15 minutes. In a 9 x 13-inch pan, place half of meat, cover with 2 tortillas and half of the Cheddar cheese. Continue with meat mixture, tortillas and Cheddar cheese. Spread sour cream on top, and sprinkle with grated cheese. Bake at 350 degrees for 25 minutes.
Yield: 6 to 8 servings

Anna Pritchett

Grilled Lamb Chops

8 rib lamb chops,
cut 1½-inch thick
1 garlic clove, cut in half
1 teaspoon thyme
1 teaspoon rosemary

½ cup dry red wine
1 tablespoon unsalted
butter
Coarse (Kosher) salt
Pepper, freshly ground

Light grill. Rub lamb chops on all sides with the garlic clove. In small saucepan, combine herbs, wine and butter. Heat until butter melts. Place chops on grill, and brush with the basting sauce. Grill about 4 inches from heat, turning once and basting occasionally with the sauce. Grill 3 to 6 minutes on each side, depending on how well done you like your meat. Season with salt and pepper. This recipe goes well with "Parslied Cherry Tomatoes With Garlic".
Yield: 6 to 8 servings

Mary Ann Blank

Leg Of Lamb With Dijon Dill Sauce

1 leg of lamb
10 cloves of garlic

1 jar Country Dijon
    Mustard
1 jar of honey

Dijon Dill Sauce:
6 tablespoons mayonnaise
4 tablespoons Country
    Dijon Mustard
4 tablespoons lemon juice

4 teaspoons fresh dill weed,
    snipped (or 1 teaspoon
    dried dill weed)

Cut garlic into thin slivers. Pierce lamb all over with knife, and insert a sliver of garlic into each puncture. Mix mustard and honey together. Roll lamb in mixture and refrigerate for at least 8 hours. Cook lamb at 300 degrees for 30 to 35 minutes per pound.

Mix sauce ingredients together to serve with lamb. (Sauce is also good with other red meat.)
Yield: 6 servings

Joan V. Stallings

Mock Veal Scallopini

3 medium onions, chopped
3 tablespoons shortening
⅔ cup pancake or biscuit
    mix
1 teaspoon salt
½ teaspoon pepper

Veal cutlets (2 pounds),
    thinly sliced or pounded
1 (10½-ounce) can beef
    consommé
1 clove of garlic, crushed
¼ teaspoon rosemary
¼ cup white wine

Lightly brown onions in shortening. Place in shallow casserole. Combine pancake mix, salt and pepper. Dredge veal in mixture. Reserve any remaining flour mixture. Brown veal on both sides in small amount of shortening in frying pan, and place on onions in casserole. Add consommé, garlic, rosemary, wine and remaining flour mixture to frying pan. Bring to boil, stirring constantly. Pour over veal. Bake at 350 degrees for 45 minutes or until veal is tender.
Yield: 6 servings

Susan Blanton

Barbara's Baked Ham

"Lee" ham (shank
    or butt end)

Cloves

Glaze (for ½ ham):
¼ cup brown sugar
¼ cup orange juice

½ teaspoon dry mustard

Remove ham from wrappings, and place in a brown paper bag. Fold the bag under, and put in broiler pan. Bake at 325 degrees for 25 minutes per pound. Take out before the last 30 minutes, and trim rind. Score and stick in cloves. Mix together glaze ingredients, spoon over ham and return to oven. Baste at least once during remaining baking time.
Yield: 15 to 20 servings

Barbara Hendrick

Nancy's Baked Ham

1 ham
½ cup sugar
2 teaspoons mustard

½ teaspoon cinnamon
1 tablespoon vinegar
Whole cloves

Wipe ham with damp cloth. Make paste with sugar, mustard, cinnamon and vinegar. Cover ham with paste, and place in a cold oven. Turn oven setting to 275 degrees. Cook 30 minutes per pound. Use this cooking method for all hams, even precooked ones.
Yield: 15 to 18 servings, dependent on size of ham

Judy Mobley

Ham Casserole

1 can cream of mushroom
    soup
½ cup milk
1 teaspoon instant onion
2 teaspoons prepared
    mustard

½ cup sour cream
2 cups ham, diced
4 ounces noodles, cooked
Buttered breadcrumbs

Mix soup, milk, onion, mustard, sour cream and ham. Heat thoroughly. Layer mixture with noodles. Top with buttered breadcrumbs. Bake at 325 degrees for 30 minutes or until bubbly.
Yield: 4 to 6 servings

Sandra Plant

Ham Loaf

1 pound lean ham, ground	½ teaspoon pepper
1 pound lean pork, ground	½ cup warm water
1 cup Rice Krispies,	½ cup brown sugar
crushed	1 teaspoon dry mustard
2 eggs, beaten	¼ cup vinegar
1 cup milk	¼ cup Worcestershire
½ teaspoon salt	sauce

Mix first seven ingredients together and pack into loaf pan. Bake at 350 degrees for 30 minutes. Reduce heat to 250 degrees and bake 1½ hours, basting frequently with sauce. To make sauce, combine warm water, brown sugar, dry mustard, vinegar and Worcestershire sauce.
Yield: 4 to 6 servings

Edna Reeves

Cajun Pork Roast

2 pound boneless single	Cooking oil
loin pork roast	

Cajun seasoning:

3 tablespoons paprika	½ teaspoon salt
½ teaspoon cayenne	½ teaspoon white pepper,
1 tablespoon garlic powder	ground
2 teaspoons oregano	½ teaspoon cumin
2 teaspoons thyme	¼ teaspoon nutmeg

Rub surface of pork lightly with oil. Rub seasoning mixture over all surfaces of pork. Place in a shallow pan. Roast in 350 degree oven for 1 hour or until meat thermometer reaches 155 degrees. Remove from oven, let rest 10 minutes. Slice and serve.
Yield: 4 to 6 servings

Caroline Frizoli

Easy Ribs

3 pounds spareribs
1 (14-ounce) bottle of
   ketchup
1¼ cups water
¼ cup vinegar
3 tablespoons brown sugar

1 tablespoon dry mustard
3 tablespoons
   Worcestershire sauce
2 teaspoons chili powder
Pinch ground cloves
Pinch garlic powder

Slice ribs into serving size pieces. Bake at 400 degrees for 30 minutes. Combine remaining ingredients, and pour over ribs. Reduce heat to 350 degrees, and bake for 1½ hours.
Yield: 2 to 4 servings

Jane Holman

Ribs - Wayne Style

3 slabs pork ribs
Dale's Steak Sauce, to taste
McCormick's Caribbean
   Jerk seasoning
McCormick's Hot Shot!
   Black and Red Pepper
   Blend

1 bottle red wine
1 onion, quartered
1 apple, quartered
1 orange, quartered
1 quart of water
Joe Kem's Barbecue Sauce

Rub 3 slabs of pork ribs with Dale's Sauce (just enough to rub all over). Sprinkle ribs with McCormick's Caribbean Jerk Seasoning and McCormick's Hot Shot! Black and Red Pepper Blend. Refrigerate for 2 to 3 hours. Prepare smoker water pan with red wine, onion, apple, orange, and water. To hot coals, add water-soaked hickory chips. Smoke ribs for 2 hours, then grill ribs over HOT coals for 5 minutes each side. Immediately wrap in aluminum foil for 30 minutes before serving. Serve with Joe Kem's Barbecue Sauce for dipping.
Yield: 10 servings

Sabrina Faison Odom

Grilled Pork Fillets With Peanut Sauce

**6 boneless pork chops
  (or venison)
2 tablespoons soy sauce**

**2 tablespoons
  Worcestershire sauce**

**Peanut Sauce:
¾ cup water
½ cup creamy peanut
  butter
2 cloves garlic, pressed
½ teaspoon curry powder**

**2 tablespoons brown sugar,
  firmly packed
2 tablespoons lemon juice
2 tablespoons soy sauce**

Pour 2 tablespoons soy sauce and Worcestershire sauce over chops. Let sit for about 30 minutes, making sure all surfaces are coated. Combine peanut sauce ingredients over medium heat until bubbling. Baste chops twice while grilling. Serve remaining as sauce.
Yield: 4 to 6 servings

Barbara B. Vereen

Pork Tenderloin

**1 whole pork tenderloin
2 to 4 slices bacon
1 tablespoon onion, grated
1 clove garlic, minced**

**1 tablespoon red wine
  vinegar
½ teaspoon sugar
½ cup soy sauce**

Wrap tenderloin with bacon. Mix remaining ingredients, and marinate tenderloin for 2 hours or longer. Bake uncovered at 300 degrees for 2 hours. This is delicious! So easy to prepare and good enough for company!
Yield: 4 to 6 servings

Jane Holman

Pork Tenderloin Cornichon

1 package pork tenderloins
   (usually 2 per package)
Salt and pepper to taste
½ cup butter
1 cup green onions,
   chopped (tops only)
½ cup red onion, chopped
2 cloves garlic, crushed

1 cup dried tomato,
   chopped coarsely and
   soaked in water to cover
1 cup white wine
½ cup French cornichon
2 tablespoons poupon
   mustard

Remove fat and any membrane from pork. Cut into medallions ½-inch thick on the diagonal. Salt and pepper to taste. Fry in melted butter until lightly browned. Remove from heat, and place on warmed serving platter. Cover loosely to keep warm. Add onions and garlic to pan juices. Sauté until translucent. Add tomatoes, juice, and white wine. Cook until slightly reduced. Add cornichon and poupon mustard. Cook until well-blended and bubbly. It will resemble a light gravy. Pour over pork medallions and serve immediately.
Yield: 4 servings

Sue Friedlander

Chicken Breasts in Cream

8 chicken breast halves,
skinned and boned
Salt and pepper
1 egg, beaten
Italian breadcrumbs
½ cup butter
¼ cup olive oil

2 cups heavy whipping
cream
½ teaspoon salt
3 or 4 plump garlic cloves,
crushed
½ pound mushrooms, sliced
½ teaspoon paprika

Season chicken breasts with salt and pepper. Dip in beaten egg, and roll in breadcrumbs. Sauté chicken in butter and olive oil until golden brown. Place in large baking dish. Over chicken breasts, pour heavy whipping cream mixed with salt and garlic. Cover with foil. At this point, you can refrigerate until ready to put in oven. Bake at 350 degrees 45 minutes to 1 hour. Add mushrooms 15 minutes before removing from oven. Dust with paprika before serving.
Yield: 8 servings

Carol Aguero

Country-Mustard Chicken

2 tablespoons Dijon
mustard
2 tablespoons low-fat
mayonnaise
2 scallions, sliced

½ teaspoon dried basil
1 clove garlic, crushed
¼ teaspoon pepper, freshly
ground
4 chicken breasts, halved

Mix mustard, mayonnaise, scallions, basil, garlic and pepper, and spread over chicken. Marinate chicken for 1 hour. Cover and bake chicken at 350 degrees for 1 hour. Baste occasionally.
Yield: 4 servings

Ann Friedlander

Chicken Bundles of Love

4 boneless, skinless chicken
  breast halves
¼ cup almond paste
4 to 6 ounces mozzarella
  cheese
¼ cup fresh breadcrumbs

½ cup butter
1 garlic clove, finely
  chopped
½ cup sherry
Pepper to taste

Preheat oven to 350 degrees. Lightly oil a large baking dish. Pound chicken breasts to flatten slightly. Spread the almond paste evenly over the breasts. Sprinkle with cheese and breadcrumbs. Roll the chicken over the filling and secure with toothpicks which form the bundles. In a large skillet, heat the butter over medium high heat. Add the garlic and cook for 1 minute, stirring constantly. Add the chicken and cook until the pieces are lightly browned, then transfer to the prepared baking dish. Add sherry to the skillet, stirring until combined. Pour the sauce over the chicken. Bake 20 to 25 minutes. Serve with wild rice and a medley of crisp cauliflower and broccoli florets.
Yield: 2 to 4 servings

Kim Jarrell

Chamber of Commerce Chicken

1 fryer, cut up
Salt and pepper
¾ cup lemon juice
1 tablespoon soy sauce

1 tablespoon
  Worcestershire sauce
Lawry's Seasoning Salt

Sprinkle chicken pieces with salt and pepper. Marinate chicken in lemon juice, soy sauce, and Worcestershire sauce several hours. This can be made the day before cooking. Sprinkle with Lawry's Seasoning Salt. Bake uncovered at 350 degrees for 1 hour.
Yield: 2 to 4 servings

Anne Norman
(Founding Member of Moultrie Service League)
*Similar recipe submitted by Harriett Whelchel

Chicken Casserole

1 box escort crackers, crumbled
1 stick butter, melted
4 chicken breasts, boiled and deboned
1 can cream of mushroom soup
1 can cream of chicken soup
1 (8-ounce) carton sour cream
1 small can water chestnuts, sliced

Pour butter over crackers. Mix well. Place ¾ of cracker mixture in baking dish. Place chicken over crackers. Mix soups, sour cream and water chestnuts. Pour over chicken. Top with remaining cracker mixture. Bake at 325 degrees to 350 degrees for 30 to 40 minutes. For variation, add ½ cup sherry wine to soup mixture.
Yield: 4 servings

Susan Newton
Similar recipe submitted by Nancy Paine

Country Captain Chicken

12 chicken breast halves
Oil
Flour
1 large onion, thinly sliced
2 green peppers, thinly sliced
1 stick margarine
4 (No. 2) cans of tomatoes
1½ teaspoons salt
1½ teaspoons pepper
½ box of raisins, plumped in hot water for 1 hour
1 cup almonds, toasted
Cooked rice

Flour and brown chicken breasts in oil. Place in large flat pan. Cook onion and peppers in margarine. Add tomatoes, salt, and pepper. Cook together for 5 minutes. Pour over chicken breasts, adding fat that chicken was browned in. Bake at 300 degrees for 2 hours or until tender. Cover pan with aluminum foil. Serve with raisins and almonds over rice.
Yield: 12 servings

Carol Ann Cannon

Chestnut Chicken Casserole

3 cups broccoli, cooked
2 cups chicken, cooked and
    cut in chunks
1 cup celery, chopped and
    cooked 1 minute in
    microwave
1 cup rice, cooked
1 can cream of mushroom
    soup
2 eggs, beaten
1 small onion, chopped

½ cup mayonnaise
¼ cup sour cream
¼ cup bell pepper, chopped
1 tablespoon MSG
¼ cup pimiento
1 small can water
    chestnuts, sliced
½ cup almonds, sliced
1 cup cornflakes, crushed
½ cup butter, melted

Line a 3-quart casserole dish with broccoli. Mix all ingredients (except cornflakes and melted butter) together, and spread on top of broccoli. Top with cornflakes and drizzle with melted butter. Bake at 350 degrees for 50 minutes.
Yield: 6 to 8 servings

Jan Smith

Chicketti

2 cups chicken, cooked and
    diced
¼ cup pimiento, drained
    and diced
¼ cup green pepper,
    chopped
⅛ teaspoon pepper

½ cup onion, chopped
1 can mushroom soup
½ cup chicken broth
½ teaspoon salt
½ pound cheese, grated
1¼ cups spaghetti, cooked
    and drained

Place diced chicken, pimiento, green pepper and onion in a 3-quart casserole. Mix together soup, broth, salt, pepper, cheese, and spaghetti. Layer on top of chicken. Bake at 350 degrees for 45 minutes.
Yield: 6 servings

Ellen Dekle Alderman

Crescent Chicken Casserole

1 package crescent rolls
2 cups chicken, cooked and
    chopped
1 cup cheese, shredded

1 can cream of chicken
    soup
1 soup can milk
1 (2-ounce) jar pimiento,
    drained and chopped

Separate crescent rolls. Mix chicken and cheese. Place 3 table-spoons of chicken mixture in each crescent roll. Roll from large end to small end. Place in lightly greased baking dish. Add soup, milk and pimiento to remaining chicken, and mix well. Pour this sauce over chicken crescents. Bake at 350 degrees for 30 minutes.
Yield: 6 to 8 servings

Jennie Estes

Biddie Clarke's Curried Chicken

½ cup onion, chopped
½ cup celery, chopped
4 tablespoons butter
⅓ cup flour
2 cups chicken stock,
    skimmed for fat
1 cup tomato juice

½ teaspoon Worcestershire
    sauce
1 teaspoon curry powder
Salt and pepper to taste
4 cups chicken, cooked and
    diced

Simmer onion and celery in butter. Add flour and mix well. Add stock gradually. Cook until smooth and thick. Add other season-ings, tomato juice and chicken. Simmer awhile. Serve over hot rice with condiments on the side (raisins, fresh or toasted coconut, crushed or broken cashews, chutney, etc.).
Yield: 6 to 8 servings

Connie Mobley
*Similar recipe submitted by Barbara Hendrick

Mimi's Chicken Curry

2 (3-pound) chickens,
   cooked and cut in large
   pieces
4 onions, chopped
¾ pound butter
1 clove garlic

6 tablespoons flour
3 tablespoons curry
2 cups whipping cream
4 chicken bouillon cubes,
   dissolved in 2 cups
   water

Sauté onion in butter. Add the whole clove of garlic. Remove when garlic is brown. Add flour and curry. Stir. Add cream and bouillon dissolved in water. Put chicken in sauce. Simmer on low about 30 minutes. Serve over rice.

Optional condiments:
1 pound bacon, crumbled
1 pint chutney
4 eggs, hard boiled (put
   whites and yolks
   separately through
   grater)

1 package of coconut,
   toasted

Arrange condiments in separate dishes. Allow guests to serve themselves.
Yield: 8 to 10 servings

Mimi Platter

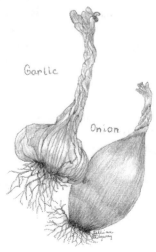

Garlic

Onion

Chicken Diabla

10 to 12 mushrooms, sliced
2 teaspoons butter
1 (8-ounce) package cream
   cheese
1 jar Dijon mustard

½ box brown sugar
8 chicken breast halves,
   deboned
Salt and pepper
Pecan pieces

Sauté mushrooms in butter until soft. Add cream cheese to butter and mushrooms. In a separate bowl, mix mustard with brown sugar. Pound chicken breasts until thin. Sprinkle with salt and pepper. Stuff chicken breasts with cream cheese mixture, and place in a baking dish. Spoon mustard sauce over top of chicken. Sprinkle with pecans. Bake at 425 degrees for 30 to 45 minutes.
Yield: 8 servings

Sally Tyndall

Chicken Divine

2 (10-ounce) packages
   frozen broccoli, cooked
6 to 8 chicken breasts,
   halved, cut in strips and
   cooked
2 cans cream of chicken
   soup
1 cup mayonnaise

Juice of one lemon
1 teaspoon curry powder
1 cup Cheddar cheese,
   shredded
½ cup soft breadcrumbs
1 tablespoon margarine,
   melted

Arrange cooked broccoli in 3-quart baking dish. Layer cooked chicken over broccoli. Combine next 4 ingredients and pour over chicken. Sprinkle cheese over mixture. Mix breadcrumbs and melted margarine, and spread over top of casserole. Bake at 350 degrees for 30 to 35 minutes. May be put together and then frozen before cooking.
Yield: 6 to 8 servings

Joan Holman

Dinner Theater Chicken

¼ cup butter
4 to 6 chicken breast
   halves, deboned
1 clove garlic, minced
1 onion, minced
Salt and pepper

2 tablespoons all-purpose
   flour
1 cup hot chicken stock
¼ cup white wine
Cooked rice

Sauté chicken in butter until well browned. Add onion, garlic, salt and pepper. Combine flour and stock. Add to chicken. Pour in wine. Cover and cook slowly for 1 hour. Serve with rice.
Yield: 6 servings

This recipe was given to me by the late Susan Sheldon, former President of the Moultrie Service League.

Diane Moore

Chicken Elegant

1 cup fresh mushrooms,
   sliced
2 tablespoons butter or
   margarine
1 can cream of shrimp soup
3 tablespoons light cream
¼ cup white wine

2 cups chicken, cooked and
   cubed
1 tablespoon parsley,
   chopped
6 party shells, prepared as
   directed

In pan, brown mushrooms in butter. Add remaining ingredients, except party shells. Heat thoroughly, stirring several times. Serve over party shells. Can also be served over rice. Garnish with parsley if desired.
Yield: 4 servings

Susan Blanton

Chicken Enchiladas

Enchilada Sauce: (makes 2½ cups)
2½ cups tomato sauce
2 tablespoons oil
1 tablespoon ground cumin
¾ teaspoon chili powder
¼ teaspoon pepper

Smothering Sauce:
1½ cups Enchilada Sauce
1¼ cups stewed tomatoes
¼ cup green chilies, drained and chopped

Chicken filling:
3 cups chicken, cooked and shredded
1 medium onion, chopped
1½ cups tomatoes, drained and stewed
¾ cup green chilies, drained and chopped
¾ cup black olives, sliced
1 teaspoon chili powder
1 teaspoon ground cumin
½ teaspoon pepper
10 (8-inch) flour tortillas
1 pound Cheddar cheese, grated
1 pound Monterey Jack cheese, grated

Preheat oven to 350 degrees. Combine tomato sauce, oil, cumin, chili powder and pepper in medium-size saucepan. Simmer for 30 minutes. Combine 1½ cups Enchilada Sauce, tomatoes and chilies to make Smothering Sauce. Combine chicken, onion, tomatoes, chilies, olives, chili powder, cumin and pepper in large saucepan or Dutch oven. Simmer for 15 minutes. Assemble by brushing inside of tortillas with 2 tablespoons Enchilada Sauce. Top each tortilla with 3 to 4 tablespoons of chicken mixture. Mix grated cheeses. Place 2 to 3 tablespoons cheese on each tortilla and roll. Place rolls, seam down, in 9 x 13-inch baking dish. Add remaining Enchilada Sauce to Smothering Sauce and pour over enchiladas. Top with remaining cheese. Bake at 350 degrees for 20 to 25 minutes. Garnish with parsley. Serve with sour cream and guacamole as toppings if desired.
Yield: 8 servings

Peggy Benner

Cheesy Chicken Enchiladas

3 chicken breasts, cooked
and chopped
2 cans cream of mushroom
soup
1 (8-ounce) carton sour
cream
1 (4-ounce) can green
chilies, drained and
chopped
½ cup onion, chopped

Salt and pepper to taste
½ teaspoon garlic powder
2 cups Cheddar cheese,
shredded
1 cup green onions,
chopped
1 package (12) corn or flour
tortillas
Vegetable oil

Combine soup, sour cream, half of the green chilies and onion. Add salt, pepper and garlic powder. Mix and cook over low heat until warm enough to melt ¾ cup of the cheese. Heat oil in small fry pan, and cook tortillas until just soft. Drain on paper towels. Spoon about 2 tablespoons of the soup mixture into the center of each tortilla. Add chicken. Sprinkle some chilies, green onions, and a little cheese, and roll tortillas tightly. Pour some of the soup mixture into a 9 x 13-inch casserole dish, then add the rolls of tortillas. Spoon remaining soup mixture over the top and use any remaining onion, chilies or cheese on top. Bake at 350 degrees partly covered with foil about 20 minutes. Uncover and continue to bake until hot and bubbly. This can be prepared in advance for freezing, or made as 2 smaller casseroles—one for now and one for later.
Yield: 6 servings

Sue Friedlander

Arlene's League Fruited Chicken

16 chicken breast halves
4 tablespoons dried
　oregano
Salt and pepper
1 cup red wine vinegar
½ cup olive oil
1 cup pitted prunes

1 cup dried apricots
⅓ jar capers, plus juice
8 bay leaves
1 cup green olives, sliced
1 cup brown sugar
1 cup dry white wine

Wash chicken. Combine all ingredients except the brown sugar and white wine. Cover and refrigerate overnight to marinate. Preheat oven to 350 degrees. Arrange chicken and marinade in a shallow pan with sides. Sprinkle with brown sugar and wine. Bake 1 hour until done. Cover immediately with foil to keep warm until serving time.
Yield: 16 servings

Debbie Cagle

King Ranch Casserole

1 can cream of mushroom
　soup
1 can cream of chicken
　soup
½ can chicken broth
½ can Rotel tomatoes,
　chopped

1 chicken, cooked and
　deboned
1 onion, chopped
1 package corn tortillas
2 cups cheese, grated

Mix soups, tomatoes and broth. Dice chicken. Place in buttered casserole, alternating with onions, tortillas and soup mixture in layers. Top with grated cheese. Bake at 350 degrees for 45 minutes. "A Texas favorite."
Yield: 6 to 8 servings

Cheryle Reeves

Creamy Chicken and Ham Medley

6 tablespoons butter or
margarine (divided)
½ cup fresh mushrooms,
sliced
⅓ cup all-purpose flour
2½ to 3 cups milk (divided)
1 cup whipping cream
1 cup Parmesan cheese,
freshly grated
½ teaspoon salt
¼ teaspoon ground black
pepper

¼ teaspoon ground nutmeg
Dash of ground red pepper
2 cups chicken, cooked and
chopped
2 cups ham, cooked and
chopped
2 (10-ounce) packages
frozen puff pastry
shells, baked
Paprika

Melt 1 tablespoon butter in a large saucepan over medium heat.
Add mushrooms, and cook until tender, stirring constantly. Remove from saucepan, and set aside. Melt remaining butter in a
saucepan over low heat. Add flour, stirring until smooth. Cook 1
minute, stirring constantly. Gradually add 2½ cups milk. Cook
over medium heat, stirring constantly, until thickened and bubbly.
Stir in whipping cream and next 5 ingredients. Cook, stirring
constantly, until cheese melts and mixture is smooth. Stir in
chicken and ham. Add enough of remaining ½ cup milk for thinner
consistency, if desired. To serve, spoon into shells, and sprinkle
with paprika.
Yield: 12 servings

Moultrie Service League Luncheon Series

Kalaris Chicken Marinade

6 chicken breast halves
3 garlic cloves, crushed
1½ teaspoons salt
½ cup brown sugar, packed
3 tablespoons grainy
    mustard (coarse ground)

¼ cup cider vinegar
Juice of 1 or 2 limes
Juice of ½ or 1 large lemon
6 tablespoons olive oil
Black pepper

Mix all ingredients and marinate chicken overnight if possible. Let stand at room temperature for 1 hour before grilling.
Yield: 6 servings

Kim Jarrell

My Original Chicken Parmigiana

8 chicken breasts, skinless
    and boneless
1 cup all-purpose flour
3 eggs, beaten
2 cups Progresso Italian
    Breadcrumbs
Cooking oil

1 (3-ounce) package
    Parmesan cheese,
    grated
2 cans Italian tomato sauce
2 tablespoons Italian
    seasoning
6 ounces mozzarella
    cheese, shredded
Cooked pasta

Dip chicken in flour, egg, and breadcrumbs in that order. In a large pan, heat oil and brown chicken on both sides until golden brown. Put chicken in a large baking dish. Sprinkle Parmesan cheese over chicken. Add both cans of tomato sauce, and sprinkle Italian seasoning over sauce. Add mozzarella cheese. Bake at 350 degrees for 20 to 30 minutes. Serve with pasta.
Yield: 8 servings

Carolyn Lodge
*Similar recipe submitted by Mary Ann Blank

Chicken Noodle Casserole

1 (8-ounce) package short
   curly noodles
3 cups chicken, cooked and
   diced
1½ cups cottage cheese

2 cups sharp Cheddar
   cheese, grated
½ cup Parmesan cheese
2½ cups mushroom sauce

Mushroom sauce:
½ stick butter
3 tablespoons flour
1 cup half and half
1 can cream of mushroom
   soup

1 jar mushrooms, sliced
   and drained
½ cup onion, diced
½ cup bell pepper, chopped

Grease 3-quart casserole dish. Prepare noodles as per package directions. Drain. Prepare mushroom sauce by melting butter and stirring in flour. Add half and half, and stir until thickens. Pour in mushroom soup, mushrooms, onion and bell pepper. Alternate noodles, chicken, mushroom sauce, cottage cheese, Cheddar cheese and Parmesan cheese. Repeat layers. This should be made one day ahead and refrigerated overnight. Bake covered with foil at 350 degrees for 45 minutes or until very hot. Uncover for the last 5 minutes.
Yield: 8 servings

Sandra Plant

Chicken Pockets

2 cups chicken, cooked and
  diced
1 (3-ounce) package cream
  cheese, softened
1 small onion, chopped
¼ to ½ cup sliced water
  chestnuts, chopped
⅓ cup mushrooms, chopped
1 teaspoon lemon pepper

2 tablespoons soft butter
1 large package crescent
  rolls
3 tablespoons butter
½ cup Pepperidge Farm
  dressing
½ cup pecans, chopped
1 can cream of chicken
  soup

Mix first 7 ingredients together. Drop large spoonful of mixture into triangle of crescent roll, fold and crease. Melt 3 tablespoons of butter. Drizzle on top of crescent rolls. Mix dressing with pecans. Dip each buttered roll in dressing mixture and place in casserole dish. Bake at 375 degrees for 15 to 20 minutes. Warm a slightly diluted can of cream of chicken soup, and use as a sauce on top of rolls when serving. For a busy day, prepare in advance and freeze before baking. Put straight in oven from freezer. For variation, substitute turkey for chicken.
Yield: 8 servings

Paula Neely
Similar recipe submitted by Rhonda Sauls

Sherried Chicken

8 boned chicken breasts
All-purpose flour
½ cup margarine
½ cup sherry

2 tablespoons soy sauce
2 tablespoons lemon juice
1 teaspoon ground ginger
¼ cup butter, melted

Flour breasts and brown in margarine. Place in shallow Pyrex dish. Stir together and heat sherry, soy sauce, lemon juice, ginger, and butter. Pour over chicken. Cover with foil and bake at 350 degrees for 1½ hours.
Yield: 8 servings

Joan Holman

Quick and Easy Chicken Pot Pie

1 package Pillsbury pie
    crusts
2 cans cream of chicken
    soup
4 to 5 chicken breast halves,
    cooked and diced

1 large can Veg-All, drained
1 small can mushrooms,
    drained
Garlic salt
Onion salt
Pepper

Lightly grease pie plate. Place one pie crust in pie plate. Mix soup, chicken, Veg-All and mushrooms. Add seasonings to taste. Place this mixture in the middle of pie crust. Mound with more in the middle and taper down to sides. Follow directions on pie crust box to assemble the second pie crust on pie plate. Cover edges of pie crust with tin-foil to prevent burning. Bake at 375 degrees for 45 minutes. Remove tin-foil and continue baking about 15 more minutes or until edges are lightly browned. Let cool for a few minutes to thicken sauce and serve.
Yield: 8 servings

Susie Mobley Cross
*Similar recipe submitted by Debbie Brown

Chicken Wild Rice Casserole

1 package wild rice
Chicken broth
3 cups chicken, cooked and
    chopped
1 can cream of celery soup
1 small jar pimientos,
    drained and chopped

1 small onion, chopped
½ cup mayonnaise
1 can sliced water
    chestnuts, drained and
    chopped

Cook wild rice in chicken broth rather than water as directed on package. Combine all ingredients and place in a casserole dish. Bake at 325 degrees for 30 minutes or until heated through.
Yield: 6 servings

Jessica Jordan

Russian Chicken

6 to 8 chicken breasts or
   pieces
1 (8-ounce) bottle Russian
   dressing
1 (8-ounce) jar apricot
   preserves

1 envelope onion soup mix
¼ cup water
1 pineapple slice for each
   chicken piece

Place chicken in Pyrex dish. Mix remaining ingredients except pineapple and pour over chicken. Cover with foil. Bake at 350 degrees for 1 hour. Uncover and place pineapple on chicken. Cook ½ hour more uncovered.
Yield: 6 to 8 servings

Kristy Allen

Chicken Ruxton

1 chicken, cooked and cut up
1 tablespoon lemon juice
1 can cream of chicken soup
1 cup sour cream
1 teaspoon salt
1 cup celery, chopped
2 eggs, hard-cooked and
   chopped

1 (3-ounce) can sliced
   mushrooms, drained
1½ cups potato chips,
   crumbled
1 small package slivered
   almonds
1 cup Cheddar cheese,
   shredded

Combine first 8 ingredients and mix together well. Pour in a casserole dish. Top with chips, almonds and cheese. Bake at 400 degrees for 25 to 30 minutes.
Yield: 8 to 10 servings

Moultrie Service League Luncheon Series

Swiss Chicken

8 chicken breast halves,
  skinned and boned
8 slices Swiss cheese
1 (10¾-ounce) can cream of
  chicken soup, undiluted

¼ cup dry white wine
¾ cup herb-seasoned
  stuffing mix, crushed
¼ cup butter, melted

Arrange chicken in greased 13 x 9-inch dish. Top each breast with cheese slice. Combine soup and wine, mixing well. Spoon sauce over chicken. Sprinkle with stuffing. Drizzle butter over stuffing. Bake at 350 degrees for 45 to 55 minutes.
Yield: 8 servings

Polly Jackson
Similar recipe submitted by JoAnn Caldwell

Texas Chicken

1 (3 to 4-pound) fryer,
  cooked and deboned
1 green pepper, chopped
1 large onion, chopped
1½ cups celery, chopped
½ cup oil
2 cups chicken stock
1 can tomato soup
1 can mushroom soup

1 clove garlic, minced
1 can sliced water
  chestnuts
Worcestershire sauce
Tabasco
1 cup stuffed olives,
  chopped
Cooked rice or Chinese
  noodles

Cut chicken into medium-sized chunks. In large pot cook pepper, onion and celery in oil until clear. Stir in chicken broth, soups, garlic and water chestnuts. Add chicken, Worcestershire sauce, and Tabasco to taste. Cook very slowly. Add olives, but do not stir much. Cook 30 minutes. Serve over rice or Chinese noodles.
Yield: 6 to 8 servings

Barbara Hendrick

Anne's Chicken Tetrazzini

8 ounces medium egg
  noodles
1 (4½-ounce) jar sliced
  mushrooms, liquid
  reserved
4 tablespoons margarine
3 tablespoons onions,
  chopped
½ teaspoon celery salt
Few grains cayenne pepper
¼ teaspoon marjoram

1 can cream of chicken soup
1 (12-ounce) can evaporated
  milk
4 cups chicken, cooked and
  cubed
2 tablespoons pimiento,
  chopped
½ cup sharp Cheddar
  cheese, grated
¼ cup Parmesan cheese,
  grated

Cook noodles until tender. Drain and rinse with hot water. Drain mushrooms saving liquid. Melt margarine in large pan. Sauté onions. Reduce heat, and add seasonings and mushroom liquid. Blend in soup, and stir until smooth. Gradually add evaporated milk. Stir until smooth and thickened. Add chicken, mushrooms and pimiento to sauce. Combine with noodles, mixing well. Place in casserole. Top with Cheddar cheese and Parmesan. Bake in preheated oven at 350 degrees for 30 minutes or until bubbly.
Yield: 6 servings

Jane H. Brown
*Similar recipe submitted by Gail Qurnell

Tomato Sage Chicken

1 cup chicken stock
1 large onion, thinly sliced
3 garlic cloves, minced
1 tablespoon white wine
   vinegar
4 chicken breasts, boneless,
   skinless and each cut
   into 3 pieces

2 (16-ounce) cans crushed
   tomatoes
2 tablespoons balsamic
   vinegar
2 tablespoons fresh sage
   leaves
Salt and freshly ground
   pepper

In 4-quart pan warm chicken stock. Add onion, garlic and wine vinegar. Simmer until softened, about 5 minutes. Add chicken pieces and continue to simmer 5 to 10 minutes until the chicken is golden on all sides. Stir in tomatoes, balsamic vinegar and sage. Cover partially, and simmer over medium heat, stirring occasionally, for 30 minutes. Uncover and cook another 5 to 10 minutes if the sauce needs to thicken. Salt and pepper to taste and mix well.
Yield: 4 servings

Harriett Whelchel

Chicken Veronique

¼ cup all-purpose flour
1 teaspoon salt
½ teaspoon pepper
8 chicken breast halves,
   skinned and boned

½ cup butter or margarine,
   melted
Leaf lettuce
1 tablespoon currant jelly
⅔ cup Madeira wine
Green or red grapes

Combine first 3 ingredients, and dredge chicken in flour mixture. Sauté chicken in butter in a large skillet until golden brown on each side. Cover, reduce heat, and cook 15 minutes or until tender. Remove chicken to lettuce lined platter, reserving pan drippings. Stir jelly and wine into pan drippings. Cook until thoroughly heated. Spoon sauce over chicken. Serve with grapes.
Yield: 8 servings

Kim Jarrell

Turkey Hash

1 (12 to 16-pound) turkey
2 cans chicken broth
3 cups celery, diced
4 cans cream of mushroom
  soup

2 cans cream of celery soup
2 cans cream of chicken
  soup
1½ (7-ounce) jars pimiento,
  drained and diced

Cook turkey, debone and cut into bite-sized pieces. Cook celery in 2 cans chicken broth. Mix undiluted soups together. (Rinse each can with just a little water to get all the soup and add this to soups.) Add celery and stock to soup mixture. Add diced pimiento to soup mixture, which should make 1 gallon of sauce. Add cut-up turkey to sauce just before serving. Heat thoroughly and serve over cornbread squares.
Yield: 10 to 12 servings

Bill Sells

Lime-Buttered Turkey Tenderloins

¼ cup butter or margarine,
  melted
¼ cup lime juice
2 teaspoons dry mustard

2 teaspoons garlic salt
2 (¾-pound) turkey breasts
Lime wedges and fresh
  parsley to garnish

Combine first 4 ingredients; divide in half, and set aside. Grill covered turkey over medium-hot coals (350 degrees to 400 degrees) 4 to 5 minutes on each side or until meat thermometer registers 170 degrees. Turn once and baste often with half of marinade. Cook remaining marinade in a small saucepan until thoroughly heated. Serve warm with sliced turkey. Garnish, if desired.
Yield: 4 to 6 servings

Harriett Whelchel

Crab Casserole

1 pound imitation
  crabmeat
1 large can chunky Veg-All
2½ cups sharp cheese,
  grated (divided)

2 to 3 tablespoons
  mayonnaise
1 cup Ritz crackers,
  crushed

Mix together crabmeat, Veg-All, 1½ cups of grated cheese and mayonnaise, adding additional mayonnaise if needed to make ingredients stick together. Spread in greased casserole dish. Top with Ritz crackers and remaining cheese. Bake at 350 degrees for 30 to 35 minutes.
Yield: 4 to 6 servings

Pam Rojas

Crab Mornay

½ cup margarine (divided)
1 medium onion, finely
  chopped
1 tablespoon green pepper,
  finely chopped
3 tablespoons pimiento,
  drained
6 tablespoons all-purpose
  flour
2 cups chicken broth
1 cup whipping cream

1 (4-ounce) package
  Gruyère cheese, grated
  (may substitute)
¼ cup Parmesan cheese,
  grated
Salt, pepper and seasoning
  salt to taste
1 pound crabmeat
1 (2½-ounce) jar sliced
  mushrooms, with juice
½ cup white wine
8 pastry shells, cooked

Sauté onion, green peppers and pimiento in 2 tablespoons of margarine. Melt remaining margarine. Add flour, stirring until it becomes a smooth paste. Pour in broth and cream, stirring constantly until thick. Add sautéed ingredients, cheeses and seasonings. Fold in crabmeat, mushrooms with juice and wine. Stir until heated through, and serve over pastry shells.
Yield: 8 servings

149

The Original Bayne Crab Gumbo

½ cup all-purpose flour
½ cup bacon drippings (or oil)
1 large onion, chopped
1 to 2 cloves garlic, minced
1 can tomatoes
½ pound okra, sliced (1 can if fresh is unavailable)
1 bell pepper, chopped
2 quarts water
1 cup tiny green butter beans
2 ears corn, cut from cob
1 tablespoon parsley, chopped
Salt, pepper and Tabasco to taste
1 bay leaf
Meat of 8 crabs

In large pot, brown flour in bacon drippings. Add onion and garlic. Stir to brown. Add tomatoes, okra and bell pepper. Cook a few minutes. Add about 2 quarts of water, and bring to a boil. Add remaining ingredients, and cook on low heat at least 1 hour, stirring often. Serve this with cooked rice and the crab claws alongside to make a beautiful meal.
Yield: 4 servings

Mica Bayne Copeland

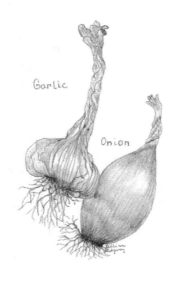

Garlic

Onion

Deviled Crab

1 pound crabmeat, well-
cleaned
2 stalks celery, chopped
1½ teaspoons onion juice
½ cup breadcrumbs
4 tablespoons butter,
melted
1 tablespoon all-purpose
flour

¼ teaspoon salt
1 teaspoon lemon juice
1 teaspoon Worcestershire
sauce
½ teaspoon mustard
Tabasco to taste (chili
sauce or ketchup may
be substituted)
Buttered breadcrumbs

Mix the first 4 ingredients together. Place in well-greased casserole dish. Make a sauce with the butter, flour, salt, lemon juice, Worcestershire, mustard and Tabasco. Pour over the crab mixture. Top with buttered breadcrumbs. Bake in 350 degree oven until heated through and breadcrumbs are browned.
Yield: 2 to 4 servings

Rhett Smith

Scalloped Oysters

1 pint oysters
2 cups cracker crumbs
½ teaspoon salt
⅛ teaspoon pepper
½ cup butter, melted

¼ teaspoon Worcestershire
sauce
1 cup milk or cream
Dash of Tabasco sauce

Drain and pick oysters clean. Combine cracker crumbs, salt, pepper and butter. Sprinkle ⅓ in a buttered casserole. Cover with layer of oysters. Repeat layer. Add Worcestershire and Tabasco to milk, and pour over contents. Sprinkle remaining crumbs over top. Bake in 350 degree oven for 30 minutes.
Yield: 6 servings

Edna Reeves

Broiled Swordfish with Mustard Sauce

¼ cup white wine
2 tablespoons spring onions, minced
¼ cup whipping cream
1 cup unsalted butter, cut into pieces (divided)
¼ cup fresh lemon juice

2 tablespoons coarse grain mustard
Salt and pepper to taste
4 (8-ounce) swordfish steaks (1-inch thick)
2 tablespoons olive oil
2 tablespoons fresh basil, parsley and/or tarragon

Boil wine and onions 3 minutes. Add whipping cream and boil for 3 minutes. Remove from heat, and whisk in 2 tablespoons of butter. Set on low heat and add remaining butter. Whisk in lemon juice, mustard, salt and pepper. Preheat broiler. Place fish in large dish and drizzle with oil. Sprinkle with herbs. Turn to coat. Let stand 5 minutes. Broil fish 3 minutes per side. Divide sauce among fish.
Yield: 4 servings

Debbie Cagle

Fish with Summer Squash Relish

Butter
½ cup green pepper, chopped
1 zucchini, sliced
¾ cup yellow squash, sliced
½ cup tomato, chopped

1 tablespoon parsley
1 tablespoon fresh basil
1 tablespoon fresh oregano
2 teaspoons brown sugar
1 pound fresh fish

Sauté vegetables with butter and seasonings in a large skillet. Remove from pan. Add more butter to skillet and sauté fish until done. Add vegetables to fish and heat.
Yield: 2 to 4 servings

Anna C. Carlton

Grilled Red Snapper

½ cup butter   2 snapper fillets
1 package Dip-idy-dill

Melt butter and add Dip-idy-dill. Simmer for 10 minutes. Remove from heat and let cool to room temperature. Place fillets on foil and place in covered grill. Baste fillets using ½ or less of Dip-idy-dill mixture. Fillets are done when fish flakes with a fork. Pour remaining Dip-idy-dill sauce over fish. (Dip-idy-dill can be found in gourmet stores, in Moultrie at Julian Bridges Florist.)
Yield: 2 servings

Polly Jackson

Grilled Salmon Mediterranean

Marinade:
1 tablespoon capers   Fresh black pepper, ground
1 tablespoon olive oil   1 pound fresh salmon
3 tablespoons white wine   fillets, ½ to ¾-inch thick
2 tablespoons lemon juice   1 teaspoon olive oil
1 clove garlic, crushed   Lemon wedges, fresh
½ teaspoon dried rosemary,   cilantro or parsley for
   crushed   garnish
¼ teaspoon salt

Place capers in a strainer, rinsing under cold water. Drain well. Combine all marinade ingredients in shallow glass dish. Arrange fish in dish. Marinate 20 minutes, turning once after 10 minutes. Brush a foil-lined baking sheet with oil, and arrange fish on sheet. Pour ½ of marinade over steaks. Broil for about 4 minutes or until slightly seared. Turn with a spatula, and pour remaining marinade over fillets. Broil another 4 minutes or until fish flakes easily with fork. Garnish with lemon slices and fresh cilantro or parsley if desired. Can substitute tuna or yellowtail for salmon.
Yield: 4 servings

Mary Campagna

Scamp With Slivered Almonds

Scamp fillets or other white flesh fish, skinless (such as Trigger or Grouper)
½ cup butter or margarine

1 egg, beaten
2 packages slivered almonds
Salt
Pepper
Flour to dust fish

Scamp is seasonal and comes from the Destin area. It is a true delicacy with a unique flavor. Melt butter in frying pan until foamy. Dip fillets in beaten egg, thinned with a little water. Allow excess to drip. Press slivered almonds on both sides and lightly sift on a little flour, salt and pepper. Slowly fry a few pieces at a time so as not to crowd. Avoid getting the pan too hot, so the almonds and butter don't burn. Fry very slowly turning only once. Cooking time will depend upon thickness of the fish.

Yield: 4 servings

Sue Friedlander

Baked Shrimp

2 pounds raw shrimp
1 cup butter
1 tablespoon salt
1 tablespoon pepper
1 tablespoon red pepper
2 large onions, sliced
3 cloves garlic, chopped
1 (11-ounce) can mandarin oranges, drained

1 cup green onion tops, chopped (optional)
3 stalks celery, chopped
2 medium bell peppers, chopped
2 hot peppers, chopped
2 lemons, sliced
2 tablespoons Worcestershire sauce

Place shrimp in deep baking pan. Put all other ingredients over shrimp, stir gently. Bake at 350 degrees for 30 minutes, stirring every 5 minutes. Serve with French bread. Place the cooked dish in the center of your table and let everyone dip their bread in the spicy sauce. Very casual - very good!

Yield: 6 servings

Nanci Lewis

Sherried Seafood

½ cup butter
1 pint half and half
5 heaping tablespoons all-
    purpose flour
1 pound sharp cheese,
    grated (divided)
2 medium cans mushrooms,
    undrained
1 cup sherry

2 pounds crabmeat
3 pounds shrimp, cooked
    and deveined
3 eggs, hard boiled
Ground pepper
Worcestershire sauce
Tabasco
Buttered cracker crumbs

Melt butter in saucepan. Stir in flour. Add half and half, stirring to make a thick cream sauce. Add ¾ of grated cheese. Then add next 5 ingredients. Season to taste with ground pepper, Worcestershire sauce and Tabasco. Top with buttered cracker crumbs and remaining cheese. Bake at 350 degrees for 35 minutes. May be prepared in advance and refrigerated. This makes a great meal served with boiled corn, green salad and rolls.
Yield: 15 servings

Bug Trimble

Katrina's Shrimp Casserole

1 cup sliced mushrooms,
    juice reserved
¼ cup margarine
1½ pounds shrimp, cooked
½ cup sharp cheese, grated

½ pint whipped cream
½ cup ketchup
1 teaspoon Worcestershire
    sauce
2 cups cooked rice

Sauté mushrooms and juice in margarine. Add shrimp and cheese. Keep over heat until cheese begins to melt. Then add cream, ketchup, and Worcestershire. Cook 1 to 2 minutes. Pour over rice in casserole dish, and bake at 350 degrees for 45 minutes.
Yield: 4 servings

Katrina McIntosh

Shrimp and Artichoke Casserole

½ pound fresh mushrooms, sliced
6 tablespoons butter (divided)
1½ pounds fresh shrimp, peeled and deveined or use a combination with crab meat or scallops
2 cans artichoke hearts, rinsed and drained, then quartered
¼ cup flour

1½ cups half and half
⅓ cup dry sherry
1 tablespoon Worcestershire sauce
Salt and ground pepper to taste
¼ teaspoon paprika
½ cup Parmesan cheese, grated
Cooked rice, white or brown

Preheat oven to 350 degrees. Sauté mushrooms in 2 tablespoons butter until soft. Layer a 9 x 13-inch casserole dish with mushrooms, artichokes and seafood. Melt remaining butter, and add flour. Cook and stir for 3 minutes. Gradually add cream, and cook until sauce is thickened. Add sherry, Worcestershire, salt, pepper and paprika. Pour over casserole and sprinkle with Parmesan. Bake 30 minutes or until bubbly hot and lightly browned. Serve over cooked rice, white or brown.

Yield: 6 servings

Sue Friedlander

Curried Shrimp

1 cup butter
1 large apple, peeled and
    chopped
1 cup celery, chopped
1 large onion, chopped
2 teaspoons curry powder
5 tablespoons all-purpose
    flour
2½ cups chicken broth
1 tablespoon lemon juice
1 cup heavy cream

Paprika
Nutmeg
Worcestershire sauce
Ginger
Salt and pepper
2 to 4 cups fresh shrimp,
    cooked and deveined
½ cup seedless raisins
2 tablespoons mango
    chutney
Cooked rice

Melt butter in skillet. Add apple, celery, onion and cook gently for 5 minutes. Sprinkle curry and flour over mixture until blended. Remove from heat. Add chicken broth and lemon juice. Then pour in cream and mix well. Return to heat and cook until thick. Sprinkle with seasonings. Add shrimp, raisins, chutney, and simmer for 15 minutes. Do not overcook. Serve with rice.
Yield: 4 to 5 servings

Mary Ann Blank

Grilled Shrimp

2 pounds jumbo shrimp,
  peeled
1 cup salad oil
1 cup lemon juice
2 teaspoons Italian salad
  dressing mix
2 teaspoons Mrs. Dash

1 teaspoon lemon pepper
1 teaspoon Worcestershire
  sauce
4 tablespoons brown sugar
¼ cup green onion,
  chopped
2 tablespoons soy sauce

Place shrimp in a large bowl. Mix oil, lemon juice, salad mix, Mrs. Dash, pepper and Worcestershire sauce. Pour over shrimp. Marinate in refrigerator for 2 to 4 hours or more, stirring occasionally. Put on skewers and grill, 10 minutes or until done, basting occasionally. Pour remaining marinade into pan. Stir in brown sugar, soy sauce and onion. Heat to boiling. Serve as a dip for shrimp.
Yield: 4 to 6 servings

Polly Jackson

Ida's Shrimp

½ pound butter
1 cup all-purpose flour
3½ cups milk
½ pint half and half
½ pint heavy cream
1½ teaspoons dry mustard
2 teaspoons dill weed
½ teaspoon curry powder
2 teaspoons Worcestershire
  sauce

1 small can Parmesan
  cheese
Dash garlic powder
Lemon pepper and salt to
  taste
5 pounds shrimp, boiled
  and cleaned
5 slices thin bacon, fried
  crisp and crumbled
2 tablespoons dry sherry

Make white sauce of butter, flour and milk, stirring constantly with wire whisk to keep from lumping. Add creams, seasonings and remainder of ingredients. Just before serving, add dry sherry. This is great served over Chinese noodles or fluffy rice.
Yield: 8 to 10 servings

Ida Murphy

Shrimp and Crab Au Gratin

4 tablespoons butter
4 tablespoons flour
1½ cups half and half
1 cup chicken stock
1 cup sharp cheese
1 teaspoon Worcestershire
  sauce
Dash of nutmeg
4 tablespoons white wine
1 teaspoon lemon juice
1 teaspoon ground thyme

1 teaspoon celery salt
Salt and pepper
1 pound crabmeat
  or 2 (6-ounce) cans lump
  crabmeat
1½ pounds fresh steamed
  shrimp, peeled and
  deveined
Cracker crumbs
Parmesan cheese
Sharp cheese, grated

Melt butter in saucepan. Add flour to make thick paste. Add half and half, chicken stock, sharp cheese and next 7 ingredients to make cream sauce. Add shrimp and crabmeat last, but do not cook. Pour in ramekins. Top with cracker crumbs, Parmesan cheese and grated sharp cheese. Cook at 350 degrees until bubbly. You can make this ahead of time and freeze.
Yield: 6 servings

Mary Ann Blank

Shrimp And Wild Rice Casserole

¼ cup bell pepper, chopped
¼ cup onion, chopped
¼ cup celery, chopped
¼ cup butter
2 pounds cooked shrimp,
  peeled and deveined

1 box Uncle Ben's Wild
  Rice, cooked according
  to directions
1 can cream of celery soup
1 cup sharp Cheddar
  cheese, grated

Sauté bell pepper, onion and celery in butter. Combine remaining ingredients, and place in casserole dish. Bake at 325 degrees for 40 minutes.
Yield: 6 to 8 servings

Sally Tyndall

Shrimp Diane

¾ cup unsalted butter (divided)
¼ cup green onions, finely chopped
¾ teaspoon salt
½ teaspoon minced garlic
½ teaspoon cayenne pepper
¼ teaspoon white pepper
¼ teaspoon black pepper
¼ teaspoon dried sweet basil leaves
¼ teaspoon dried thyme leaves

⅛ teaspoon dried oregano leaves
6 tablespoons shrimp stock (recipe follows)
1¾ pounds medium shrimp, peeled and deveined (shells reserved)
½ pound mushrooms, cut into thick slices
3 tablespoons fresh parsley, finely chopped
Cooked pasta

Melt ½ cup butter over high heat. When almost melted, add green onions and the seasonings. Stir well. Add shrimp, and sauté just until they turn pink, about one minute. Add mushrooms and 2 tablespoons of the stock; then add the remaining 4 tablespoons butter in chunks and continue cooking. Before butter chunks are completely melted, add parsley, then remaining 2 tablespoons of the stock. Continue cooking until all ingredients are mixed thoroughly, and butter sauce is the consistency of cream. Serve immediately in a bowl over pasta with French bread on the side.

Shrimp Stock:
2 quarts cold water
1 medium onion, unpeeled and quartered
1 large clove garlic, unpeeled and quartered

1 rib celery
1½ to 2 pounds rinsed shrimp shells (or heads)

Place all ingredients in a large saucepan. Bring to a boil, then gently simmer at least 4 hours or more. Replenish the water as needed to keep about 1 quart of liquid in the pan. Strain, cool and

(Continued on next page)

(Shrimp Diane, continued)

refrigerate until ready to use. If you are short on time, then simmer 20 to 30 minutes. This is far better than no stock at all or substituting water for stock. Freeze and use later.
Yield: 2 servings

Mary Ann Blank

Dr. Bayne's Shrimp Rémoulade

4 pounds medium shrimp
1½ cups mayonnaise
5 boiled eggs, chopped
   (reserve 1 for garnish)
3 tablespoons parsley,
   chopped
3 tablespoons green
   pepper, chopped
1 teaspoon garlic, minced
9 stuffed olives, chopped

¼ cup celery, chopped
2½ tablespoons white
   onion, chopped
3 teaspoons horseradish
1½ teaspoons
   Worcestershire sauce
2½ teaspoons dry mustard
Salt to taste
Shredded lettuce

Cook shrimp in boiling salted water for 5 minutes. Allow shrimp to cool, then shell and devein. Chill until ready to serve. Mix remaining ingredients, and serve over shrimp on a bed of shredded lettuce. Garnish with reserved egg. For a complete meal, serve with garlic bread and dessert.
Yield: 6 servings

Mica Bayne Copeland

Bayne's Squirrel and Dumplings

3 gray squirrels
1 cup buttermilk
¼ teaspoon baking powder
2 tablespoons oil

1 teaspoon salt
All-purpose flour
Butter
Pepper

Boil squirrels until meat falls off the bone. For dumplings, mix buttermilk, baking powder, oil and salt. Add enough flour to make a stiff dough. Roll paper thin, and cut in strips one inch by three inches. Put meat back in pot and bring to a rolling boil. Drop dumplings one by one, adding lumps of butter and dashes of pepper. Push dumplings down, and continue adding more as water comes up. After all dumplings have been put in, cover and simmer 15 minutes. This recipe is also good with rabbit, or a combination of squirrel and rabbit.

Yield: 6 to 8 servings

Mica Bayne Copeland

Christmas Eve Quail

6 to 8 quail, (1½ to 2 birds
   per serving)
Flour, seasoned with salt
   and pepper
Butter
1 clove garlic, minced
½ pound mushrooms, sliced

¼ cup shallots, minced
¼ cup white wine
2 cups heavy cream
Salt and pepper to taste
Fresh thyme or dried if
   fresh unavailable

Dredge birds in seasoned flour and brown in butter. Transfer to warm oven. Add garlic, mushrooms and shallots to pan. Sauté 3 to 5 minutes. Add wine, and cook 2 more minutes. Then stir in cream. Season with salt and pepper. Return birds to pan. Cover and cook 15 minutes. Remove lid and reduce heat. Spoon sauce over quail, and garnish with fresh thyme or dried if fresh is not available. I serve this on a croûte or shredded potato basket.
Yield: 4 servings

Carol Ann Cannon

Quail with Rice

8 quail
¼ cup butter or margarine
1 cup carrots, shredded
½ cup onion, sliced
1 teaspoon dry parsley,
   or ½ cup fresh parsley,
   chopped

3 cups chicken broth
1 cup rice, uncooked
½ teaspoon salt
4 slices bacon, halved
Pepper to taste

Melt butter in skillet. Add quail and cook on both sides until brown. Remove quail and set aside. Sauté carrots, onions and parsley in drippings until tender. Add chicken broth, rice, salt and pepper to vegetables. Stir well. Arrange quail on top, and put a slice of bacon on each quail. Cover and cook over low heat for 30 minutes or until tender. Remove bacon to serve.
Yield: 4 servings

Kathy Heard

Stuffed Cornish Hens

2 tablespoons onion,
chopped
⅓ cup rice, uncooked
2 tablespoons butter,
melted
1 tablespoon lemon juice
½ cup cream of celery soup
1 teaspoon chives

1 teaspoon parsley flakes
¾ cup water
1 chicken bouillon cube
2 (1 to 1½ pounds each)
Cornish Hens
Salt and pepper to taste
Melted butter

Sauté onions and rice in butter for 5 minutes or until onion is transparent and rice is golden. Add next 6 ingredients, and bring to a boil. Cover and reduce heat to medium low. Cook 25 minutes. Remove giblets from hens. Rinse in cold water and pat dry. Sprinkle inside with salt and pepper. Stuff hens with rice mixture and close cavities with toothpicks. Place in shallow baking pan with breast side up. Brush hens with butter. Cover and bake at 375 degrees for 30 minutes. Uncover and bake 1 hour, basting with butter.
Yield: 2 servings

Kathy Heard

Complementary
Choices
Rice, Pasta & Eggs

Complementary Choices

Rice, Pasta, and Eggs

Creating the Setting

Well-known local artist, Lynwood Hall, whose oil painting appears on the front cover (for biographical sketch, see page 6), captured the ambiance of a warm Southern setting with this pen and ink drawing in the dining room of Mr. and Mrs. Roy Zess, also of Moultrie.

Combined for your Setting

Just as an artist adds subtle touches to complement his subject, so your selective strokes will add to your setting. Whether a simple side dish, such as a rice pilaf, to enhance the main course or a heaping mound of seafood lasagna over a beachside chat, these recipes are guaranteed to keep your compliments coming!

Black Beans and Yellow Rice

1 small onion, thinly sliced
1 clove garlic, minced
1 tablespoon light olive oil

1 (15-ounce) can black
  beans, drained
1 (5-ounce) package yellow
  rice

Sauté onion and garlic in olive oil until onion is tender. Pour in beans and heat thoroughly. Cook rice according to package directions. Serve beans on top of rice. (If using for a salad, mix thoroughly and chill. You may need to add a small amount of olive oil.) This recipe can be served hot as a side dish or cold as a salad.
Yield: 4 servings

Cooka Hillebrand

Broccoli Cheese Rice

1 small onion, chopped
1 package frozen broccoli
1 tablespoon butter
½ cup long grain rice,
  cooked

1 can cream of mushroom
  soup
1 small jar Cheese Whiz
¼ cup milk

Sauté onion and broccoli in butter. Add all other ingredients and pour into greased casserole dish. Bake at 350 degrees for 30 minutes.
Yield: 8 to 10 servings

Cathy Mobley

Broccoli-Wild Rice Combo

1 (6-ounce) package long-
  grain and wild rice mix
2 ~~1~~ can cream of chicken
  soup, undiluted
2 ~~1~~ (10-ounce) package frozen
  chopped broccoli,
  thawed
1 (8-ounce) can sliced water
  chestnuts, drained

½ 1 cup Cheddar cheese,
  shredded
½ cup celery, sliced
½ cup onion, chopped
½ cup milk
1 (2-ounce) jar sliced
  pimiento, drained
½ cup chow mein noodles,
  coarsely crushed

S + P to taste

Cook rice according to package directions, using 2 cups water. Combine rice and next 8 ingredients, stirring well. Spoon mixture into a lightly greased 2-quart casserole. Bake, uncovered at 350 degrees for 35 to 40 minutes. Sprinkle with crushed chow mein noodles, and bake an additional 5 minutes. May be made ahead, covered, and refrigerated for up to 2 days.
Yield: 8 to 10 servings

Jessica Jordan

Brown Rice

1 cup raw rice
2 cans beef consommé
1 can cream of onion soup
1 can sliced mushrooms,
  juice reserved

1 shake garlic salt
Worcestershire sauce
1 stick butter

Combine all ingredients except butter. Slice stick of butter and stir into other ingredients. Put in a 2-quart casserole dish. Bake 45 minutes at 400 degrees. Stir occasionally. Do not cover.
Yield: 8 to 10 servings

Donna Marshall
*Similar recipe submitted by Rhonda Sauls

Red Beans and Rice

1 pound red kidney beans
8 to 10 cups water (may add
  more while cooking)
2 to 3 chunks lean ham
1 onion, chopped
1 clove garlic, chopped
  (optional)

2 tablespoon celery,
  chopped
2 tablespoons parsley
1 large bay leaf
Green onions, chopped
  (optional)
Salt and pepper to taste

Rinse and discard undesirable beans. Cover with water. Add ham chunks, onion, garlic, celery and parsley. Add bay leaf, salt and pepper. Cook for 1½ to 2 hours or until beans are soft enough to mash. Mash 4 to 5 tablespoons of beans through strainer and add back to bean mixture. Serve over rice with sprinkles of chopped green onions (optional). For variation, you may use a meat seasoning such as Goya ham seasoning or beef bouillon cubes.
Yield: 8 to 10 servings

Cherie Anne Whiddon

Rice in Cream Sauce

2 tablespoons butter
1 clove garlic, minced
2 tomatoes peeled, chopped
  and seeded
1 teaspoon basil

¼ cup water
½ cup cream
1 cup cooked rice
¾ cup frozen green peas
½ cup Parmesan cheese

Sauté garlic in butter. Add tomatoes, basil and water. Cook down for about 5 to 10 minutes. Add cream to thicken. Add rice, peas, and Parmesan cheese. Stir together. You may substitute orzo pasta for the rice, and you may add other vegetables.
Yield: 8 to 10 servings

Mary Ann Blank

Wild Rice

2 boxes Uncle Ben's Wild
    Rice (using seasoning
    packet)
1 small jar artichoke hearts
¼ cup green spring onions,
    chopped
¼ cup almonds, sliced
1 cup white wine
1 can water chestnuts,
    sliced
2 celery stalks, diced
1 can mushrooms, sliced
½ cup butter
1 teaspoon white pepper

Mix all of the above in a mixing bowl. Pour into a 3-quart buttered casserole dish. Cover and bake at 350 degrees for 1 hour, adding water if necessary while cooking.
Yield: 8 to 10 servings

Paula Neely

Laura Keith's Straw and Hay

1 (4-ounce) package white
    linguine, uncooked
1 (4-ounce) package green
    linguine, uncooked
½ cup butter
½ cup ham, cut in thin
    strips
¾ cup peas, cooked
⅓ cup pitted black olives,
    sliced
1 small jar mushrooms,
    sliced
1 small jar pimiento,
    drained and sliced
1 egg, well beaten
1 cup whipping cream
1 cup Parmesan cheese,
    freshly grated
Parsley

Cook linguine in boiling, salted water until tender. Drain and return to pot. Stir in butter. Add ham, peas, olives, mushrooms, and half of the pimiento. In a small bowl, combine egg and cream. Slowly add this mixture to warm linguine, stirring well. Add half of Parmesan. Stir over medium-high heat until mixture thickens slightly. Do not let eggs curdle. Serve garnished with parsley and the remaining pimiento and cheese.
Yield: 4 to 6 servings

Laura Keith

Lasagna

1 pound lean ground beef
¾ cup onion, chopped
1 (16-ounce) can tomatoes
2 (6-ounce) cans tomato
   paste
2 cups water
3 tablespoons dried parsley
   (divided)
2 teaspoons salt
1 teaspoon sugar

1 teaspoon garlic powder
½ teaspoon pepper
½ teaspoon oregano
½ package lasagna noodles
1 pound cottage cheese
2 cups Parmesan cheese,
   grated (divided)
1 (8-ounce) package
   mozzarella cheese,
   grated

Cook beef with onion and drain off fat after cooking. Add tomatoes, paste, water, 1 tablespoon of parsley, salt, sugar, garlic powder, pepper and oregano. Simmer, uncovered about 30 minutes, stirring occasionally. Cook noodles in lightly salted water and drain. Mix cottage cheese with one cup of the Parmesan cheese and the remaining 2 tablespoons parsley. In 3-quart casserole dish, layer ½ the noodles, sauce, cottage cheese mixture, and mozzarella. Repeat layers, and top with rest of Parmesan. Bake at 350 degrees for about 45 minutes. Let stand for 15 minutes.
Yield: 6 to 8 servings

This recipe came from Judy Cole and was included in the 1986 First Methodist MYF youth cookbook.

Lynn Acuff

Laura Keith's Seafood Lasagna

Seafood Sauce:
3 tablespoons olive oil
1 large Vidalia or yellow
    onion, chopped
4 cloves garlic, minced
5 cups canned tomatoes
    (plum packed in puree)
½ cup dry white wine
½ cup fresh basil, chopped
1½ teaspoons fennel seeds
Salt and fresh ground
    pepper to taste

1 cup heavy cream
2 tablespoons Pernod
    (anise flavored liqueur)
2 pounds medium-sized
    shrimp, shelled,
    deveined and poached
    briefly
2 pounds scallops, poached
    briefly
1 package lasagna noodles

Filling:
3 cups ricotta cheese
1 (8-ounce) package cream
    cheese, at room
    temperature
2 eggs
1 (10-ounce) package
    spinach; cooked,
    drained and chopped
1 pound lump crabmeat,
    with all shell removed

1 sweet red pepper, diced
1 bunch green onions,
    sliced
½ cup fresh basil, chopped
Salt and pepper to taste
1½ pounds mozzarella
    cheese, thinly sliced
    (6 cups grated)

To make the sauce, heat the oil in a large skillet over medium-high heat. Add the onion and garlic. Sauté for 5 minutes. Add the tomatoes with the puree, and cook for 5 minutes more. Stir in wine, basil, fennel seeds and salt and pepper to taste. Simmer uncovered over medium heat for 45 minutes, stirring occasionally. Stir the cream into the sauce and then the Pernod. Stir in the shrimp and scallops. Simmer 5 minutes. Remove from heat. Preheat the oven to 350 degrees. Cook lasagna noodles in boiling salted water until tender but firm. Drain and cool under cold running water.

(Continued on next page)

(Laura Keith's Seafood Lasagna, continued)

For filling, beat the ricotta, cream cheese and eggs in a mixing bowl until smooth. Stir in the spinach, crabmeat, red pepper, green onions, basil, salt and pepper. To assemble, butter a 4-quart rectangular baking pan. Spread a thin layer of the sauce on the bottom of the pan. Cover with a layer of noodles. Top with half the filling, then half the seafood sauce. Cover the sauce with a layer of mozzarella. Place another layer of noodles over the mozzarella, and spread with the remaining filling. Top with another layer of mozzarella. Add a final layer of noodles and then the remaining seafood sauce. Cover with the remaining cheese. Bake the lasagna until bubbling and browned, about 50 minutes. Do not cover. Let stand for 10 minutes before serving.
Yield: 10 to 12 servings

Laura Keith

Macaroni Special

1 small package macaroni
1 large can mushrooms
1 pound American cheese, grated
1 can peas
6 to 8 saltine crackers, crushed

1 stick margarine
Salt and pepper to taste
1 can tomatoes, chopped and liquid reserved
½ pint whipping cream
1 cup tomato juice

Cook macaroni in salted water until tender. Cook can of mushrooms in juice until tender. Drain peas. Crush crackers. In 4½-quart baking dish, alternate layer of macaroni, cheese, peas, and mushrooms. Sprinkle in cracker crumbs. Dot with margarine. Salt and pepper to taste. Have macaroni, cheese and crackers on top of last layer. Pour the tomatoes with reserved liquid over the top. Pour in the cream and tomato juice. Cook at 250 degrees for 4 hours.
Yield: 8 to 10 servings

Edna Reeves

Lasagna with Spinach and Cheese

1 pound ground beef
1 large onion, chopped
1 green pepper, chopped
1 (8-ounce) package fresh
   mushrooms, sliced
1 teaspoon oregano
1 bay leaf
1 clove garlic, minced
Salt to taste
1 large can stewed
   tomatoes
1 (15-ounce) can tomato
   sauce

1 (12-ounce) can tomato
   paste
1 (10-ounce) package frozen
   spinach
1 pound cottage cheese
1 egg
1 (16-ounce) package
   lasagna noodles, cooked
   per directions
1 (12-ounce) package
   mozzarella cheese

Brown ground beef with onions and peppers. Add mushrooms, seasonings, tomatoes, tomato sauce and tomato paste. Bring to a boil and simmer until done, approximately 1 hour. Prepare spinach and cheese filling by cooking package of spinach as directed. Drain, and add cottage cheese and egg. In two large casserole dishes, evenly layer in the following order: sauce, noodles, spinach and cheese filling, noodles, sauce and top with mozzarella cheese. Bake at 350 degrees for about 30 minutes or until cheese bubbles and begins to brown. Makes two large dishes.

Yield: 8 to 10 servings per dish

Polly Boetcher

Orzo with Pine Nuts and Feta Cheese

1 pound orzo (rice-shaped
    pasta, also called riso)
2 tablespoons olive oil
⅓ pound feta cheese,
    crumbled

⅓ cup pine nuts, toasted
Salt and pepper to taste
Fresh parsley, chopped

Bring large pot of salted water to boil. Add orzo and boil until just tender (about 6 minutes) but still firm to bite. Stir occasionally. Drain well. Return to pot. Add oil and toss to coat. Mix in feta and pine nuts. Season to taste with salt and pepper. Sprinkle with parsley.
Yield: 6 servings

Harriett Whelchel

Pasta Greek Salad

1 (8-ounce) package pasta
1 (8-ounce) package Feta
    cheese
1 cup ripe olives, sliced
½ cup light olive oil

2 tablespoons Balsamic
    vinegar
2 garlic cloves, minced
Salad peppers (optional)

Cook pasta according to package directions; drain and blanch in cold water. Crumble feta cheese, and add to pasta along with olives. Mix olive oil, vinegar and garlic with a wire whisk. Pour over salad and mix well. Add peppers if desired.
Yield: 6 servings

Cooka Hillebrand

Pasta Primavera

12 spears asparagus,
cut on the diagonal at
2-inch lengths
¼ pound sugar snap peas
or snow peas, ends and
strings removed
¼ cup olive oil
¼ cup butter (divided)
3 cloves of garlic, pressed
and crushed
1 large zucchini, cut in
3-inch Julienne strips
1 large yellow squash,
cut in thin rounds

1 sweet red pepper,
cut in 3-inch strips
6 mushrooms, thinly sliced
½ pound proscuitto ham,
cut in Julienne strips
8 fresh leaves of basil, cut
in Julienne strips or 1
teaspoon of dried basil
Salt and pepper to taste
Red pepper flakes to taste
Parmesan cheese, grated
1 pound linguine, partially
cooked

Blanch asparagus and peas for 1 minute. Refresh under cold water and dry. In large frying pan, add olive oil, ½ of butter and garlic. When it starts to sizzle, add vegetables. Cook until they are hot, but still crisp. Add proscuitto, basil, salt, pepper, and red pepper. Toss barely cooked pasta with remaining butter. Add vegetables and sprinkle with cheese.
Yield: 6 to 8 servings

Kim Jarrell

Paula's Pasta Salad

1 (16-ounce) box vermicelli
   or angel hair pasta
¾ cup olive oil
4 tablespoons McCormick's
   steak seasoning
4 tablespoons fresh lemon
   juice
Dash of Tabasco
3 tablespoons mayonnaise
Black pepper to taste

1 can black olives, sliced
1 jar of pimiento, sliced
8 green onions, tops and
   bottoms, sliced
1 box frozen green peas,
   thawed
Optional: broccoli,
   asparagus or other
   vegetables of choice

Break pasta into fourths and cook according to package directions. Pour into colander. Rinse with cold water and allow to drain. Mix olive oil, steak seasoning, lemon juice, Tabasco, mayonnaise, and black pepper. Beat with a wire whisk. Add drained black olives and pimiento to pasta. Toss in green onions and green peas (or optional vegetables). Add sauce. Better if prepared the day before. Refrigerate.
Yield: 6 to 8 servings

Jan M. McLean

Roasted Pepper and Capers

1 (7-ounce) jar roasted red
   peppers, drained and
   sliced
3 tablespoons olive oil
2 tablespoons fresh parsley,
   chopped
2 tablespoons capers

1 teaspoon garlic, minced
½ teaspoon oregano
½ teaspoon salt
½ teaspoon white pepper
½ teaspoon butter, softened
1 box corkscrew pasta,
   cooked

Combine red peppers, olive oil, parsley, capers, garlic, oregano, salt, pepper and butter. Let stand 30 minutes and toss with cooked pasta.
Yield: 4 to 6 servings

Debbie Cagle

Shrimp And Green Noodles

1 (6-ounce) package	½ teaspoon Dijon mustard
spinach noodles	1 tablespoon chopped
2 pounds shrimp, peeled	chives
½ cup butter	4 tablespoons dry sherry
1 (10¾-ounce) can cream of	1 cup sour cream
mushroom soup	¾ cup sharp Cheddar
1 cup mayonnaise	cheese, grated

Cook noodles. Line casserole dish with noodles forming a nest. In a large frying pan, sauté shrimp in butter until pink, about 5 minutes. Cover center of dish with shrimp. Combine remaining ingredients except cheese. Pour over shrimp and noodles. Sprinkle cheese on top. Bake at 350 degrees for 30 minutes.
Yield: 6 servings

Nancy Paine
*Similar recipe submitted by Lisa Saunders

Shrimp Spaghetti

¼ pound butter, melted	1 large can sliced
All-purpose flour	mushrooms
1 can chicken broth	1½ pounds cooked shrimp,
1 cup Swiss cheese, grated	drained and peeled
Garlic powder to taste	1 carton sour cream
Touch of cayenne pepper	½ pound spaghetti
	Parmesan cheese

Add enough flour to melted butter in saucepan to make a thick paste. Stir in chicken broth to make thick white sauce. Melt in Swiss cheese. Season with garlic powder and cayenne pepper. Add mushrooms, shrimp and sour cream. Cook spaghetti and drain. Spread spaghetti in shallow baking dish, and pour shrimp sauce over. Sprinkle with Parmesan cheese. Bake at 350 degrees for 30 minutes or until heated through.
Yield: 4 to 6 servings

Skillet Macaroni and Cheese

1 (8-ounce) package of ziti
  or elbow macaroni
2 tablespoons butter or
  margarine
2 tablespoons all-purpose
  flour
½ teaspoon dry mustard
Dash pepper

1¾ cups milk
1 (8-ounce) package sharp
  Cheddar cheese,
  shredded
1 (2-ounce) jar pimiento
1 tablespoon parsley,
  chopped

Cook macaroni as label directs and drain. In skillet over medium heat, melt butter or margarine. Stir in flour, mustard, and pepper until blended. Cook 1 minute. Gradually add in milk, stirring constantly, until thickened and smooth. Remove skillet from heat. Stir in cheese until melted. Stir macaroni into cheese sauce. Add pimiento and parsley. Heat thoroughly over low heat.
Yield: 6 servings

Donna Taylor

Spaghetti Salad

1 pound spaghetti
1 jar McCormick Salad
  Supreme
1 (16-ounce) jar Wishbone
  Italian Dressing
1 onion, chopped

3 large tomatoes, chopped
3 stalks celery, chopped
1 green pepper, chopped
Sliced black olives,
  optional

Cook and drain spaghetti. Mix Salad Supreme and dressing in a large bowl. Add spaghetti and let cool. Mix in vegetables. Chill 24 hours, stirring occasionally. This keeps well in the refrigerator for several days.
Yield: 12 servings

Donna Taylor
*Similar recipe submitted by Sandy Hooks

Spaghetti Pie

1 pound ground beef
1 cup onion, chopped
½ cup green pepper,
   chopped
1 (1-pound) can tomatoes,
   chopped
1 small can tomato paste
1 teaspoon oregano
1 teaspoon salt
1 teaspoon sugar
½ teaspoon garlic salt

6 ounces spaghetti
2 tablespoons butter
2 eggs, beaten
⅓ cup Parmesan cheese,
   grated
1 (8-ounce) carton cottage
   cheese
1 (4-ounce) package
   mozzarella cheese,
   grated

Brown meat with onions and green pepper. Add tomatoes, tomato paste, oregano, salt, sugar, and garlic salt. Simmer until thoroughly heated. Cook spaghetti. Drain well. Add butter, eggs, and Parmesan cheese. Pour into a deep dish pie pan, making a well in the center of the spaghetti. Put cottage cheese into the center, leaving a one-inch border of spaghetti mixture showing. Pour meat sauce over the cottage cheese. Bake in 350 degree oven for 30 minutes. Sprinkle with the mozzarella cheese and return to oven until cheese melts.
Yield: 6 to 8 servings

Susan Newton

Southwestern Pasta Salad

1 (16-ounce) package penne
   pasta
Creamy Southwestern
   Salad Dressing (recipe
   follows)
Lettuce leaves
1 (15-ounce) can black
   beans, rinsed and
   drained

1 (8¾-ounce) can whole
   kernel corn, rinsed and
   drained
1 sweet red pepper,
   chopped
3 green onions, sliced
¼ cup fresh cilantro,
   chopped
Fresh cilantro sprigs for
   garnish

Cook pasta according to package directions. Drain. Rinse with cold water. Drain. Combine pasta and 1¾ cups Creamy Southwestern Salad Dressing. Toss gently. Chill. Spoon pasta mixture onto a lettuce-lined serving platter. Top with black beans and layer next 4 ingredients so that the previous layer is always showing around the edge. Garnish, if desired. Serve with remaining dressing on the side.
Yield: 6 to 8 servings

Creamy Southwestern Salad Dressing:
1 (8-ounce) carton sour
   cream (nonfat,
   if desired)

1 (16-ounce) jar mild, thick
   and chunky salsa
½ teaspoon ground cumin
2 cloves garlic, minced

Combine all ingredients. Chill.
Yield: 2¾ cups

Sally Tyndall

Brunch Casserole

1½ pounds mild bulk
   sausage
3 cups milk
9 eggs, beaten
1 teaspoon salt
Black pepper to taste

1½ teaspoons dry mustard
1½ pounds sharp Cheddar
   cheese, grated
3 slices of bread, trimmed
   and cubed

Brown sausage and drain. Mix milk, eggs, salt, pepper and mustard. Add sausage, cheese and bread. Mix well. Refrigerate overnight. Spray a 3-quart casserole dish with Pam. Pour in sausage and egg mixture. Bake at 350 degrees for 1 hour. Cut in squares to serve.
Yield: 10 servings

Bug Trimble
*Similar recipes by Lanelle Rogers and Donna Taylor

Eggs Delmonico

1 can cream of chicken
   soup
1 small jar pimiento,
   minced
¼ cup medium cheese,
   grated (or 4 to 5 slices
   of cheese)

4 eggs, hard cooked and
   chopped
Buttered toast slices
Paprika, optional
Parsley, optional

Heat soup over low heat. Stir in pimiento and cheese. Carefully fold in chopped eggs. Continue cooking over low heat until cheese has melted. Serve immediately over hot, buttered toast. Sprinkle with paprika and garnish with parsley.
Yield: 4 servings

Ellen Alderman

Ham and Cheese Pie

Deep dish pie crust	2 eggs
Shaved ham	1 (8-ounce) carton sour
1 cup mozzarella cheese, grated	cream

Alternate two layers of ham and cheese in pie shell. Mix eggs and sour cream together. Pour over top. Bake at 425 degrees for 30 minutes. Cool in oven for 15 minutes before serving.
Yield: 6 servings

Cindy Tyus

Jo's Cheese Soufflé

6 to 8 slices bread, cut in squares	2 cups milk
2 pounds medium Cracker Barrel Cheese, shredded	3 eggs, beaten

Place bread in bottom of 2-quart casserole. Put cheese on top. Mix milk and eggs together and pour over cheese. Let sit overnight in refrigerator. Bake at 350 degrees for 30 to 40 minutes.
Yield: 8 servings

Judy Mobley

Mexican Deviled Eggs

8 eggs, hard cooked	2 tablespoons green onions, chopped
½ cup sharp Cheddar cheese, grated	1 tablespoon sour cream
¼ cup mayonnaise	¼ teaspoon pepper
¼ cup salsa, medium or hot	

Slice eggs in half lengthwise. Put yolks in medium-sized bowl. Add remaining ingredients. Mix thoroughly. Mound mixture into whites. Refrigerate.
Yield: 16 servings

Donna Taylor

Favorite Quiche

5 eggs
2 (13-ounce) cans low fat
    evaporated milk
1 teaspoon salt
½ teaspoon black pepper
1 pound bacon, crumbled
1 cup ham, ground in
    blender or food processor

1 cup Cheddar cheese,
    grated
A few drops Worcestershire
    sauce
A few drops Tabasco sauce
2 unbaked pie crusts

Combine all ingredients and pour into pie shells. Bake at 375 degrees for 40 minutes or until knife comes out clean. For variation: use ½ cup Cheddar cheese and ½ cup Swiss cheese; or add 1 package of frozen spinach, chopped and uncooked, to egg and milk mixture.
Yield: 8 servings

Cherie Anne Whiddon

Quiche Lorraine with Broccoli and Tomato

4 slices bacon
½ cup green onion,
    chopped
½ cup Swiss Cheese, grated
½ cup sharp Cheddar
    cheese, grated
1 deep dish pie shell

¼ cup broccoli, chopped
¼ cup tomato, chopped
4 eggs, slightly beaten
2 cups half and half
½ teaspoon salt
Dash of cayenne pepper

Sauté bacon until crisp. Drain all but 1 teaspoon fat. Add onion and sauté. Sprinkle crumbled bacon, onion, and cheeses into pie crust. Add broccoli and tomato bits. Combine eggs, half and half and seasonings. Pour into crust. Bake at 450 degrees for 10 minutes. Reduce heat to 325 degrees and bake for 45 minutes to 1 hour.
Yield: 8 to 10 servings

Connie Fritz

Hamburger Quiche

1 pound ground beef
⅓ cup onion, chopped
⅓ cup bell pepper, chopped
½ cup mayonnaise
½ cup milk
2 eggs

1½ cups Cheddar cheese,
    grated
1 tablespoon corn starch
Salt and pepper to taste
1 unbaked pie shell

Brown ground beef in skillet with onions and bell pepper. Drain fat. Blend all remaining ingredients. Stir until smooth. Add to ground beef. Turn into unbaked pie shell. Bake at 350 degrees for 35 to 45 minutes.
Yield: 6 to 8 servings

Rhonda Sauls
*Similar recipe submitted by Farolyn Mobley

Spinach Quiche

1 pound bacon, cooked and
    crumbled
1 cup Swiss cheese or
    mozzarella, grated
¾ cup Cheddar cheese,
    grated
4 eggs, beaten
2 cups milk
2 tablespoons self-rising
    flour

1 small onion, chopped fine
¾ teaspoon salt
⅛ teaspoon pepper
1 teaspoon parsley, minced
    and crushed
1 package spinach, thawed
    and drained
Paprika
2 unbaked pie crusts

Prick bottom and sides of pie shells. Bake at 425 degrees for 6 to 8 minutes. Let cool. Mix remaining ingredients, except paprika together and pour into pie shells. Bake at 425 degrees for 15 minutes. Reduce heat to 300 degrees, and bake for 40 minutes more. Sprinkle quiche tops with paprika.
Yield: 2 pies

Ava English

185

Sue's Quiche

4 eggs
½ cup sour cream
⅓ pound bacon, fried and
    crumbled

1 (4-ounce) package any
    cheese of your choice,
    grated
1 teaspoon paprika
1 teaspoon parsley flakes
1 deep dish pie shell

Beat eggs slightly. Stir in sour cream. Add bacon, cheese (reserve a small amount), paprika and parsley. Stir until well blended. Pour into pie shell. Bake at 400 degrees for 20 minutes. Sprinkle top with reserved cheese. Bake for 5 minutes more. Let stand 5 minutes before cutting. For variation: add ham, onions, green peppers, mushrooms or a combination of your favorites.
Yield: 8 servings

Sandy Hooks

Dorothy Zuck's Zucchini Pie

1 stick butter
4 cups zucchini, sliced
1 cup onion, chopped
2 eggs, beaten
1 (8-ounce) package
    Monterey Jack cheese,
    shredded
1 tablespoon parsley flakes

½ teaspoon salt
½ teaspoon pepper
¼ teaspoon garlic powder
¼ teaspoon basil
¼ teaspoon oregano
2 teaspoons mustard
1 deep dish pie shell

Melt butter and sauté zucchini and onion. Stir in eggs and cheese. Add seasonings. Pour mixture in pie shell and cover with foil. Bake at 375 degrees for 30 minutes. Let stand before slicing.
Yield: 8 servings

Polly Jackson

Primary Selections
Fruit & Vegetables

K. FLOWERS
95

Primary Selections

Fruit and Vegetables

Creating the Setting

Kathy Perryman Flowers, instructor at the Colquitt County Arts Center, drew this pen and ink "Cluster of Grapes" (for biographical information, see page 44). Kathy also provided the paint brush and spoon sketches used on each divider page.

Combined for your Setting

Tints, shades and hues of color help to create an incredible vegetable study for your menu planning. Vegetables, like the basic primary colors, are essential to maintain balance, yet limitless in the options provided to ensure a wonderful presentation. Dabble with the following choices.

Cheesy Apple Casserole

2 (20-ounce) cans sliced
   apples
1 stick butter, sliced
1 cup sugar

¾ cup plain flour
1 (8-ounce) package
   Velveeta cheese, grated

Drain apples and spread in a greased and buttered 12 x 8-inch glass baking dish. Combine butter, sugar, flour and cheese. Drop on apples. Bake at 350 degrees for 30 minutes.
Yield: 6 to 8 servings

Debbie Cagle
*Similar recipe submitted by Farolyn Mobley

Hot Curried Fruit

1 large can pineapple
   chunks
1 large can pears
1 large can peaches

1 jar spiced apples
1 stick margarine
1 cup light brown sugar
¼ teaspoon curry powder

Drain pineapple, pears and peaches well. Quarter pears and peaches. Arrange pineapple, pears and peaches in a 9 x 13-inch glass dish. Rinse spiced apples; quarter and place with other fruit. Melt margarine. Add light brown sugar and curry powder. Bring to light boil, stirring constantly for one minute. Pour over arranged fruit. Bake at 325 degrees for 30 to 45 minutes.
Yield: 12 servings

Hot Pineapple Casserole

1 (20-ounce) can pineapple
   chunks, drained
½ cup sharp cheese, grated
¼ cup sugar

3 tablespoons flour
10 to 12 Ritz crackers,
   crushed
½ stick butter, melted

Combine cheese, sugar, and flour. Add to pineapple chunks, mixing well. Pour into 1½-quart casserole. Top mixture with crushed Ritz crackers. Drizzle with melted butter. Bake at 350 degrees for 20 to 25 minutes.
Yield: 4 to 6 servings

Marsha McLean

Asparagus With Cream Sauce

2 pounds fresh asparagus
1 tablespoon butter
1½ tablespoons all purpose
   flour
½ cup chicken broth
½ cup half and half

2 tablespoons Dijon
   mustard
1 teaspoon lemon juice
¼ teaspoon freshly ground
   pepper
Pimiento rose and parsley
   sprigs for garnish

Snap off tough ends of asparagus. Remove scales from stalks with knife or vegetable peeler, if desired. Cover and cook asparagus in a small amount of water for 6 to 8 minutes until crisp tender. Drain. Arrange on a serving dish and keep warm. Melt butter in saucepan on low heat. Add flour, stirring until smooth. Cook one minute, stirring constantly. Gradually add chicken broth and half and half. Cook over medium heat, stirring constantly until thickened and bubbly. Stir in mustard, lemon juice, and pepper. Spoon over asparagus. Garnish.
Yield: 8 servings

Patti Wells

Asparagus Vinaigrette

2 pounds medium, fresh
   asparagus, stems
   broken
1 teaspoon salt, or to taste
1 generous teaspoon Dijon-
   style mustard

Scant ½ teaspoon black
   pepper
2 tablespoons balsamic
   vinegar
3 tablespoons vegetable oil
2 tablespoons olive oil

Bring large pan of well salted water to boil. Put asparagus in and return to a boil. Cook until just tender, about 8 to 10 minutes. Drain and refresh under cold water. Arrange the cooked asparagus on a platter or individual plates. Whisk together the remaining ingredients and spoon vinaigrette over all. Top with an additional grind of pepper. This may all be done earlier in the day. Even people who hate asparagus love this!!
Yield: 6 servings

Kim Jarrell

Baked Beans

8 wieners, thinly sliced
1 cup onion, chopped
2 tablespoons butter
2 teaspoons dry mustard
1½ teaspoons allspice
½ teaspoon black pepper

1 (28-ounce) can B&M
   Baked Beans
½ cup ketchup
¼ cup brown sugar
1 (10-ounce) package
   Cheddar cheese, grated

Preheat oven to 350 degrees. Brown wieners, onion, and spices in butter. Mix together everything except the cheese. Pour half of the mixture in the casserole and sprinkle with half the cheese. Repeat each layer. Bake 30 minutes.
Yield: 6 to 8 servings

Jane Holman

Green Bean Casserole

4 strips of bacon
½ cup onion, chopped
½ cup bell pepper, chopped
½ cup celery, chopped

2 cans French cut beans,
  drained
1 jar mushrooms, sliced
1 can tomato soup

Fry bacon strips crisp, remove and drain. In the drippings brown onion, bell pepper, and celery. Pour over beans and mix. Add jar of sliced mushrooms. Pour into casserole and spread with tomato soup. Top with crumbled bacon. Bake uncovered at 350 degrees for 30 to 45 minutes, until bubbly.
Yield: 8 servings

Patti Wells

Swiss Green Bean Casserole

4 (10-ounce) boxes frozen
  French-style green
  beans
2 tablespoons flour

1 pound Swiss cheese
1½ cups sour cream
1 onion, diced
Salt and pepper to taste

Topping:
4 tablespoons butter

¾ to 1 cup cornflakes

Cook beans by package directions, drain well. Melt remaining ingredients in top of a double boiler, stirring. In casserole, place layer of beans, then layer of cheese sauce. Continue layering, ending with cheese sauce on top. Bake at 350 degrees for 30 minutes. Top with buttered cornflakes, return to oven and brown.
Yield: 12 to 14 servings

Peggy Benner

Butter Bean Casserole

1 (10-ounce) package frozen
    butter beans,
    or 1 (16-ounce) can
    butter beans, drained
2 cups chicken broth
2 tablespoons corn starch

¼ cup broth or water
1 teaspoon blue cheese
½ cup Cheddar cheese,
    grated
1 (2.8-ounce) can French
    fried onions

Cook butter beans in 2 cups broth and season to taste. When done, spoon beans into a 1½-quart casserole. In a saucepan, thicken broth with corn starch dissolved in ¼ cup broth or water. Add blue cheese and Cheddar cheese, stirring until melted. Pour sauce over beans, and top with onions. Bake at 375 degrees until casserole is bubbling hot. Very tasty.
Yield: 6 servings

JoAnn M. Caldwell

Cheryl's Bean Casserole

1 can white shoepeg corn,
    drained
1 can kidney beans,
    drained
1 can baked beans, drained

1 can chili (no beans)
½ cup chili sauce
2 teaspoons Worcestershire
    sauce
1 medium onion, diced

Combine all ingredients. Pour into a 2-quart casserole. Bake at 350 degrees for one hour or until bubbly.
Yield: 8 to 10 servings

Cheryl Friedlander

Broccoli Cheese Dish

2 (10-ounce) packages
  frozen chopped broccoli,
  cooked and drained
1 (10¾-ounce) can
  mushroom soup
2 eggs, well beaten

1 cup mayonnaise
1 cup Cheddar cheese,
  grated
2 tablespoons dried onion
Salt and pepper to taste

Mix all ingredients together. Put in any dish with a cover or lid.
Bake at 350 degrees for 45 minutes. Note: I always remove cover,
and cook another 10 or 15 minutes if I double this recipe.
Yield: 6 servings

Susan Newton
*Similar recipe submitted by Lynn Acuff

Mrs. Pippin's Broccoli Casserole

2 packages frozen broccoli
Garlic salt
1 egg
1 stick garlic cheese, grated
1 cup mushroom soup

1 can sliced mushrooms,
  drained
Sliced almonds
Cracker Crumbs
2 to 3 tablespoons butter,
  melted

Cook broccoli in garlic-salted water. Drain. Add beaten egg, cheese,
mushroom soup and mushrooms. Pour into casserole. Top with
sliced almonds, cracker crumbs, and butter. Bake at 400 degrees
for 30 minutes.
Yield: 6 servings

Debbie Cagle

My Grandmother's Broccoli Casserole

2 (10-ounce) packages
   frozen broccoli
1 stick butter, not
   margarine (divided)

1 (8-ounce) package
   Velveeta cheese, cut in
   small pieces
½ package Ritz crackers,
   crumbled

Cook and drain broccoli. Add ½ stick of butter and Velveeta to broccoli. Stir until both are melted. Pour into a casserole dish. Melt remaining butter, and add to crumbled crackers. Top broccoli with cracker mixture. Bake at 350 degrees until well heated, about 15 to 30 minutes.
Yield: 6 to 8 servings

Sandy Hooks

Sesame Broccoli

1 pound fresh broccoli
1 tablespoon salad oil
1 tablespoon red wine
   vinegar

1 tablespoon soy sauce
4 teaspoons sugar
1 tablespoon sesame seeds,
   toasted

Cook or steam broccoli until tender and drain. In small saucepan, combine oil, vinegar, soy sauce, sugar and sesame seeds. Heat to boiling. Pour sauce over broccoli, turning to coat. Serve hot.
Yield: 4 servings

Susan Blanton

Cabbage Casserole

1 medium cabbage,
   chopped
1 can celery soup
½ cup sour cream
1 medium onion, chopped

1 small jar pimiento
½ cup water
Ritz crackers
1 cup cheese, grated

Cook cabbage and cool. Mix next 4 ingredients with ½ cup of water. Place ½ of cabbage in casserole dish. Crumble Ritz crackers over cabbage. Add ½ soup mixture and ½ cup grated cheese. Repeat layers. Heat in 350 degree oven until hot.
Yield: 8 to 10 servings

Bill Sells

Carrot Casserole

1 pound carrots
1 small onion, finely
   chopped
1 teaspoon prepared
   mustard

4 saltine crackers,
   crumbled
⅔ cup Cheddar cheese,
   grated
½ cup mayonnaise
Salt to taste

Cook carrots until done. Blend well with a potato masher. Add remaining ingredients to carrots, and bake at 375 degrees for 30 minutes.
Yield: 4 to 6 servings

Susan Blanton

Calloway Gardens' Carrot Soufflé

3 tablespoons butter,
   melted
3 tablespoons flour
1 cup hot milk
¼ teaspoon salt
3 eggs

2 cups carrots, cooked and
   mashed
1 teaspoon vanilla
3 tablespoons sugar
½ teaspoon nutmeg

In a mixing bowl, blend butter and flour. Add milk and mix until
smooth. Add remaining ingredients. Pour mixture into a greased
casserole. Bake at 350 degrees for 40 minutes.
Yield: 6 servings

Debbie Brown

Glazed Carrots

1 package baby carrots
5 tablespoons butter
¼ cup sugar

2½ tablespoons water
Salt and pepper to taste

Put all ingredients in a covered skillet or saucepan. Bring to a boil.
Reduce heat to low, and cook 15 to 20 minutes or until desired
tenderness. Uncover and cook until liquid evaporates, and carrots
are glazed.
Yield: 6 servings

Kathy Heard

Herbed Carrots And Onions

1 cup carrots, sliced
   diagonally
1 small onion, sliced
Pinch of dry rosemary
   leaves, crushed
Pinch of marjoram leaves

Pinch of thyme
Pinch of salt
Pinch of pepper
1 teaspoon margarine
1 tablespoon fresh parsley

Place carrots and onion in a vegetable steamer. Place rack over boiling water in a Dutch oven. Sprinkle with herbs, salt and pepper. Cover and steam 10 to 15 minutes. Spoon into serving dish and stir in margarine. Sprinkle with parsley.
Yield: 2 servings

Angela Castellow

Zesty Carrots

8 carrots, peeled and cut in
   strips
2 tablespoons onion, grated
2 tablespoons horseradish
½ cup mayonnaise

1 teaspoon salt
¼ teaspoon pepper
⅓ cup buttered
   breadcrumbs
Paprika

Cook carrots until tender. Place in baking dish. Mix mayonnaise, onion, horseradish, salt and pepper. Spread over carrots. Top with breadcrumbs. Bake at 375 degrees for 15 minutes. Sprinkle with paprika.
Yield: 4 to 6 servings

Marilyn Huber

Corn And Bean Casserole

1 (16-ounce) can French
   style green beans,
   drained
1 (16-ounce) can whole
   kernel corn, drained
1 (10¾-ounce) can cream of
   celery soup, undiluted

1 (2-ounce) jar diced
   pimiento, drained
½ cup onion, chopped
½ cup commercial sour
   cream
½ cup herb seasoned
   stuffing mix
1 stick margarine

Mix first 6 ingredients together. Pour into a 2-quart casserole dish. Melt margarine in a pan and add stuffing mix. Stir to combine. Spread over top of vegetables. Bake at 350 degrees for 40 to 45 minutes.
Yield: 6 to 8 servings

JoAnn M. Caldwell

Corn Pudding Casserole

1 (16-ounce) can cream-
   style corn
1 (16-ounce) can whole
   kernel corn

1 stick butter, melted
1 box Jiffy muffin mix
1 (8-ounce) carton sour
   cream

Mix all ingredients together well. Pour into a greased soufflé dish. Bake at 350 degrees for 30 minutes.
Yield: 6 to 8 servings

Lynne Stone

Curried Cauliflower

1 (10½-ounce) can cream of
   mushroom soup
1 cup Cheddar cheese,
   shredded
⅓ cup Hellmann's
   mayonnaise
1 teaspoon curry powder

1 large head cauliflower,
   broken into florets
¼ cup fine dry
   breadcrumbs
2 tablespoons margarine,
   melted

In a medium bowl, stir together soup, cheese, mayonnaise, and
curry powder until well blended. Cook cauliflower and drain. Place
in a 2-quart casserole, and pour sauce over. In a small bowl, mix
together breadcrumbs and margarine. Sprinkle over top. Bake
uncovered at 350 degrees for 30 minutes or until hot and bubbly.
Yield: 6 to 8 servings

Barbara Hendrick

Elegant Fried Eggplant

1 medium eggplant
½ cup flour
2 eggs, well beaten
¼ cup milk
1 cup saltine cracker
   crumbs

¼ to ½ cup oil
2 tomatoes, sliced ¼-inch
   thick
1 (8-ounce) package
   Monterey Jack cheese,
   sliced

Clean and cut the unpeeled eggplant into ¼-inch slices. Coat the
slices with flour. Mix eggs and milk. Dip eggplant into mixture,
then coat with cracker crumbs. Fry the eggplant in oil until it is
lightly browned and tender. Leave the eggplant in pan. Add a slice
of tomato and a slice of cheese to each piece. Cover the pan, and
place on low heat until the cheese melts.
Yield: 6 servings

Cooka Hillebrand

Pam Yocom's Green Enchilada Casserole

1 dozen corn tortillas
Oil
1 cup light cream
1 (10¾-ounce) can cream of
    chicken soup

1 small can green chilies,
    chopped
½ cup onions, finely
    chopped
1 cup Cheddar cheese,
    grated

Fry tortillas in hot oil until they bubble. Mix cream, soup and green chilies, and heat. Place in dish, alternating a tortilla topped with onions and cheese, and soup mixture until all is used. Bake at 350 degrees for 30 to 40 minutes.
Yield: 6 to 8 servings

Ellen Dekle Alderman

Baked Potatoes

6 cups potatoes, cooked
    and diced
2 cups cottage cheese,
    creamed
2 tablespoons flour
1 cup sour cream

¼ cup green onions,
    chopped
1 clove garlic, very finely
    grated
½ cup sharp cheese, grated

Mix potatoes and cottage cheese with flour. Add next three ingredients. Place in 1-quart buttered casserole dish. Sprinkle cheese on top. Bake at 350 degrees for 30 minutes or until bubbly. Let sit 20 minutes before serving. Easy and may be frozen.
Yield: 12 servings

Sandra Plant

Fabulous Potatoes

2 pounds frozen hash brown
   potatoes
½ cup butter, melted
1 teaspoon salt
1 can cream of chicken soup

2 cups Cheddar cheese,
   grated
½ cup onion, chopped
2 cups sour cream

Pour melted butter over frozen hash browns and mix. Add remaining ingredients and stir well. Place in 13 x 9-inch buttered casserole dish, and bake at 350 degrees for 45 minutes.
Yield: 10 servings

Martha Reeves

Sliced Baked Potatoes

4 medium potatoes
1 teaspoon salt
3 tablespoons butter, melted
3 tablespoons fresh herbs,
   chopped (parsley, chives,
   thyme or sage; use 3
   teaspoons dried herbs if
   fresh are unavailable)

4 tablespoons Cheddar
   cheese, grated
1½ tablespoons Parmesan
   cheese

Peel potatoes if the skin is tough, otherwise just scrub and rinse. Cut potatoes into thin slices but not all the way through. (Use the handle of a spoon to prevent knife from cutting all the way through.) Put potatoes in a baking dish, and fan them slightly. Sprinkle with salt, and drizzle with butter. Sprinkle with herbs. Bake at 425 degrees for about 50 minutes. Remove from oven. Add cheeses. Bake potatoes for another 10 to 15 minutes or until lightly browned, cheeses are melted, and potatoes are soft inside.
Yield: 4 servings

Farolyn Mobley

Potato Latkes

2 tablespoons flour
½ teaspoon baking powder
2 teaspoons corn starch
1 teaspoon salt
¼ teaspoon pepper

2 eggs, well beaten
1 onion, grated and drained
6 raw potatoes, grated and
   drained
Oil for frying

Combine first 5 ingredients. Beat eggs in large bowl. Add onion and potatoes. Stir in dry ingredients and mix well. Drop by spoonful into hot oil. Turn once until brown and crisp. Serve with applesauce or sour cream.
Yield: 6 servings

Ann Friedlander

Sweet Potato Casserole

3 cups sweet potatoes,
   cooked until soft and
   drained
¾ cup sugar (or to taste)
2 eggs

1 teaspoon vanilla
½ cup evaporated milk
½ cup butter (or less)
1 teaspoon cinnamon

Topping:
1 cup brown sugar
⅓ cup flour

⅓ cup butter, melted
1 cup pecans, chopped

Mix hot potatoes with remaining ingredients (excluding topping). Place in buttered casserole. For the topping, mix sugar and flour with butter. Fold in nuts. Spread on top of potatoes. Bake at 400 degrees approximately 30 minutes or until firm.
Yield: 8 to 10 servings

Deryl Beadles
*Similar recipes submitted by Ellen Alderman,
Terrie Moody, Lee Willis and Evoline McLean

Marshmallow Sweet Potato Balls

2 cups sweet potatoes,
   boiled and peeled
1 egg
½ teaspoon salt

½ teaspoon nutmeg
8 marshmallows
Crushed cornflakes
Oil

Rice potatoes, then add egg and seasonings. Roll marshmallows in sweet potato mixture to form a ball, then roll them in crushed cornflakes. Fry them in hot oil until brown, not more than 2 to 3 minutes. Serve warm.
Yield: 8 servings

Barbara B. Vereen

Posh Squash

2 pounds yellow squash,
   sliced
1 cup mayonnaise
1 cup Parmesan cheese,
   grated
1 small onion, chopped

2 eggs, beaten
½ teaspoon salt
¼ teaspoon pepper
½ cup soft breadcrumbs
1 tablespoon butter or
   margarine

Cook squash, covered, in boiling salted water for 10 to 15 minutes or until tender. Drain and cool slightly. Combine mayonnaise, cheese, onion, eggs, salt, and pepper. Stir until well combined. Add squash, stirring gently. Pour squash mixture into a lightly greased 1½-quart casserole. Combine breadcrumbs and butter. Spoon over squash mixture. Bake at 350 degrees for 30 minutes.
Yield: 6 servings

This recipe was given to me by the late Joyce Parrish Gammage, former President of the Moultrie Service League.

Barbara Hendrick

Split Squash

Small fresh squash	Margarine
Cavender's Greek	Breadcrumbs or cracker
Seasoning	crumbs
Parmesan cheese	

Par boil squash. Cut lengthwise, and place on cookie sheet, cut side up. Sprinkle with Cavender's, Parmesan cheese and breadcrumbs. Dot with margarine. Broil in oven until slightly brown.
Yield: 6 servings

Mary Ann Blank

Squash Casserole

2 pounds squash	1 onion, chopped fine
½ cup butter	1 small carton sour cream
½ package Pepperidge Farm	1 can water chestnuts,
Herb Stuffing mix	sliced thin
(divided)	Salt and pepper to taste
1 can cream of chicken soup	

Steam squash until slightly tender. Mix butter with ½ of the stuffing mix, and place in the bottom of a buttered casserole dish. Stir together soup, onion, sour cream and seasonings. Add to squash. Pour into casserole, and top with remaining stuffing mix. Bake at 350 degrees for 25 to 30 minutes.
Yield: 6 to 8 servings

Mary Catherine Turner
*Similar recipes submitted by Sandy Hooks and Karen Willis

Cheesy Squash Casserole

2 cups squash, cooked and
    drained
1 stick margarine
1 egg

1 cup milk
7 tablespoons flour
2 cups cheese, grated

Melt margarine in hot, cooked squash. Add egg, milk and flour. Mix well. Add cheese to mixture. Bake at 350 degrees for 35 to 45 minutes.
Yield: 6 servings

Cindy Tyus

Squash Soufflé

2 pounds yellow or
    zucchini squash
1 box Jiffy corn muffin mix
3 eggs
½ cup milk
1 medium onion, grated

1 cup sour cream
½ teaspoon dill weed
1¾ cups sharp Cheddar
    cheese, grated
Paprika

Mix all ingredients, except ¾ cup of cheese and paprika. Pour into a 13 x 9-inch pan. Sprinkle with remaining cheese and paprika. Bake at 400 degrees for 1 hour.
Yield: 6 servings

Arlene Schreiber

Baked Tomatoes

Tomatoes
Italian seasoning
Bottle of Italian salad
   dressing

Mozzarella cheese, grated
Italian breadcrumbs

Butter 2-quart casserole dish. Peel and slice enough tomatoes to cover bottom of dish by overlapping tomato slices. Sprinkle Italian seasoning over tomato slices, and cover with Italian dressing. Top with mozzarella cheese and breadcrumbs. Let marinate for 20 to 30 minutes. Bake uncovered in 350 degree oven for approximately 20 minutes.

Yield: 10 servings

Alyce McCall

Tomato Casserole

½ cup onion, chopped
½ cup green pepper,
   chopped
2 teaspoons margarine
2 large cans peeled
   tomatoes, quartered
½ teaspoon garlic salt
¼ teaspoon thyme

¼ teaspoon basil
   (½ teaspoon Italian
   seasoning can be
   substituted for the
   thyme and basil)
Salt and pepper to taste
⅓ to ½ cup Ritz crackers,
   crushed
Sharp Cheddar cheese

Sauté onion and pepper in margarine or oil until just tender. Add tomatoes with juice and seasonings. Cook over medium heat about 5 minutes. Add enough of the crushed Ritz crackers to bind together. Allow a few minutes for the liquid to be absorbed, before adding more. Pour into casserole dish, and bake at 350 degrees for about 30 minutes. Top with cheese (and additional cracker crumbs if desired), and bake until cheese is bubbly.

Yield: 4 to 6 servings

Mary Campagna

Oven "Fried Green Tomatoes"

12 saltine crackers,
   crumbled
⅓ cup Parmesan cheese

Salt and pepper to taste
4 to 5 green tomatoes,
   sliced but not peeled

Mix together first 3 ingredients. Dredge tomatoes in mixture. Place on cookie sheet, sprayed with Pam. Bake at 450 degrees for 30 minutes, turning once after 20 minutes.
Yield: 8 servings

Harriett Whelchel

Parslied Cherry Tomatoes With Garlic

1 pint cherry tomatoes, cut
   in half
2 garlic cloves, minced
¼ teaspoon salt
2 tablespoons extra virgin
   olive oil

2 teaspoons fresh lemon
   juice
⅓ cup fresh parsley,
   coarsely chopped

Toss the tomatoes with garlic, salt, oil and lemon juice. Stir in parsley just before serving. This recipe goes well with grilled lamb chops.
Yield: 4 to 6 servings

Mary Ann Blank

Tomato Pie

Pie crust (Pillsbury All
   Ready crusts)
3 or 4 tomatoes, thickly
   sliced
3 or 4 spring onions,
   chopped including tops

1 teaspoon sweet basil
Salt and pepper to taste
1 cup mayonnaise
1 cup sharp cheese, grated

Prepare pie crust according to instructions, prick and bake. Put tomatoes and onions in baked crust. Mix mayonnaise, cheese and seasonings. Spread evenly over tomatoes and onions. Bake at 350 degrees for 30 minutes. Cool 5 minutes before slicing in wedges.
Yield: 8 servings

Martha Beard Payne
*Similar recipe submitted by Jane Holman

Turnip Green Casserole

1 can turnip greens,
   chopped
1 can cream of celery soup
½ cup mayonnaise
2 eggs, beaten

2 tablespoons wine vinegar
1 teaspoon horseradish
1 teaspoon sugar
Water chestnuts (optional)
Breadcrumbs

Mix ingredients together in order listed. Pour into casserole and top with breadcrumbs. Bake at 350 degrees for 30 to 40 minutes. So easy and so good! People who do not like turnip greens love this.
Yield: 4 to 6 servings

JoAnn M. Caldwell

Roasted Summer Vegetables

1½ pounds fresh ripe tomatoes, peeled and thinly sliced
1 pound red onions, cut into wedges
1½ pounds new potatoes, cut into wedges
1 pound zucchini, cut into 1½-inch chunks
2 stalks of celery, cut into 1½-inch chunks
⅓ cup parsley, minced
1½ tablespoons fresh dill
1 teaspoon fresh mint
2 teaspoons garlic, minced
Salt and pepper to taste
¼ cup olive oil

Preheat oven to 400 degrees. Place rack in the upper third of oven. Grease a 9 x 18-inch baking dish. Spread half the tomatoes over bottom of the baking dish. Scatter the onions, potatoes, zucchini and celery over the tomatoes. Arrange remainder of tomatoes over the top. Sprinkle with parsley, dill, mint, garlic, salt, pepper and oil. Bake 30 minutes. Remove from oven and stir. Bake an additional 30 minutes. The vegetables should be charred slightly to combine the flavors.
Yield: 8 servings

Cooka Hillebrand

Baked Vegetables

4 baking potatoes, washed
4 medium sweet onions,
    whole
4 medium carrots, cut in
    large pieces

4 stalks of celery, cut in
    large pieces
2 cups Crisco oil
1 stick margarine
Salt and pepper to taste

Place whole potatoes, onions and prepared carrots and celery in Dutch oven. Pour Crisco oil over the above. Cut up butter and add. Sprinkle with salt and pepper. Cover and bake in 200 to 250 degree oven for 3 hours or until done. To serve, remove from liquid. Very good with steak.
Yield: 4 servings

Marsha McLean

Vidalia Onion Pie

1½ sticks butter (divided)
1 cup saltines, crumbled
3 cups Vidalia onions,
    coarsely cut
3 eggs, beaten

¾ cup milk, scalded
Salt and pepper to taste
¾ cup Cheddar cheese,
    grated

In a large pie plate, melt ½ stick of butter. Press in saltines. Sauté onions in one stick of butter until just tender. Pour on top of saltines. Add eggs, milk, salt and pepper. Top with cheese. Bake at 350 degrees for 30 minutes.
Yield: 6 to 8 servings

Sandra Plant

Broiled Zucchini

3 small zucchini, cut
    lengthwise
1 to 2 tablespoons butter,
    melted

Salt and pepper
3 tablespoons Parmesan
    cheese, grated
Paprika

Place zucchini, cut side up, in a lightly greased broiler pan. Brush tops of zucchini with melted butter. Sprinkle with salt, pepper, cheese and paprika. Broil 6 to 8 inches from heat for 12 minutes or until tender.
Yield: 3 servings

Jill Lazarus
*Similar recipe submitted by Debbie Cagle

Abstract Collections
Beverages, Dressings, Sauces
& Miscellaneous

Abstract Collections

Beverages, Dressings, Sauces and Miscellaneous

Creating the Setting

"Muscadines On A Brick Wall," a watercolor by Moultrie's Randy Gibbs, typifies a spring setting. Gibbs studied art at Abraham Baldwin Agricultural College and Valdosta State College before enlisting in the U. S. Army. Returning home to Moultrie, he retired the artist brush to raise a family and operate a heavy equipment construction company. In 1989, Gibbs was commissioned by a plantation owner in Coolidge, Georgia, to do a mural for the dome of Woodhaven Plantation, which has been featured in Southern Living. And from that point, art became his profession. Painting from his backyard art studio, Gibbs' works have been displayed regionally as well as outside of Georgia. He received national recognition for his 1993 print, "The Last Boll Weevil," and now has commissioned work in private collections throughout the United States and abroad.

Combined for the Setting

Here's the adventuresome area for self-expression. As an artist experiments with new techniques before presenting his work of art, so you can deviate from the norm with a spicy sauce or an inexplicable chutney. Don't shy away from any of these creative mediums.

Banana-Pineapple Punch

6 ripe bananas
1 (12-ounce) can frozen
   lemonade
2 (12-ounce) cans frozen
   orange juice
3 cups sugar

1 (46-ounce) can
   unsweetened pineapple
   juice
6 cups water
1 (2-liter) 7-Up

Mash bananas with lemonade. Add next four ingredients. Add 7-Up just before serving.
Yield: 50 servings

Amanda Statom

Betty Hall's Eggnog

1 envelope unflavored
   gelatin
4 tablespoons water
1 cup milk

4 eggs, separated
1¾ cups sugar
1 cup bourbon
2 pints whipping cream

Chill bowl and beaters. Dissolve gelatin in cool water. Bring milk to boiling point. Pour milk into gelatin and stir. Let cool. Beat egg yolks until thick and light yellow. Add sugar and continue beating. Add bourbon and mix well on low. Add cooled gelatin mixture to egg mixture. Refrigerate until it starts to congeal, about 1 hour. May need to stir. Beat egg whites until stiff and lose gloss. Whip cream until stiff. Fold egg whites and cream together. Add bourbon and egg mixture. Preparation time: 2 to 2½ hours.
Yield: 10 to 12 servings

(Traced to Betty Hall through Ellen Peters, Judy Dixon, Jan McLean and in turn given to me.)

Jane H. Brown

215

Coffee Punch

1 quart boiling water
8 tablespoons instant coffee
2 cups sugar
1 tablespoon vanilla
1 (5½-ounce) can Hershey's
  chocolate syrup

2 quarts cold water
2 quarts milk
2 quarts vanilla ice cream
2 quarts coffee ice cream

Mix boiling water with instant coffee, sugar, vanilla, and chocolate syrup. Then add cold water and milk. Refrigerate overnight. Pour over ice cream about 30 minutes before serving. Break up ice cream and stir occasionally while waiting to serve.
Yield: 40 servings

(Given to me by Anna Elizabeth Taylor and given to her by Ruth Shepherd)
Cherie Anne Whiddon
*Similar recipe submitted by Debbie Cagle

Nell Dekle's Slush Punch

2 (46-ounce) cans pineapple
  juice
2 (46-ounce) cans orange
  juice

½ (8-ounce) bottle Real
  lemon juice
2 cans water
5 cups sugar
1 (2-liter) ginger ale

Mix and freeze first 5 ingredients. To serve, let thaw to slushy stage and add ginger ale.
Yield: 40 servings

Ellen Dekle Alderman

Hot Apple Cider

1 gallon apple juice
¾ cup sugar
1 teaspoon whole cloves

1 teaspoon allspice
1 stick of cinnamon
½ lemon (sliced)

Mix all ingredients. Simmer for 20 minutes or longer. Serve warm.
Yield: 16 cups

Judy Mobley

Orange Eye-Opener

1 small can frozen orange
   juice
1½ cups milk
½ cup water

10 to 12 ice cubes
1 tablespoon sugar
1 teaspoon vanilla

Place all ingredients in blender and blend.
Yield: 4 servings

Cooka Hillebrand

Whiskey Sours

3 (6-ounce) cans lemonade concentrate (undiluted)

**18 ounces bourbon
1 (2-liter) bottle ginger ale**

Mix and pour into wine-size stemware.
Yield: 8 servings

Sandra Plant

Wine Cooler

**4 cups grapefruit juice
3 cups wine**

1½ cups diet ginger ale

Mix all ingredients together.
Yield: 8 servings

Nell Brown

Mama V's Italian Dressing

1 cup tarragon vinegar
1 cup orange juice
1 cup lemon juice
1 cup oil
2 tablespoons salt

1 package Good Seasons
   Italian Dressing Mix
4 cloves garlic, split
1 tablespoon celery seed

Mix in quart jar and shake well. Chill.
Yield: 1 quart

Joan V. Stallings

Poppy Seed Dressing

1½ cups sugar
2 teaspoons dry mustard
2 teaspoons salt
⅔ cup vinegar

3 tablespoons onion juice
2 cups salad oil, not olive
   oil
2 tablespoons poppy seeds

Mix all ingredients in blender except salad oil and poppy seeds.
Blend three minutes. Add oil while blending on low speed. Toss in
poppy seeds and stir.
Yield: Approximately 3 cups

Debbie Cagle

Spinach Salad Dressing

1 cup oil
⅔ cup sugar
½ teaspoon dry mustard

1 small onion, finely
   chopped
½ teaspoon salt
⅓ cup vinegar

Combine all ingredients except vinegar in blender. Mix well. Add
vinegar while blending for one minute. Serve over fresh salad.
Yield: 2 cups

Gail Qurnell

Fruit Salad Dressing

1 egg
½ cup sugar
Juice of 1 lemon

½ cup mayonnaise
½ cup whipping cream

In a small saucepan, beat the egg. Add sugar and lemon juice. Stir over low heat about 5 minutes, until thick. Cool thoroughly. Before serving, stir in mayonnaise and fold in whipped cream. Serve on any fruit salad.
Yield: 1½ cups

Vegetable or Fruit Dressing

¾ cup salad oil
¼ cup red wine vinegar
1 tablespoon lemon juice
1 teaspoon onion, grated
1 clove of garlic
¼ teaspoon dry mustard

1 teaspoon salt
1¼ teaspoons sugar
2 dashes of Tabasco
3 tablespoons ketchup
1 cup mayonnaise
2 teaspoons poppy seed

Mix together, shake well.
Yield: 1 pint

Marie Saunders

Homemade Mayonnaise

2 eggs
1 teaspoon salt
2 cups or less of canola oil

Juice of 1 to 2 lemons
2 teaspoons mustard or to taste

Beat eggs and salt in blender on high until pale. Slowly add oil. After mayonnaise is made, stir in lemon juice and mustard by hand. For best results, chill blender, eggs and oil.
Yield: 2 cups

Lee Willis
*Similar recipe submitted by Koala Fokes

Cooked Dressing for Chicken Salad

2 eggs, beaten
⅔ cup sugar
2 level tablespoons all-
    purpose flour
½ cup water

½ cup vinegar
½ teaspoon salt
2 tablespoons butter or
    margarine

Beat eggs and sugar. Mix the flour in the water, and add vinegar. Combine egg and flour mixtures in a saucepan. Add salt and cook until thick, stirring constantly. Set aside and allow to cool. Add butter or margarine and stir. Cool and add to your favorite chicken salad.
Yield: 1 pint

Mary Beard
(Founding Member of Moultrie Service League)

Durkee Bar-B-Q Sauce

1 stick margarine
2 bottles Durkee Famous
    Sauce
1 tablespoon yellow
    mustard

⅓ cup fresh lemon juice
⅓ cup sugar (more to taste)
1 tablespoon vinegar
Salt and pepper to taste
¾ cup or more water

Melt margarine in saucepan. Add Durkee sauce and mustard, stirring until smooth. Add lemon juice, sugar, vinegar, salt and pepper. Water may vary according to desired thickness of sauce.
Yield: sauce for 3 to 4 chickens

Wonderful on chicken, served with extra sauce on the side.

Mary Campagna

Aioli (Garlic Sauce)

4 large cloves fresh garlic
3 large egg yolks
1 teaspoon dry mustard
¼ teaspoon salt
¼ teaspoon white pepper

1 cup olive oil
   (or ½ vegetable oil
   and ½ olive oil)
1½ teaspoons fresh lemon
   juice

Put first five ingredients in blender or food processor. Slowly add
½ cup oil. Scrape down sides and add lemon juice. Slowly add
remaining oil. Wonderful on vegetables, chicken or fish. I sometimes top with toasted breadcrumbs or almonds.
Yield: 1⅓ cups

Barbara B. Vereen

Hot Mustard Sauce

⅓ cup Coleman's dry
   powdered mustard
⅓ cup vinegar

1 egg
⅓ cup sugar
Mayonnaise to taste

Soak mustard and vinegar overnight. Beat egg with sugar. Put all
ingredients except mayonnaise in a double boiler. Stir constantly,
until sauce begins to thicken. Remove from heat. Let cool. Add
mayonnaise to taste. Store in the refrigerator. Great with ham and
other meats.
Yield: 1 cup

Mary Katherine Turner

Microwave White Sauce

3 tablespoons butter
3 tablespoons flour
¼ teaspoon salt

⅛ teaspoon pepper
1 cup milk

Place butter in 1-quart glass measure. Microwave at high (100 percent) for 30 seconds or until melted. Stir in flour, salt, and pepper. Microwave at high for 45 seconds. Slowly add milk, beating mixture with whisk. Continue microwaving at high for 2 minutes or until thickened, stirring once. (For basic cheese sauce, stir in ½ cup grated sharp Cheddar cheese and beat until smooth.)
Yield: 1 cup

Barbara Fallin

Sweet and Spicy Mustard

5 tablespoons dry mustard
½ cup sugar
1 tablespoon all purpose
    flour
½ teaspoon salt

Dash red pepper
2 eggs, beaten
½ cup vinegar
1 tablespoon butter

Combine first 5 ingredients, blending thoroughly. Add eggs and vinegar. Place over boiling water in a double boiler. Cook, stirring constantly until thick. Add butter. Stir until melted. Store in the refrigerator.
Yield: 1 pint

Arlene Schreiber

Marinade for Beef or Pork

1½ cups salad oil
¾ cup soy sauce
¼ cup Worcestershire
    sauce
2 teaspoons dry mustard
2¼ teaspoons salt

1 teaspoon pepper
½ cup wine vinegar
½ teaspoon fresh parsley,
    chopped
2 cloves garlic, minced
½ cup lemon juice

Mix all ingredients together in a glass container. Marinate meat in sauce 12 to 24 hours in the refrigerator. Great for shish-kabobs.
Yield: 3½ cups

Lisa Horkan

Blueberry Sauce

½ cup sugar
2 tablespoons corn starch
Dash of salt
½ cup water

1 pint blueberries
1 tablespoon lemon juice
1 teaspoon lemon rind,
    grated

Combine sugar, corn starch and salt in pan. Stir in water. Add blueberries, bring to a boil. Simmer until it thickens slightly, about 4 minutes. (Sauce will not be too thick.) Remove from heat, add lemon juice and rind. Chill.
Yield: 2 cups

Paula Neely

Fudge Sauce

3 (1-ounce) squares
   unsweetened chocolate
Handful of semi-sweet
   chocolate pieces
2 cups confectioners sugar,
   sifted

1 (5⅓-ounce) can
   evaporated milk
3 tablespoons butter
⅛ teaspoon salt
1 teaspoon vanilla

Melt chocolate. Gradually add sugar. Add milk and cook until smooth, stirring constantly. Add butter and salt. Cook until butter is melted, stirring occasionally. Add vanilla. Serve warm or store in refrigerator. Reheat in double boiler before using. If too thick, thin with evaporated milk, cream or hot water.
Yield: 6 to 8 servings

Mrs. William E. Smith, Sr.

Praline Sauce

1 cup brown sugar, firmly
   packed
½ cup half and half
½ cup butter

½ cup pecans, finely
   chopped and toasted
½ teaspoon vanilla extract

Combine sugar, half and half, and butter in a small saucepan. Bring to a boil over medium heat, stirring constantly. Boil one minute. Remove from heat. Stir in pecans and vanilla. Serve warm or store in refrigerator. Great over ice cream.
Yield: 2 cups

Paula Neely

Bread and Butter Pickles

1 gallon cucumbers, thinly
  sliced
1 large onion, thinly sliced
1 teaspoon turmeric
1 teaspoon mustard seed

1 teaspoon celery seed
4 cups sugar
4 cups vinegar
¼ cup salt

Pack, alternating cucumbers and onions, into large mouth gallon jar. On top put the turmeric, mustard seed, and celery seed. Bring the sugar, vinegar and salt to a rolling boil. Pour this mixture into jar over cucumbers. Shake jar every hour for the next 24 hours. Must be stored in refrigerator.
Yield: 1 gallon

Mary Jo Stone

Chutney

2 cans apple pie slices
  or 12 apples, sliced
2 cans whole tomatoes or
  12 tomatoes, chopped
6 onions, chopped
2 green peppers, chopped
2 quarts dark pickling
  vinegar
2 teaspoons salt
2 ounces crystallized
  ginger
1 teaspoon each cloves,
  cinnamon, allspice

1½ tablespoons ground
  ginger
3 cloves garlic, thinly sliced
Lemon with rind, thinly
  sliced
½ cup dry mustard
2 teaspoons curry powder
2 pounds light brown sugar
Red pepper to taste
1 pint dark corn syrup
2 boxes currants
2 boxes raisins

Combine all ingredients, except currants and raisins. Simmer 3 or 4 hours. Add currants and raisins. Set covered overnight in pot. If not thick enough, cook more in the morning. Store in jars.
Yield: Approximately 15 half-pint jars

Becky Duggan

Chutney for Pork Tenderloin

¾ cup onion, chopped
2 tablespoons butter
1 cup red plum preserves
½ cup brown sugar, packed
¾ cup water
2 tablespoons lemon juice

⅓ cup chili sauce
¼ cup soy sauce
2 tablespoons Dijon
  mustard
3 drops Tabasco

Sauté onions in butter. Add remaining ingredients. Simmer for one hour or until thickened. Serve warm. Best if thick when serving.
Yield: 10 servings

Gail Qurnell

Glazed Apples

2 cups sugar
2 cups water
1½ dozen small, firm,
  uniform-sized apples,
  peeled and cored

Lemon juice
Red vegetable coloring or
  red cinnamon candy
  (both, if color is needed)
Butter

To make syrup, boil sugar and water for a few minutes. Add coloring and/or cinnamon candy to achieve desired color. Once peeled and cored, roll each apple in lemon juice. Immediately place apples in the syrup. Cook a few apples at a time in order to keep well turned. After apples are done, bake with a little butter inside. Spread the syrup, in which they were cooked, over them. Delicious apples are pretty for garnishing meat platters. Pear halves may also be prepared in the same manner.
Yield: 1½ dozen apples

Mrs. Love Felton

Hot Pepper Jelly

¼ to ½ cup hot peppers,
 finely ground
¾ cup bell peppers, ground
 (approximately 3)
6½ cups sugar

1½ cups apple cider
 vinegar
1½ boxes Certo (3 silver
 pouches)

Bring peppers, sugar, and vinegar to a hard boil, stirring with wooden spoon. Cool for 5 minutes. Add Certo. Mix. Add a few drops of green or red food coloring. Put into 8-ounce jars and seal.
Yield: 8 (8-ounce) jars

Mary Katherine Turner

Lake Pines Orange Preserves

8 oranges
4 cups sugar
½ cup vinegar
12 whole cloves

3 sticks cinnamon, broken
 in half
1 small can pineapple
 chunks, liquid reserved
1 (8-ounce) jar red cherries

Cover whole oranges with water. Let boil about 30 minutes. Do not overcook. (Check for doneness by sticking with long fork. If oranges spew, they are ready.) Drain. Pour cold water over oranges and let cool. Cut up oranges and save juices. Mix sugar, vinegar, and all juices. Add cloves, cinnamon, pineapple, and oranges. Cook slowly for 3 to 4 hours. Add cherries near end of cooking time. Leave overnight in pot. Pour in jars.
Yield: 10 (4-ounce) jars

Becky Duggan

Peach Chutney

4 cups (about 3 pounds)
   peaches, chopped
½ cup white vinegar
¼ cup lemon juice
1 cup golden raisins
⅓ cup onion, chopped
¼ cup preserved ginger,
   slivered

1 teaspoon allspice
½ teaspoon cinnamon
½ teaspoon cloves
½ teaspoon ginger
1 tablespoon salt
1 (1¾-ounce) box Sure-jell
4¼ cups sugar (2 pounds)

Combine all ingredients except Sure-jell and sugar in a large pot and mix well. Stir in Sure-jell. Bring to a rolling boil over high heat, stirring constantly. Add sugar. Bring to boil again. Boil hard for 5 minutes. KEEP STIRRING! Remove from heat. Stir for 10 minutes to cool slightly and prevent fruit from rising to top. Pour into sterilized jars and process to seal.
Yield: 8 (8-ounce) jars

Diane Moore

Pear Honey Preserves

12 cups pears, crushed and
   grated
1 cup crushed pineapple

10 pounds, minus 3 cups
   sugar
Juice of 5 lemons
1 (15-ounce) package Certo

Combine all ingredients except Certo and bring to a rolling boil. Boil one minute. Add Certo. Boil one more minute. Place into clean 8-ounce jelly jars. Immediately place seals on jars and rims. As soon as the seal has sealed, tighten the rim.
Yield: 13 (8-ounce) jars

Lanelle Rogers

Candied Grapefruit or Orange Peel

4 grapefruit shells or 6
   orange shells
1 teaspoon salt

3 cups sugar (divided)
1 cup water

Cut peel into strips ¼-inch wide from stem to blossom end. Put in saucepan and add salt. Cover with water. Boil 15 minutes. Pour off water. Add fresh water. Boil 20 minutes. Change water again, and boil another 20 minutes. Drain thoroughly. Cover with 2½ cups sugar and 1 cup water. Simmer, stirring continually to prevent scorching, until syrup has boiled away. Spread on waxed paper. Roll each piece in remaining sugar.
Yield: 4 dozen

Becky Duggan

Spiced Raisins

2⅔ cups water
1½ cups sugar
¾ cup vinegar
1 cup pineapple juice
½ to 1 teaspoon nutmeg

½ to 1 teaspoon allspice
½ to 1 teaspoon ground
   cloves
2 cups seedless raisins
Prepared mustard

Combine water, sugar, vinegar, pineapple juice, and spices. Heat to boiling. Add raisins. Simmer until syrup is thickened and raisins are spiced and plump. Add prepared mustard to enhance the flavor. A family favorite that is good served with baked ham.
Yield: 2 to 3 cups

Mrs. Love Felton

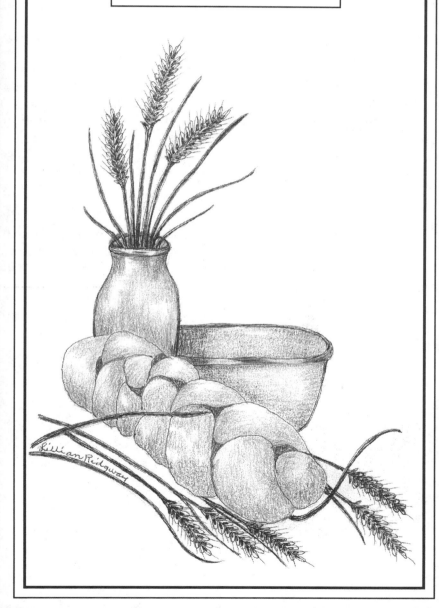

Warm Textures
Breads

Lillian Ridgway

Warm Textures

Breads

Creating the Setting

Moultrie artist Lillian Ridgeway (see biographical sketch on page 64) created this pen and ink drawing, "Grain Goodness." Ridgeway is noted for her attention to detail, as exhibited in her magnolia featured on our menu pages.

Combined for the Setting

Bread offers the soft texture and warmth vital to a truly enjoyable setting. This medium varies to complement each meal, from an informal breakfast meeting to afternoon tea. Envision not only the form, but the delightful flavors that will greet you in these next few pages.

Apple Bread

½ cup butter
1 cup sugar
2 eggs
½ teaspoon salt
1 teaspoon soda

2 tablespoons buttermilk
2 cups all-purpose flour
1 teaspoon vanilla
2 cups apples, peeled,
    cored, and chopped

Topping:
2 tablespoons butter
2 tablespoons sugar

2 tablespoons flour
2 teaspoons cinnamon

Cream butter and sugar. Add eggs one at a time, mixing after each. Add salt. Dissolve soda in buttermilk and add to mixture. Add remaining ingredients and mix. Pour into loaf pan. Prepare topping by mixing butter, sugar, flour, and cinnamon. Crumble on top of loaf. Bake at 350 degrees for 1 hour.
Yield: 1 loaf

Nell Brown

Applesauce Muffins

1 cup butter, softened
2 cups sugar
2 eggs
2 cups applesauce
4 cups all-purpose flour
2 teaspoons baking soda

1 teaspoon salt
1 tablespoon cinnamon
2 teaspoons allspice
½ teaspoon ground cloves
1 cup pecans, chopped

Cream butter. Add sugar, beating well. Add eggs one at a time, beating well after each addition. Add applesauce, mixing well. Sift together flour, baking soda, salt, cinnamon, allspice, and cloves. Add to creamed mixture, stirring well. Stir in pecans. Fill greased miniature muffin pans about ¾ full. Bake at 350 degrees for 14 minutes or until light brown. Batter may be made ahead and refrigerated until needed. Full-sized muffin tin may be used which will increase cooking time.
Yield: 7 dozen

Jessica Jordan

Baby Broccoli Muffins

1 (10-ounce) package frozen
   chopped broccoli
1 (7½-ounce) box corn
   muffin mix

4 eggs, beaten
1 stick margarine, melted
¾ cup cottage cheese
1 large onion, chopped

Preheat oven to 425 degrees. Grease miniature muffin tins. Cook broccoli according to package directions. Drain well. Mix corn muffin mix, eggs, margarine, cottage cheese, onion, and broccoli. Put in tins and bake 10 to 12 minutes.
Yield: 5 to 6 dozen

Paula Neely

Banana Bread

1 cup Crisco shortening
2 cups sugar
2 eggs
2 cups bananas, mashed
3 cups all-purpose flour

1 teaspoon salt
1 teaspoon soda
¼ cup buttermilk
1 teaspoon vanilla

Cream shortening and sugar, adding sugar slowly to shortening. Add eggs one at a time, mixing after each. Add bananas and vanilla, mixing well. Mix in flour and salt. Combine soda and buttermilk and add to mixture. Spray 1 large tube pan or 2 loaf pans with Pam. Pour into pans. Bake at 350 degrees for 1 to 1½ hours.
Yield: 1 tube pan or 2 loaves

Cherie Anne Whiddon

Banana-Pecan Coffee Cake

¾ cup pecans, chopped
¼ cup brown sugar, packed
1 teaspoon cinnamon
1½ cups self-rising flour
¾ cup sugar

1½ cups ripe bananas,
  mashed (about 3)
⅓ cup vegetable oil
2 eggs
1 teaspoon vanilla

Preheat oven to 350 degrees. Lightly grease 9-inch square baking pan. Mix pecans, brown sugar, and cinnamon and set aside. Stir flour and sugar until well mixed. Combine bananas, oil, eggs, and vanilla and mix until blended. Add liquid ingredients to flour mixture and stir just until moistened. Spread half of batter into prepared pan and sprinkle with half of brown sugar mixture. Top with remaining batter and sprinkle with remaining brown sugar mixture. Bake for 35 to 40 minutes until toothpick inserted in center comes out clean. Cool in pan for 10 minutes before serving.
Yield: 8 to 9 servings

Marsha McLean

Banana Muffins

1½ sticks margarine or
  butter
1½ cups sugar
4 eggs

1 cup bananas, mashed
1 pound or 12 ounces
  vanilla wafers, crushed
1 cup nuts, chopped

Cream margarine and sugar. Add eggs and remaining ingredients. Bake at 350 degrees in greased muffin pans. Fill pans full. Bake for 15 minutes for small muffins; 20 to 25 minutes for large muffins.
Yield: 5 dozen small or 1½ dozen large muffins

Paula Neely

Blueberry Lemon Bread

¼ cup plus 2 tablespoons
   butter or margarine,
   softened
1 cup sugar
2 eggs
2½ cups all-purpose flour

1 teaspoon baking powder
Pinch of salt
½ cup milk
2 teaspoons lemon rind,
   grated
1 cup fresh blueberries

Glaze:
½ cup confectioners' sugar

3 tablespoons lemon juice

Cream butter. Gradually add sugar, beating at medium speed of an electric mixer until well blended. Add eggs, one at a time, mixing well after each. Combine flour, baking powder, and salt. Add to creamed mixture alternately with milk beginning and ending with flour mixture. Stir in lemon rind and fold in blueberries. Pour batter into a greased 8 x 4 inch loaf pan. Bake at 350 degrees for 55 minutes or until a wood pick inserted in center comes out clean. Prepare glaze by mixing confectioners' sugar and lemon juice until smooth. Cool bread slightly. Poke holes in top with a toothpick and pour glaze over. Make a delicious lemon bread by deleting blueberries.
Yield: 1 loaf

Arlene Schreiber
*Similar recipe submitted by Caroline Frizoli

Bran Muffins

6 cups of 100% bran cereal
2 cups boiling water
2 cups sugar
5 cups flour
5 teaspoons soda
2 teaspoons salt

1 teaspoon cinnamon
4 eggs or 1 carton
   Eggbeaters
1 cup oil
1 quart buttermilk
1 box raisins

In a bowl, combine 2 cups of bran cereal and water. Let stand. In separate bowl combine remaining cereal, sugar, flour, soda, salt, and cinnamon. Add eggs, oil, and buttermilk, mixing well. Add reserved cereal and water, mixing well. Stir in raisins. Bake in greased muffin pans at 400 degrees for 20 minutes. Bake in mini-muffin pans for 10 minutes. Batter keeps in refrigerator for up to 6 weeks.
Yield: 5 to 6 dozen

Ann Friedlander
*Similar recipes submitted by Cathy Mobley and Caroline Frizoli

Carrot Muffins

½ cup oil
2 cups brown sugar
4 eggs
2 cups flour
2 teaspoons baking powder

1 teaspoon salt
2 teaspoons lemon juice
2 teaspoons vanilla
2 cups carrots, grated

Combine oil and brown sugar and mix well with mixer for about 5 minutes. Add eggs and mix. Sift together flour, baking powder and salt. With mixer on lowest speed, add to mixture. Add lemon juice and vanilla. Add carrots. Spoon batter into well-greased muffin tins, and bake for 30 minutes at 350 degrees.
Yield: 2 dozen

Diane Moore

Broccoli-Cheddar Rolls

1 (16-ounce) loaf frozen
  bread dough, thawed
1 (10-ounce) package frozen
  chopped broccoli,
  thawed and drained
  well
1 cup (4 ounces) Cheddar
  cheese, shredded

1 egg, beaten
2 tablespoons instant
  minced onion
1 teaspoon onion salt
2 tablespoons butter or
  margarine, melted

Roll dough into a 12-inch square on a lightly floured surface. Combine broccoli and next 4 ingredients, stirring well. Spread mixture evenly over dough, leaving a ½-inch border. Starting on one side, roll dough tightly, jelly roll fashion. Moisten seam edge of dough with water; press securely to seal, turning seam side down. Cut roll into 8 slices. Cut each slice almost in half again, cutting to within ½-inch of bottom. Gently open out halves, invert, and place on a lightly greased baking sheet. Brush with melted butter. Cover and let rise in a warm place for 45 minutes or until double in bulk. Bake at 375 degrees for 18 to 20 minutes or until golden brown.
Yield: 8 rolls

Ava English

Cornbread

3 eggs
2 cups buttermilk
1 teaspoon baking soda
1 cup flour

2 cups plain cornmeal
2 teaspoons salt
2 teaspoons baking powder
1 tablespoon sugar

Beat eggs with buttermilk and soda. Add other ingredients. (Add ¾ cup water to make a thinner batter.) Bake in 2 hot, well-greased pans or iron skillets at 375 degrees for 20 minutes. Cook until dry, but not brown.
Yield: 24 servings

Elaine Redding

Cranberry Nut Bread

2 cups sifted all-purpose
  flour
1 cup sugar
1½ teaspoons baking
  powder
1 teaspoon salt
½ teaspoon baking soda

¼ cup margarine
1 teaspoon orange peel,
  grated
¾ cup orange juice
1 egg, well beaten
1 cup cranberries, chopped
½ cup nuts, chopped

Stir flour, sugar, baking powder, salt, and baking soda together. Cut in margarine. Add orange peel, orange juice, and egg. Stir just to moisten. Fold in cranberries and nuts. Bake in greased and floured loaf pan at 350 degrees for 60 minutes. May be baked for 45 minutes in 3 small loaf pans.
Yield: 1 large or 3 small loaves

Mary Stapleton

Helen Whitney's Pumpkin Bread

3 cups sugar
4 eggs
1 cup oil
3½ cups all-purpose flour
2 teaspoons salt
1 teaspoon baking powder
2 teaspoons soda

1 teaspoon cinnamon
1 teaspoon allspice
1 teaspoon ginger
½ teaspoon ground cloves
1 cup pumpkin, packed
1 cup minced meat
⅔ cup water

Mix sugar, eggs, and oil. Add dry ingredients that have been sifted together. Add pumpkin and minced meat. Pour in water. Grease and flour large Bundt pan. Bake 45 minutes to 1 hour at 350 degrees. Wrap bread in plastic wrap while still warm. May also be baked in miniature loaf pans.
Yield: 1 Bundt cake or 14 miniature loaves

Judy Mobley
*Similar recipe submitted by Sandy Hooks

Golden Holiday Bread

¾ cup milk
½ cup butter or margarine
½ cup water (divided)
3 cups all-purpose flour
   (divided)
¾ cup sugar (divided)
1 package dry yeast

½ teaspoon salt
3 egg yolks
1 cup golden raisins
¼ cup sugar
¼ cup water
2 tablespoons lemon juice

Combine milk, butter, and ¼ cup water in a small saucepan. Cook over low heat until butter melts, stirring occasionally. Cool to 120 to 130 degrees. Combine 1½ cups flour, ½ cup sugar, yeast, and salt in a large mixing bowl. Gradually add liquid mixture to flour mixture, beating at low speed with an electric mixer. Beat an additional 2 minutes at medium speed. Add ½ cup flour and egg yolks, and beat 2 minutes at high speed. Gradually stir in remaining flour and raisins (dough will be sticky). Cover, and let rise in a warm place (85 degrees) free from drafts for 1 hour. (Dough will not double in bulk.) Punch dough down. Spoon in a greased 12-cup Bundt pan. Cover and let rise in a warm place, free from drafts, about an hour. Bake at 350 degrees for 35 minutes or until golden brown. Remove bread from pan immediately. Combine ¼ cup sugar, ¼ cup water, and lemon juice stirring until sugar dissolves. Brush glaze over warm bread. Let cool completely on a wire rack.
Yield: 1 loaf

Miller Beer Bread

3 tablespoons sugar
3 cups self-rising flour

1 (12-ounce) can Miller beer

Stir ingredients together. Place in greased loaf pan. Bake at 400 degrees for 30 to 40 minutes.
Yield: 1 loaf

Sandy Hooks

Duke's Corn Bread

1½ cups Duke's Mayonnaise
1 (17-ounce) can whole
   kernel corn, undrained

2 eggs
1 (12-ounce) box corn
   muffin mix

Combine all ingredients and pour into a greased 2-quart baking dish. Bake at 350 degrees for 35 to 40 minutes.
Yield: 10 to 12 servings

Sandra Plant

Old-Fashioned Soft Gingerbread

½ cup butter, softened
½ cup sugar
1 egg
1 cup unsulfured molasses
1 cup sour milk or
   buttermilk
1¾ teaspoons soda

2¾ cups unbleached all-
   purpose flour
2 teaspoons powdered
   ginger
1 teaspoon cinnamon
¼ teaspoon ground cloves
½ teaspoon salt

Preheat oven to 350 degrees. Beat the butter and sugar until fluffy. Add egg and beat well. Combine molasses, milk, and soda. Sift together flour, spices, and salt. Add the two mixtures to the butter mixture alternately, beating continuously. Pour into a greased 9x9-inch baking/serving dish. Bake for 30 to 35 minutes. Bread is done if no imprint is left after pressing the surface with a fingertip. Serve warm with any of the following toppings: sweet whipped cream, whipped cream cheese mixed with crystallized ginger, marshmallow fluff, or sweet butter.
Yield: 9 to 12 servings

Connie Fritz

Nell Dekle's Baked Dressing

1 package stuffing crumb
   mix (herb or plain)
1 onion, chopped
1 egg
1½ to 2 soup cans of water
   or broth

½ teaspoon salt
½ teaspoon sage
½ teaspoon pepper
1 small can cream of
   chicken soup
½ soup can water or milk

Combine first 7 ingredients. Use part or all of the water or broth, depending on moistness desired in dressing. Put in greased casserole dish. Thin cream of chicken soup with ½ can of water or milk. Pour on top of casserole. Bake at 350 degrees for 30 minutes.
Yield: 6 to 7 servings

Ellen Dekle Alderman

Orange Blossoms

4 eggs, well beaten
¾ cup water
¾ cup Wesson Oil

1 package Duncan Hines
   Yellow Cake Mix
1 package lemon instant
   pudding

Icing:
2 teaspoons Wesson Oil
⅓ cup plus 2 teaspoons
   orange juice

1 box 4x confectioners'
   sugar
Yellow food coloring

To eggs, add water, Wesson Oil, cake mix, and lemon pudding. Beat for 3 minutes. Spray Pam in 4 small muffin tins. Fill half full. Bake at 350 degrees for 12 minutes on middle rack of oven. Prepare icing by combining oil, orange juice, confectioners' sugar, and food coloring. While muffins are hot, dip the tops into the icing or spread icing on tops of muffins with a knife. These also freeze well.
Yield: 8 dozen

Pam Rojas

Orange French Toast

2 eggs
½ cup orange juice
1 teaspoon brown sugar

5 to 6 slices French bread,
    cut ¼-inch thick
1 to 2 teaspoons oil
Maple syrup

Beat eggs, juice, and sugar until combined. Dip bread in mixture. Let stand 30 seconds. Put oil in skillet and cook bread slices on medium heat for 2 to 3 minutes on each side until brown. Serve with maple syrup.

Yield: 2 to 3 servings

Polly Boetcher

Oyster Dressing Stuffing

1 cup cooked corn bread
    with 3 strips bacon fried
    crisp and crumbled into
    batter before cooking
4 slices white bread,
    toasted
1 package Pepperidge
    Farm dressing
Chicken stock
2 sticks butter (divided)
2 large onions, chopped
3 stalks celery, chopped

¼ bell pepper, chopped
3 or 4 green onions,
    chopped
1 bay leaf
½ teaspoon thyme
¼ teaspoon rosemary
½ teaspoon oregano
2 pinches nutmeg
Salt to taste
Pepper to taste
2 pints oysters

Put all breads in large bowl and soak with enough chicken stock to moisten. Fry onions, celery, bell pepper, green onions, and spices in 1 stick of butter. Add vegetables to bread mixture, along with salt and pepper to taste. Check oysters for shells and fry in remaining butter until edges of oysters curl. Add bread mixture to oysters, and fry again until flavors are blended, about 10 minutes. Use to stuff turkey. May be done ahead and frozen without oysters.

Yield: 16 servings

Refrigerator Rolls

6 to 6½ cups all-purpose
   flour (divided)
½ cup sugar
1 teaspoon salt
2 tablespoons yeast

½ cup butter, softened
2 cups medium-warm tap
   water
1 egg
Salad oil

Early in the day or up to 1 week ahead, combine 2¼ cups flour, sugar, salt, and yeast. Add ½ cup softened butter. With mixer at low speed, gradually add 2 cups medium warm tap water. Add egg; increase speed to medium and beat 2 minutes. Beat in ¾ cup flour and continue beating for 2 minutes. Stir in additional flour (about 2½ cups) with spoon. Knead until smooth and elastic. Shape into ball and place in large, greased bowl. Let rise until doubles, about 1½ hours. Punch down; turn dough over and brush with oil. Cover with plastic and refrigerate, punching down occasionally until ready to use. Two hours before serving, grease pan. Shape 30 rolls. Cover and let rise. Bake at 425 degrees for 15 to 20 minutes.
Yield: 30 rolls

Nanci Lewis
*Similar recipe submitted by Mary Ann Blank

Spoon Bread

1 pint whole milk
¾ cup corn meal
1 teaspoon salt

3 egg yolks, well beaten
3 tablespoons butter
3 egg whites, beaten

Scald milk and stir in corn meal and salt. Cook until thick. Add egg yolks and butter. Last fold in egg whites and place in a well-buttered baking dish. Set in a pan of water and cook at 375 degrees for 35 minutes or until done.
Yield: 8 to 10 servings

Deryl Beadles

Sea Island Company
Corn Bread Muffins

6 ounces butter
4 ounces sugar
4 eggs
4 ounces bacon, diced
1 (12-ounce) can cream
   style corn
4 ounces Cheddar cheese,
   shredded

4 ounces Jack cheese,
   shredded
8 ounces pastry flour
8 ounces yellow corn meal
4 tablespoons baking
   powder
1 teaspoon salt

Preheat oven to 350 degrees. Cream butter and sugar. Add eggs one at a time, mixing after each. Add remainder of ingredients and mix until well incorporated. Fill well-greased muffin tins half way. Bake for approximately 20 minutes.
Yield: 2 dozen

Judy Mobley

Zucchini Bread

3 cups flour
2 teaspoons soda
1 teaspoon salt
½ teaspoon baking powder
1 tablespoon cinnamon
¾ cup nuts, chopped
3 eggs

2 cups sugar
1 cup vegetable oil
2 teaspoons vanilla
2 cups zucchini, shredded
1 can pineapple, drained
   (optional)

Combine dry (first 5) ingredients and nuts. Beat eggs. Add sugar, oil and vanilla beating until creamy. Stir in zucchini and pineapple. Add dry ingredients and stir until moistened. Spoon batter into 2 well-greased and floured loaf pans. Bake at 350 degrees for 55 minutes.
Yield: 2 loaves

Amanda Statom

Sour Cream Coffee Cake

¼ cup pecans, chopped
2 tablespoons brown sugar,
    firmly packed
2 teaspoons ground
    cinnamon
1 cup butter
1 cup sugar

2 eggs
2 cups all-purpose flour
1 teaspoon baking powder
1 teaspoon soda
1 (8-ounce) carton sour
    cream

Glaze:
1¼ cups confectioners'
    sugar, sifted

1 tablespoon water
¼ teaspoon vanilla

Combine pecans, brown sugar, and cinnamon. Stir well and set aside. Cream butter and gradually add sugar, beating until fluffy. Add eggs and beat well. Combine flour, baking powder, and soda. Add to cream mixture alternately with sour cream, beginning and ending with flour mixture. Spoon half of batter into a greased and floured 10-inch Bundt pan. Sprinkle half of pecan mixture over batter. Repeat layers. Bake at 375 degrees for 35 to 40 minutes. Cool in pan. Prepare glaze with powdered sugar, water, and vanilla, mixing well. Drizzle glaze over cake. Store overnight in airtight container.
Yield: 12 to 16 servings

Rhonda Sauls

Final Touches
Cakes, Candy, Cookies, Desserts & Pies

Final Touches

Cakes, Candy, Cookies, Desserts and Pies

Creating the Setting

Kelly Jones, active member of the Moultrie Service League, provided this pen and ink drawing of an afternoon tea setting in the home of Mr. and Mrs. Jack Gay of Moultrie. Kelly, formerly of Ocilla, Georgia, is married to Lynn Jones, Jr., and they have two young sons, Trey and Braxton. Kelly graduated from Valdosta State University in 1993 with her B.S. in Education. She received no formal art training during her education, but has recently enjoyed occasional painting classes at the Colquitt County Arts Center under the direction of Kathy Flowers. She also provided the sample art used in **Beginning Strokes**, our children's section. Kelly is creative and energetic, as well as involved in civic activities, serving as President of the Moultrie Junior Woman's Club.

Combined for the Setting

Celebrate your ability to combine all of the mediums necessary for a masterpiece by adding the irresistible final touch. Careful attention to detail is required for some of these favorites. However, with only a few minutes, your setting can be remembered by the scrumptious grand finale. *Bon Appetite!*

Caramel Cake

12 ounces Crisco	1¼ cups milk
5 eggs	1 teaspoon baking powder
3 cups cake flour	½ teaspoon salt
3 cups sugar	1 teaspoon vanilla

Icing:

2 cups brown sugar (1½ cups light and ½ cup dark)	½ cup milk
2 teaspoons vanilla	
2 sticks margarine	1 box 4X sugar

For cake, sift together dry ingredients. Cream sugar and Crisco; add eggs. Alternate milk and dry ingredients. Pour in 4 (9-inch) pans which have been greased and floured. Bake at 350 degrees for 30 minutes.

For icing, melt margarine and brown sugar; add milk and boil 5 minutes. Cool and add vanilla and sugar. Beat and spread.
Yield: 4 layer cake

Karen Willis

Watergate Cake

1 box yellow cake mix	1 cup oil
1 box pistachio instant pudding mix	1 cup ginger ale or tonic water
3 eggs	1 cup nuts, chopped

Glaze:

Confectioner's sugar	Milk
A drop of vanilla	

Combine first six ingredients. Mix on medium speed for 2 minutes. Pour into greased and floured 9 x 13-inch or Bundt pan. Bake at 350 degrees for 45 minutes or until done. Cool completely. Decorate if desired, making glaze of medium-thick consistency.
Yield: 16 servings

Caroline Frizoli

Lynn Acuff's Mother's Caramel Cake

1 cup Crisco
3 cups sugar
7 or 8 eggs

3 cups all-purpose flour
½ pint whipping cream
1 tablespoon vanilla

Cream Crisco and sugar. Add 4 eggs, one at a time. Add 1 cup of flour. Add rest of eggs, one at a time and 1 more cup of flour. Add last cup of flour, alternately with whipping cream. Add vanilla. Bake at 350 degrees for 25 to 30 minutes in greased and floured pans.
Yield: Three 13 x 9-inch or 4 round layers.

Brown Caramel Cake Icing:
4½ cups sugar (divided)
2 sticks butter
1 cup whole milk

6 tablespoons light Karo syrup

Turn on 2 burners of stove. In skillet on first burner, brown ½ cup of the sugar until brown as desired. In medium-sized saucepan on the other burner, bring remaining ingredients to a boil. Add browned sugar to saucepan, and return to boiling. Boil for 2 minutes. Remove from heat, and beat until creamy. Spread between layers, top and sides. Note: To frost a pound cake, reduce recipe by one-half.
Yield: Frosting for 3 long or 4 round layers

Elizabeth Odom

Carrot Cake

2 cups sugar
1½ cups Wesson Oil
4 eggs
2 cups flour

2 teaspoons salt
2 teaspoons baking soda
2 teaspoons cinnamon
3 cups carrots, grated

Icing:
1 (8-ounce) package cream
    cheese
1 stick margarine

1 box 4X sugar
1 cup pecans, grated
Pecan halves

Beat sugar and oil; add eggs one at a time. Mix together dry ingredients and add to sugar mixture. Stir in carrots. Bake in 3 9-inch pans which have been floured and greased. Bake at 350 degrees for 20 minutes. Mix together icing ingredients and spread on each layer. Top cake with pecan halves.
Yield: 3 layer cake

Karen Willis

Yellow Layer Cake

3 cups sugar
½ cup Crisco
¼ cup butter or margarine
5 eggs, at room
    temperature

3 cups sifted all-purpose
    flour
1 teaspoon baking soda
1½ cups buttermilk
1 teaspoon vanilla

Cream together sugar, Crisco and butter until light and fluffy. Add eggs, one at a time, beating well after each. Add baking soda to buttermilk and dissolve. Add flour and buttermilk alternately to creamed mixture, mixing well after each addition, and ending with flour. Add vanilla and mix. Pour into 4 (9-inch) cake pans that have been greased, floured and bottoms lined with waxed paper. Bake at 350 degrees, 20 to 25 minutes until done. Good with any frosting or filling.
Yield: 4 layer cake

Paula Neely

Laura Keith's Heavenly Coconut Cake

2 fresh coconuts
4 cups all-purpose flour
2⅔ cups sugar
5½ teaspoons baking
   powder

2 teaspoons salt (divided)
6 egg whites
2 cups heavy cream
3 teaspoons vanilla

Reserve coconut milk and grate coconuts. Set aside. Sift flour, sugar, baking powder and 1½ teaspoons salt. Repeat sifting. Beat egg whites with remaining ½ teaspoon salt until stiff. Whip cream until stiff and fold lightly into whites with whisk. Alternately add in thirds, dry ingredients, coconut milk and vanilla. Pour into 4 greased and floured 9-inch cake pans. Bake at 350 degrees for 20 minutes. Cool.
Yield: 4 layer cake

Coconut Syrup:
1 cup water
½ cup sugar

½ cup coconut

Combine water and sugar in small saucepan. Boil 5 minutes. Add coconut. Mixture will be thin.

Frosting:
4½ cups granulated sugar
1 cup water
6 tablespoons light corn
   syrup

6 egg whites
⅓ cup confectioner's sugar

Combine granulated sugar, water and corn syrup. Boil syrup until it reaches the soft ball stage (234 to 240 degrees). Beat 6 egg whites until stiff. With mixer on, add hot syrup in a steady stream. Continue mixing while adding confectioner's sugar.

(Continued on next page)

(Laura Keith's Heavenly Coconut Cake, continued)

To assemble, spread first layer with coconut syrup. Cover with a thick layer of frosting then cover with a layer of grated coconut. Repeat until layers are stacked, then frost entire cake and cover with grated coconut.
Yield: Frosting for 4 layer cake

Laura Keith

Italian Cream Cake

1 stick margarine	1 teaspoon soda
½ cup shortening	1 cup buttermilk
2 cups sugar	1 teaspoon vanilla extract
5 egg yolks	1 cup chopped pecans
2 cups cake flour	5 egg whites, stiffly beaten

Cream margarine and shortening; add sugar and beat until mixture is smooth. Add egg yolks and beat well. Combine flour and soda and add to creamed mixture alternately with buttermilk. Stir in vanilla; add chopped pecans. Fold in stiffly beaten egg whites. Pour batter into three greased and floured 8-inch cake pans. Bake at 350 degrees for 25 minutes. Cool. Frost with Cream Cheese Frosting.
Yield: Three 8-inch layers

Cream Cheese Frosting:

1 (8 ounce) package cream cheese (softened)	1 box powdered sugar
½ stick margarine	1 teaspoon vanilla extract
	Chopped pecans

Beat cream cheese and margarine until smooth; add sugar and mix well. Add vanilla extract and beat until smooth. Spread between layers and on top and sides of cake. Sprinkle top with pecans.
Yield: Enough for three 8-inch layers

Rhonda Sauls

Hummingbird Cake

3 cups all-purpose flour
1 teaspoon baking soda
½ teaspoon salt
2 cups sugar
1 teaspoon ground
   cinnamon
3 large eggs, well beaten
   with whisk or fork

¾ cup Wesson oil
1½ teaspoons vanilla
1 (8-ounce) can crushed
   pineapple, undrained
1¾ cups bananas, mashed
1 cup pecans, chopped

Combine first 5 ingredients in a large bowl. Add eggs, oil and vanilla, stirring until dry ingredients are moistened. Do not beat. Stir in pineapple, bananas and pecans. Pour batter into 3 greased and floured 9-inch round cake pans. Bake at 350 degrees for 23 to 28 minutes or until a wooden pick inserted in center comes out clean. Cool in pans on wire racks for 10 minutes. Remove from pans, and let cool completely on wire racks. Spread Cream Cheese Frosting between layers and on top and sides of cake.
Yield: 3 layer cake

Cream Cheese Frosting:
½ cup butter, softened
1 (8-ounce) package cream
   cheese, softened
1 (16-ounce) package XXXX
   powdered sugar, sifted

1 teaspoon vanilla
½ cup pecans, chopped
   (optional)

Beat butter and cream cheese at medium speed with an electric mixer. Reduce blender speed to low and gradually add powdered sugar. Beat at medium speed until light and fluffy. Stir in vanilla and pecans.
Yield: Frosting for 3 layer cake

Connie Mobley

Lemon Cheese Cake

Cake:

1 cup butter
3 cups sugar
3 cups flour, sifted
4 whole eggs
4 egg whites

½ pint whipping cream
1 teaspoon vanilla extract
½ teaspoon lemon extract
¼ teaspoon almond extract

Filling:

2 cups sugar
6 tablespoons corn starch
2½ cups water
Dash of salt
½ cup butter

1 teaspoon vanilla extract
4 egg yolks
¼ cup water
5 ounces lemon juice

For cake, cream butter and sugar; add eggs, one at a time. Alternate flour and cream. Add flavorings. Grease and flour 5 (9-inch) round cake pans. Use 1½ cups batter per pan. Bake at 350 degrees for 20 to 25 minutes. Cool 10 minutes and remove from pans.

For filling, combine sugar, corn starch, lemon juice, water and salt. Cook until hot; add butter and egg yolks mixed with water. Add vanilla. Allow lemon filling to cool, and ice and fill cake. Refrigerate until time to serve.
Yield: 5 layer cake

Elaine Redding

Luscious Lemon Cake

Lemon Curd Filling:

1 cup sugar
Peel of two large lemons,
   removed with zester
5 egg yolks

½ cup fresh lemon juice
½ cup unsalted butter,
   melted

Combine sugar and lemon zest in food processor until peel is finely minced. Add egg yolks and lemon juice. Blend for 5 seconds. With machine running pour melted butter through feed tube and blend. Transfer mixture into heavy non-aluminum saucepan. Cook over medium low heat, stirring constantly until curd is thickened and starts to boil, about 5 minutes. Remove from heat and cool. Refrigerate thoroughly before using.
Yield: 1⅔ cups filling

Cake Layers:

1¼ cups sugar
Peel of one lemon, removed
   with zester
3 eggs
¾ cup unsalted butter
¾ cup sour cream
¼ cup plus 2 tablespoons
   orange juice

2 tablespoons fresh lemon
   juice
1½ teaspoons lemon extract
1¾ cups cake flour
2 teaspoons baking powder
¾ teaspoon baking soda
¾ teaspoon salt

Cream butter and sugar. Add lemon peel. Add eggs, one at a time, mixing well. Sift flour, baking powder, baking soda, and salt together. Combine sour cream, orange juice, lemon juice, and lemon extract. Add sour cream mixture alternately with flour mixture. Divide batter among three 8-inch round cake pans which have been lined with parchment paper and buttered. Bake in 350 degrees oven until cake just begins to pull away from sides of pans, about 20 minutes. Transfer to wire racks. Let cool 10 minutes in pans. Invert onto racks and let cool. To frost, set one layer on serving platter. Spread evenly with half of Lemon Curd Filling. Top with second

(Continued on next page)

(Luscious Lemon Cake, continued)

layer and spread with remaining filling. Add top layer. Cover top and sides of cake with frosting.
Yield: 3 layer cake

Lemon Buttercream Frosting:

3 cups powdered sugar
Peel of one lemon, removed
  with zester
Pinch salt
5 tablespoons unsalted
  butter

4 to 5 tablespoons sour
  cream
2 tablespoons Lemon Curd
  Filling
¼ teaspoon lemon extract

Combine sugar, peel and salt in food processor until peel is finely minced. Add butter, 4 tablespoons sour cream, Lemon Curd Filling and extract. Mix 5 seconds. Add remaining sour cream if mixture is too thick. Refrigerate until firm enough to spread, about 10 to 15 minutes.
Yield: 2 cups

Diane Moore

Bishop's Cake

1½ cups sifted flour
1½ teaspoons baking
  powder
¼ teaspoon salt
⅔ cup semi-sweet chocolate
  pieces
2 cups walnuts, coarsely
  chopped

1 cup dates, finely snipped
1 cup glacéed cherries,
  halved
3 eggs
1 cup sugar
½ cup dark rum

Preheat oven to 325 degrees. Grease Bundt pan. Sift flour with baking powder and salt. Add next four ingredients. Stir until well coated. Set aside. Beat eggs in large mixing bowl. Gradually add sugar and rum. Add reserved mixture. Bake for one hour. Cool in pan on wire rack.
Yield: 12 to 16 servings

Becky Duggan

Strawberry Jello Cake

1 package white cake mix
1 package strawberry Jello
½ cup cold water
½ cup Wesson oil

3 eggs
1½ cups strawberries,
  mashed

Mix cake mix, Jello, and water. Add oil. Add eggs, one at a time. Add strawberries. Pour into 3 greased and floured cake pans. Bake at 325 degrees for 45 minutes. Cool.
Yield: 3 layer cake

Frosting:
1 stick butter or margarine
1 box 10X confectioner's
  sugar

Strawberry juice
Strawberries, mashed
  (optional)

Melt butter. Mix in confectioner's sugar. Add enough strawberry juice (and mashed strawberries if desired) to make spreading easy.
Yield: Frosting for 3 layers

Jessica Jordan

Applesauce Fruitcake

2 cups sugar
1 cup butter
4 eggs, well beaten
2 cups applesauce
4 cups all-purpose flour
2 cups pecans, chopped
2 cups raisins

2 teaspoons baking soda
2 teaspoons cinnamon
1 teaspoon ground cloves
1 teaspoon nutmeg
¼ pound candied cherries
¼ pound candied pineapple
  (chopped)

Cream sugar with butter. Add eggs. Add applesauce with flour. Add remaining ingredients. Bake at 275 degrees in large greased and floured tube pan, for 1½ to 2 hours. Good for the holiday season.
Yield: 15 to 20 servings

Rhett Smith

Erin's Caramel Icing

1 stick butter
1 small can evaporated
   milk

3 cups sugar (divided)
1 teaspoon vanilla
   (optional)

Mix butter, milk and 2½ cups sugar in large boiler. Melt remaining
½ cup sugar in skillet and pour into first mixture. Cook until soft
ball stage. Whip before spreading. Add vanilla, if desired.
Yield: Icing for one cake

Rhett Smith

Mrs. Smith's Chocolate Fudge Icing

2 cups sugar
4 to 5 tablespoons cocoa
½ cup butter

½ cup milk
½ teaspoon vanilla

Mix first four ingredients together. Boil hard until soft ball stage
(from 2 to 5 minutes). Add vanilla. Beat until creamy. Use to frost
Devil's Food Cake or yellow cake.
Yield: Icing for 1 cake

Rhett Smith

Best Cheesecake

Crust:

1 cup all-purpose flour
¼ cup sugar
1 teaspoon lemon peel, grated

¼ cup butter, softened
1 egg yolk
½ teaspoon vanilla

(These ingredients are easier to work with if doubled.) Stir together flour, sugar, and lemon peel. Blend in butter, egg yolk and vanilla. Mix with fingers until dough holds together. Press one cup of dough on bottom of a greased 9 x 3-inch springform pan. Cover remaining dough and set aside. Bake at 400 degrees until lightly browned, about 8 to 10 minutes. Cool on wire rack. Press reserved dough around sides of pan to height of 2½ inches, joining sides to baked bottom crust.

Filling:

5 (8-ounce) packages cream cheese, softened
1¾ cups sugar
3 tablespoons all-purpose flour

2 teaspoons lemon peel, grated
2 teaspoons vanilla
5 eggs
2 egg yolks
¼ cup whipping cream

Beat together cream cheese, sugar, flour, lemon peel and vanilla at high speed until fluffy. Add eggs and egg yolks, one at a time, beating well after each. Blend in cream. Pour filling into crust. Bake at 400 degrees for 10 minutes. Reduce heat to 250 degrees, and bake an additional 1 to 2 hours. Test center for doneness. Cool on wire rack. Spread cooled raspberry topping over. Refrigerate for eight hours.

Raspberry Topping:

1 (12-ounce) package frozen raspberries, liquid reserved

Water
2 tablespoons sugar
2 tablespoons corn starch

(Continued on next page)

260

(Best Cheesecake, continued)

Drain berries, reserving syrup. Add water to syrup to make ½ cup. Stir together sugar and corn starch. Stir in reserved liquid. Cook over medium heat until mixture boils and thickens. Stir in raspberries. Cool. Note: This is the biggest, best cheesecake that I have ever tasted! It always gets raves! Very much worth the effort.
Yield: 16 servings

Jane Holman

Cheesecake

Crust:
1¾ cups Graham cracker
   crumbs
1 stick margarine, melted

¾ cup sugar
2 teaspoons cinnamon
   (optional)

Filling:
3 (8-ounce) packages
   Philadelphia Brand
   Cream Cheese, softened
1 cup sugar
2 tablespoons all-purpose
   flour

1 tablespoon lemon juice
2 teaspoons lemon rind,
   grated
4 eggs

In bowl, combine Graham cracker crumbs, melted margarine, sugar and cinnamon. Press into bottom and 2½ inches up side of an 8 or 9-inch springform pan. Set aside. Combine cream cheese, sugar, flour, lemon juice and rind, mixing at medium speed on electric mixer until well blended. Add eggs, one at a time, mixing well after each addition. Pour over crust. Bake at 300 degrees for 1 hour and 15 minutes. Loosen cake from rim of pan. Cool before removing rim of pan. Cherry pie filling may be spooned over cooled cheesecake or use a smooth layer of sour cream, garnished with strawberries or other fruit.
Yield: 16 servings

Joy Matthews

Miniature Cheese Cakes

10 graham crackers,
  crushed
1 (8-ounce) package cream
  cheese, softened

¾ cup sugar
3 eggs, separated
1 (8-ounce) carton sour
  cream

Topping:
2½ tablespoons sugar
1 teaspoon vanilla

Cherry or blueberry pie
  filling

Butter the sides and bottoms of 4 miniature muffin tins. Sprinkle with graham cracker crumbs and shake to coat. Beat together the cream cheese and ¾ cup sugar. Add egg yolks, one at a time, beating well. Beat the egg whites until very stiff and fold into cream cheese mixture. Spoon filling into muffin tins almost to the top and bake in upper third of a preheated 350 degree oven for 10 minutes. Remove from oven and cool. Cakes will sink in the middle. Mix together the sour cream, sugar, and vanilla. Drop about 1 teaspoon of sour cream mixture in the center of each little cake. Bake 5 minutes in 400 degree oven. Cool before removing from pans. To facilitate removal from pans, loosen sides with sharp knife. Top each with blueberry or cherry pie filling.
Yield: 4 dozen

Judy Mobley
*Similar recipe submitted by Diane Moore

Chocolate-Bottom Cupcakes

1 (8-ounce) package cream
   cheese, room
   temperature
1 egg, beaten
1⅔ cups sugar (divided)
⅝ teaspoon salt (divided)
1 (6-ounce) package
   chocolate chips

1½ cups all-purpose flour
¼ cup cocoa
1 teaspoon baking soda
⅓ cup oil
1 teaspoon vanilla
1 cup water
1 tablespoon vinegar
⅔ cup nuts, chopped

Blend cream cheese, egg, ⅓ cup sugar, ⅛ teaspoon salt and chips.
Set aside. Sift together flour, one cup sugar, cocoa, baking soda and
salt. Mix oil, vanilla, water and vinegar. Add dry ingredients. Beat
well. Fill 18 paper-lined cupcake tins about one-third full with the
chocolate batter. Drop 1 heaping tablespoon of cheese mixture on
top of cupcake batter. Mix nuts and remaining ⅓ cup sugar, and
sprinkle over all. Bake in a preheated 350 degrees oven for 30 to 35
minutes or until cakes test done.
Yield: 1½ dozen

Sharon B. Adcock

Chocolate, Chocolate Chip Cake

1 package Devil's Food
   Chocolate Cake mix
1 (6-ounce) package instant
   chocolate pudding
1 cup sour cream

1 cup vegetable oil
4 eggs, beaten
½ cup warm water
1 (12-ounce) package
   chocolate chips

Preheat oven to 350 degrees. In a large bowl, mix together the cake
and pudding mix, sour cream, oil, eggs and water. Stir in chocolate
chips and pour batter into a well-buttered, nonstick, 12-cup Bundt
pan. Bake for 50 to 55 minutes or until top is springy to the touch.
Do not overbake! Cool and remove from pan. Serve plain or sprinkle
with powdered sugar.
Yield: 16 servings

Donna Marshall

Mimi's Cupcakes

1 cup butter
2 cups sugar
4 eggs
3 cups all-purpose flour
½ teaspoon salt

1 teaspoon baking powder
1 cup milk
1 teaspoon vanilla
  flavoring

Cream butter, and add sugar gradually. Add eggs one at a time, beating well after each addition. Sift flour, salt, and baking powder together, alternately with milk and flavoring. Pour batter into individual cupcake baking cups in muffin pan. Fill ½ to ⅔ full of batter. Bake at 350 degrees for 15 to 20 minutes. Cool completely before frosting.
Yield: 2 dozen

Mimi's Strawberry Icing:
⅓ cup Crisco or butter
¼ teaspoon salt
½ teaspoon lemon juice
½ small packet strawberry
  Kool-Aid

3½ cups confectioner's
  sugar (divided)
¼ cup milk

Combine Crisco or butter, salt, lemon juice, and Kool-Aid. Add 1 cup sugar. Stir in milk and remaining sugar alternately. Mix until smooth and creamy.
Yield: Icing for 2 dozen cupcakes

Judy Mobley

Hot Chocolate Texas Cake

2 cups sugar
2 cups all-purpose flour
1 stick margarine
½ cup Crisco
1 cup water

2 heaping tablespoons
  cocoa
½ cup buttermilk
2 eggs
1 tablespoon soda
1 tablespoon vanilla

Sift sugar and flour together. Set aside. Put next 4 ingredients in saucepan, and bring to a rapid boil. Take off heat and pour hot mixture over sugar and flour. Mix well. Add buttermilk, eggs, soda, and vanilla. Mix well. Pour into greased 11 x 16-inch pan. Bake at 400 degrees for 20 minutes. Batter will be thin. Start to make icing 5 minutes before cake is done.

Icing:
1 stick butter
4 tablespoons cocoa
6 tablespoons milk

1 box powdered sugar,
  sifted
1 tablespoon vanilla
1 cup nuts, chopped
  (optional)

Melt butter, and add cocoa and milk. Bring to a boil. Remove from heat and add sugar. Blend well. Add vanilla and nuts. Leave cake in pan and pour icing over hot cake.
Yield: 16 servings

Sandy Hooks
*Similar recipe submitted by Lisa Horkan

Chocolate Upside Down Cake

1 box chocolate cake mix
1 cup sugar

3 tablespoons cocoa
¾ cup boiling water

Prepare chocolate cake mix as directed on box, but only use half of batter for this recipe. Pour batter into 8 or 9-inch square pan. (Use other half of batter for making cupcakes.) Mix sugar and cocoa and pour over batter. Then pour boiling water on top of sugar mixture. Bake at 350 degrees for approximately 20 minutes, depending on size of pan. May be served with Cool Whip or ice cream.
Yield: 6 to 9 servings

Marsha McLean

Mother's Old Fashioned Pound Cake

1 pound pure butter
1 dozen large eggs
3½ cups sugar
4 cups White Lily all-
purpose flour, measure
after sifting

1 teaspoon baking powder
1½ teaspoons vanilla
1½ teaspoons lemon
flavoring

Leave butter and eggs out overnight. Gradually cream butter and sugar. Sift flour at least twice, adding ¼ teaspoon baking powder to each cup flour. Beginning and ending with flour, gradually blend flour and 2 eggs at a time with creamy mixture. Add vanilla and lemon flavorings. Pour into two 10-inch tube pans, greased and lightly floured. Bake at 325 degrees for 1 hour. Take out of oven. Place upside down on heavy duty foil. As soon as the cake falls onto foil, wrap the cake with the foil. Let cool. This cake freezes well. Also can use 16 x 4 x 4-inch long tube pan, cooking for 1½ hours or until cake pulls away from pan.
Yield: 24 servings per cake

Jane H. Brown
*Similar recipe submitted by Lynne Stone

Chocolate Pound Cake

1 cup butter, softened
½ cup shortening
3 cups sugar
5 eggs
3 cups all-purpose flour
½ teaspoon salt

½ teaspoon baking powder
7 tablespoons cocoa
1 teaspoon vanilla
1 cup milk
1 cup nuts, chopped

Cream butter, shortening and sugar. Add eggs, one at a time, beating well after each. Combine flour, salt, baking powder and cocoa. Add dry ingredients to creamed mixture. Mix well. Add vanilla and milk. Beat well; add nuts. Bake in greased and floured tube pan at 275 degrees for 2 hours.

Chocolate Icing:
1 stick butter
3 tablespoons cocoa
6 tablespoons buttermilk

1 box powdered sugar
1 teaspoon vanilla
1 cup nuts, chopped

Bring butter, cocoa and buttermilk to a boil. Add sugar, vanilla and nuts.
Yield: 16 servings

Angela Castellow
*Similar recipes submitted by Lee Willis and Sandy Hooks

Cream Cheese Pound Cake

3 sticks butter
1 (8-ounce) package cream
    cheese
3 cups sugar
6 eggs
1 teaspoon vanilla
    flavoring

½ teaspoon coconut
    flavoring
¼ teaspoon almond
    flavoring
3 cups all-purpose flour
½ teaspoon baking powder

Cream butter and cream cheese. Add sugar and eggs, beating well after each addition. Add flavorings, flour and baking powder. Bake in 9-inch tube pan at 325 degrees for 1½ hours. Test for doneness.
Yield: 16 servings

(Variation: 8 ounces of sour cream may be substituted for the cream cheese.)

Jennie Estes
*Similar recipes submitted by Sharon Adcock,
Susan Newton, Cindy Tyus and Ava English

Ava's Vanilla Icing For
Cream Cheese Pound Cake

1 (8-ounce) package cream
    cheese
½ stick butter, softened

1 teaspoon vanilla
1 box XXXX sugar

Blend cream cheese and butter. Add vanilla. Gradually blend sugar with creamy mixture.
Yield: Icing for 1 pound cake

Ava English

268

Marbled Pecan Pound Cake

½ cup butter, softened
½ cup plus 1 tablespoon
   shortening
3 cups sugar
5 large eggs
3 cups all-purpose flour
½ teaspoon baking powder

¼ teaspoon salt
1 cup milk
1 teaspoon vanilla
1 (1-ounce) square
   unsweetened chocolate
½ cup pecans, chopped

Beat butter and ½ cup shortening at medium speed with an electric mixer, about 2 minutes or until creamy. Gradually add sugar, beating at medium speed 5 to 7 minutes. Add eggs, one at a time, beating just until yellow disappears. Combine flour, baking powder, and salt. Add to butter mixture, alternately with milk, beginning and ending with flour mixture. Mix at low speed just until blended after each addition. Stir in vanilla. Combine chocolate and 1 tablespoon shortening in a small, heavy saucepan. Cook over low heat, stirring constantly, until chocolate melts. Remove 2 cups batter, and add chocolate mixture, stirring until blended. Pour ⅓ of remaining plain batter into a greased and floured 10-inch tube pan. Top with ½ of chocolate batter. Repeat layers, ending with plain batter. Gently swirl batter with a knife to create marble effect, and sprinkle with pecans. Bake at 350 degrees for 1 hour and 10 minutes or until a wooden pick inserted in center comes out clean. Cool in pan on a wire rack for 10 to 15 minutes. Remove from pan and let cool completely on a wire rack.
Yield: 16 servings

Rhonda Sauls

Whipping Cream Pound Cake

1 cup butter or margarine
3 cups sugar
6 eggs
3 cups all-purpose flour,
    sifted

½ pint whipping cream
1 teaspoon vanilla
½ teaspoon lemon extract
¼ teaspoon almond extract

Cream butter and sugar; add eggs, one at a time. Alternate flour and cream. Add flavorings. Grease and flour a Bundt pan or 2 loaf pans. Bake at 325 degrees for 1¼ hours.
Yield: 16 to 20 servings

Elaine Redding

Rum Cake

1 cup pecans, chopped
1 (18-ounce) yellow cake
    mix with pudding
3 eggs

½ cup cold water
½ cup oil
½ cup dark rum

Preheat oven to 325 degrees. Grease and flour a 10-inch tube pan, lined with nuts. Mix all cake ingredients together. Pour batter over nuts. Bake for 1 hour. Cool. Invert on a serving plate. Prick top and sides.

Glaze:
¼ pound butter
¼ cup water

1 cup sugar
½ cup dark rum

Melt butter in saucepan. Stir in water and sugar. Boil 5 minutes. Remove from heat and add rum. Drizzle glaze evenly over top sides of cake.
Yield: 12 to 16 servings

Polly Jackson
*Similar recipe submitted by Mary Stapleton

Pumpkin Cake With Cream Cheese Icing

4 eggs
2 cups sugar
1 cup oil
2 cups all-purpose flour

2 teaspoons baking soda
½ teaspoon salt
2 teaspoons cinnamon
2 cups pumpkin

Beat the eggs together with the sugar until light and well blended. Add salad oil, continuing to beat. Sift dry ingredients together. Thoroughly mix into the egg mixture. Add pumpkin and blend well again. Pour into well-greased and floured 9-inch tube pan. Bake at 350 degrees for 55 minutes. Let stand in pan for 10 minutes before turning over on rack to cool. When cool, frost with Cream Cheese Icing.

Cream Cheese Icing:
1 (8-ounce) package cream cheese, softened
1 stick butter, softened

1 (1-pound) box confectioner's sugar
1 teaspoon vanilla
1 cup pecans, broken

Mix all ingredients together. Beat until ready to spread.
Yield: 12 servings

Sharon Adcock

Pumpkin Roll

3 eggs
1 cup sugar
⅔ cup pumpkin, cooked or
   canned
1 teaspoon lemon juice
¾ cup all-purpose flour
1 teaspoon baking powder

½ teaspoon salt
2 teaspoons cinnamon
1 teaspoon ginger
½ teaspoon nutmeg
1 cup nuts, chopped
Powdered sugar

Beat eggs for 5 minutes. Gradually beat in sugar. Stir in pumpkin and lemon juice. Combine flour, baking powder, salt and spices. Fold into pumpkin mixture. Pour batter into a greased and floured jellyroll pan. Sprinkle with nuts. Bake 15 minutes at 350 degrees or until cake springs back when touched. Sprinkle powdered sugar on towel. Loosen edges of cake and immediately invert warm cake onto towel. Roll cake up in towel beginning with narrow edge. Cool cake completely. Unroll cake and spread with filling to within ½-inch of edges. Reroll cake and chill. Keep refrigerated.

Pumpkin Roll Filling:
¼ cup butter, softened
6 ounces cream cheese,
   softened

1 cup powdered sugar
½ teaspoon vanilla

Combine ingredients and beat until smooth.
Yield: 10 to 12 servings

Paula Neely

English Toffee

2 tablespoons instant coffee
2 tablespoons water
2 cups sugar
1½ cups butter
1½ cups almonds, toasted

1 cup semi-sweet chocolate
   bits, melted
½ cup almonds, toasted and
   finely chopped

Combine coffee, water, sugar and butter. Cook over low heat, stirring until mixture boils. Continue cooking until mixture reaches 280 degrees or medium crack stage, without stirring. Remove from heat. Fold in 1½ cups of almonds. Spread thinly on greased cookie sheets. Cool. Spread melted chocolate over cooled toffee. Sprinkle remaining almonds over all. Let chocolate set. Break into pieces. A delightful gift for that special friend.
Yield: 2 dozen

Sandra Plant

Chocolate Meringues

2 egg whites
⅛ teaspoon cream of tartar
1 teaspoon vanilla
⅛ teaspoon salt

¾ cup sugar
1 (6-ounce) package semi-
   sweet chocolate pieces
¼ cup nuts, chopped

Combine first four ingredients and beat until very soft peaks form. Gradually add sugar until very stiff peaks form. Fold in chocolate pieces and nuts. Drop on foil wrapped cookie sheet. Bake at 300 degrees for 25 minutes or less.
Yield: 4 dozen

Mary Jo Stone

Meringues

6 egg whites
¼ teaspoon cream of tartar
1 tablespoon vinegar

2 teaspoons vanilla
2 cups sugar

Beat egg whites until foamy. Add cream of tartar. Beat. Add vinegar and continue beating until stiff. Add vanilla. Beat again until stiff. Add sugar gradually, while continuing to beat. Pour onto a greased cookie sheet. Bake at 300 degrees for 45 minutes or until lightly browned. Recipe makes 18 meringues which can be cut in half. Meringues can be filled with ice cream, topped with fruit or a favorite sauce.
Yield: 18 servings

Mrs. William E. Smith, Sr.

Nell Dekle's Pecan Confections

1 egg white
1 cup light brown sugar
¼ teaspoon salt
1 tablespoon flour

1 cup pecans, coarsely
  chopped
1 cup pecan halves

Preheat oven to 300 degrees. In a small bowl, beat egg white to a stiff froth at medium speed. Gradually beat in brown sugar, salt and flour. Stir in chopped pecans. On a greased cookie sheet, drop mixture by half teaspoonfuls, lightly pressing a pecan half into top of each. Bake confections for 15 minutes. Let cool partially on cookie sheet. Remove to wire racks to completely cool. Store in covered container.
Yield: 6 dozen

Ellen Dekle Alderman

Turtles

1 package caramels
2 tablespoons evaporated
  milk

3 cups pecans halves
One pan dipping chocolate

Combine caramels and milk in a microwave-safe bowl. Cook on high until melted. Keep an eye on the mixture and stir occasionally. Do not overcook! Remove from microwave. Stir in pecans. Drop by scant teaspoonfuls onto a cookie sheet that will fit into your freezer. Place in freezer overnight or until frozen. Melt dipping chocolate according to package directions. Remove caramel and nuts from freezer. Dip into chocolate. Place on waxed paper. Let set.
Yield: 5 dozen

Lanelle Rogers

Blond Brownies

1⅓ sticks margarine,
  melted
1 box dark brown sugar
3 eggs, well beaten
2¾ cups all-purpose flour
2½ teaspoons baking
  powder

½ teaspoon salt
2 cups nuts, chopped
1 (6-ounce) package semi-
  sweet chocolate morsels
2 teaspoons vanilla

Melt margarine. Add sugar and eggs. Sift flour, baking powder and salt. Add to sugar mixture. Stir in nuts, chocolate morsels and vanilla. Spread in 9 x 13-inch pan. Bake at 300 degrees for 20 to 25 minutes.
Yield: 2½ dozen

Debbie Friedlander

Chocolate Brownies

1 cup butter
2 squares baking chocolate
1 cup sugar
1 cup flour

1 cup nuts, chopped
2 eggs, beaten
20 large marshmallows,
    cut into quarters

Melt together butter and chocolate. Add sugar, flour, nuts and eggs. Mix well. Pour into rectangular pan (approximately 11 x 7-inch). Bake in preheated 325 degree oven for 25 minutes. Remove from oven and put marshmallows on top while still hot. Let cool.

Icing:
2 tablespoons butter
1 square baking chocolate
1½ cups confectioners'
    sugar, sifted

4 tablespoons evaporated
    milk
1 teaspoon vanilla
Pinch of salt

Melt butter and chocolate. Add remaining ingredients. Mix until creamy. Spread on brownies. Let set up before cutting. Cut into 1½-inch squares.
Yield: 3 dozen

Note: I use this recipe quite often omitting the marshmallows. Cut very small for a tea or large for a party. Will freeze.

Barbara Hendrick

Chocolate-Caramel "Killer Brownies"

1 (14-ounce) bag caramels
⅔ cup evaporated milk
  (divided)
1 (18½-ounce) package
  German chocolate cake
  mix

¾ cup butter or margarine,
  softened
1 cup nuts, chopped
1 (6-ounce) package semi-
  sweet chocolate morsels

Combine caramels and ⅓ cup evaporated milk in top of a double boiler. Cook, stirring constantly, until caramels are completely melted. Remove double boiler from heat. Combine dry cake mix, remaining ⅓ cup of milk, butter and nuts. Stir until dough holds together. Press ½ of cake mixture into a greased 9 x 13 inch baking pan. Bake at 350 degrees for 6 minutes. Sprinkle chocolate morsels over crust. Pour caramel mixture over chocolate morsels, spreading evenly. Crumble remaining cake mixture over caramel mixture. Return to oven. Bake 15 to 18 minutes. Cool. Chill 30 minutes. Cut into small bars.

Yield: 5 dozen

Jan Smith
*Similar recipe submitted by Laura Keith

Pam's Iced Brownies

1 cup butter, softened
1 cup sugar
4 eggs
16 ounces chocolate syrup

1 cup plus 1 tablespoon all-
purpose flour
¾ cup pecans, chopped

Cream butter and sugar. Add eggs one at a time and beat well. Add chocolate syrup and flour. Stir in nuts. Bake 20 to 25 minutes at 350 degrees in 9 x 13-inch pan. Be careful not to overcook! Ice while brownies are still hot.

Icing:
6 tablespoons butter
6 tablespoons milk
1½ cups sugar

½ cup chocolate chips
½ cup pecans, chopped

Boil butter, milk and sugar for 1 minute, stirring at full boil for 45 seconds to 1 minute. Add chocolate chips. Beat with mixer until smooth and just beginning to harden. Add nuts. Spread icing on brownies in pan. Cut into 2-inch squares.
Yield: 2 dozen

Pam Rojas

German Chocolate Brownies

1 package German
   chocolate squares,
   melted
½ cup margarine, softened
1 cup sugar

1 egg
1 cup all-purpose flour
1 teaspoon salt
1 teaspoon vanilla
1 cup pecans, chopped

Preheat oven to 350 degrees. Melt chocolate over low heat or in top of double boiler. Cream together margarine and sugar. Add egg and beat well. Blend in melted chocolate. Stir in flour, salt, vanilla and pecans. Blend thoroughly. Spread into greased 8-inch square pan, and bake at 350 degrees for 35 to 40 minutes. Cool thoroughly before cutting and removing from pan.
Yield: 1 to 1½ dozen

Angela Castellow

The Best Lemon Squares

Crust:
1 package lemon "pudding
   in the mix" cake mix
1 cup butter, softened

1 cup nuts, chopped
1 egg, beaten

Filling:
1 (8-ounce) package cream
   cheese

2 eggs, beaten
1 box confectioners' sugar

Combine crust ingredients and press into 9 x 13-inch metal pan. Beat cream cheese; add eggs and confectioners' sugar. Pour over crust layer. Bake at 350 degrees for 45 minutes. Cool completely before cutting. Cut into 1½-inch squares. Tip: line metal pan with heavy-duty aluminum foil. When squares are done, remove foil liner on to a cutting board. Trim edges and cut on the diagonal for prettier squares. For special occasions, sprinkle with powdered sugar and top with a fresh raspberry.
Yield: 2½ dozen

Laura Keith

Mrs. Jeter's Lemon Squares

Crust:
1 cup butter, room
temperature
½ cup sugar

2 cups all-purpose flour,
fork-stirred

Lemon Filling:
5 tablespoons all-purpose
flour
1 teaspoon baking powder
2 cups sugar
4 extra large eggs

¼ to ½ teaspoon lemon
rind, grated
½ cup lemon juice
Confectioner's sugar

Crust: In medium bowl using hand mixer at medium speed, cream butter and sugar. Gradually add flour. Blend. Spread in greased 15 x 10 x 1-inch jellyroll pan. Preheat oven to 350 degrees. Bake 20 to 25 minutes or until brown around the edges. Let crust cool.

Lemon Filling: Blend flour and baking powder. Add 2 cups of sugar and blend. Slightly beat eggs with hand mixer at medium speed. Add flour-sugar mixture. Beat until blended. Add lemon rind and lemon juice. Beat until blended. Pour over crust. Bake at 350 degrees for 18 to 20 minutes or until filling is brown and set. Place on wire rack to cool. Sprinkle with confectioner's sugar. Cut into 1 x 1-inch squares.

Yield: 12½ dozen

Jane H. Brown
Similar recipe submitted by Mary Campagna

Lemon Glazed Date Sticks

½ cup all-purpose flour
½ teaspoon baking powder
¼ teaspoon salt
1 egg, beaten
⅓ cup sugar

1 tablespoon butter, melted
1 (8-ounce) package
    chopped dates
½ cup pecans, chopped

Glaze:
1 tablespoon milk
1 tablespoon butter
1 teaspoon lemon juice

1 teaspoon lemon rind,
    grated
1 cup confectioners' sugar,
    sifted

Sift flour, baking powder and salt together. Set aside. To egg, add sugar gradually and butter. Stir in chopped dates and pecans. Add reserved flour mixture. Turn into 8-inch square greased pan and spread thinly. Bake at 325 degrees for 25 to 30 minutes. Prepare glaze by mixing milk, butter, lemon juice, lemon rind, and confectioners' sugar. While warm, spread with glaze. Cut into bars.
Yield: 1 to 1½ dozen

Barbara Fallin

Mama Bates Butter Balls

1 cup butter
¼ cup sugar
2 cups flour

1 teaspoon vanilla
1 cup nuts, chopped
¼ box powdered sugar

Cream butter and sugar. Add flour, vanilla and nuts. Drop by teaspoon on cookie sheet. Bake at 325 degrees for 20 minutes. Roll in powdered sugar.
Yield: 4 dozen

Cathy Mobley

Maple Squares

½ cup butter
1 cup all-purpose flour
2 tablespoons brown sugar
2 eggs, well beaten
1½ cups brown sugar
2 tablespoons flour

1 teaspoon baking powder
½ teaspoon salt
½ cup coconut
½ cup nuts, chopped
1 teaspoon vanilla

Combine butter, 1 cup flour and brown sugar. Mix well and pat into greased 8 or 9-inch square pan. Bake at 350 degrees for 15 minutes or until slightly brown. Let cool. Combine remaining ingredients. Mix well and pour over crust. Bake 30 minutes at 350 degrees. When cool, cover with maple icing.

Maple Icing:
½ box 10X powdered sugar
2 tablespoons butter or
   margarine, softened

2 to 3 tablespoons milk
1 teaspoon maple flavoring

Beat sugar and butter. Add milk and flavoring, mixing well.
Yield: 2 to 3 dozen

Cathy Mobley

Mother's Fruit Bars

2 cups pecans, chopped
½ cup butter
1 cup brown sugar
2 eggs

1¼ cups all-purpose flour
2 teaspoons vanilla
½ pound candied cherries
½ pound candied pineapple

Grease a 9 x 12-inch baking pan well. Flour nuts and place in bottom of pan. Cream butter and sugar. Add eggs, flour, and vanilla. Beat well. Spread batter over nuts in pan. Sprinkle fruit over batter in pan, then press into batter. Cook at 275 degrees for 45 minutes to 1 hour. Let cool and cut into 2-inch squares or bars.
Yield: 2 dozen

Laura Keith

Peanut Butter Squares

1 cup butter or margarine
1 cup chunky peanut butter
2 cups graham cracker
   crumbs

2 cups confectioners' sugar,
   sifted
1 cup semi-sweet chocolate
   morsels
2 tablespoons shortening

Combine butter and peanut butter in a 2-quart glass bowl. Cover with a paper towel and microwave at high 1½ minutes. Stir in graham cracker crumbs and powdered sugar. Press mixture into an 11 x 7½ x 1½-inch dish. Combine chocolate morsels and shortening in a 2-cup glass measure. Microwave at medium speed for 2 minutes or until chocolate melts. Spread over peanut butter mixture. Chill and cut into squares.
Yield: 4 dozen

Chocolate Chip Cookies

2 cups butter
2 cups sugar
2 cups brown sugar
4 eggs
2 teaspoons vanilla
4 cups all-purpose flour
5 cups oatmeal, pulverized

1 teaspoon salt
2 teaspoons baking soda
2 teaspoons baking powder
2 (12-ounce) bags chocolate
   chips
1 (8-ounce) Hershey bar,
   finely grated

Cream butter and sugars. Add eggs and vanilla. Combine dry ingredients. Add to creamed mixture. Add chocolate chips and Hershey bar. Bake at 350 degrees for 15 minutes on ungreased cookie sheet. Do not overcook! They are grand!
Yield: 12 to 13 dozen

Donna Marshall
*Similar recipe submitted by Jane Holman

Super Chocolate Chunk Cookies

1 cup butter or margarine,
  softened
1 cup sugar
½ cup brown sugar, firmly
  packed
2 eggs
2 teaspoons vanilla

2 cups all-purpose flour
1 teaspoon baking powder
½ teaspoon salt
1 (12-ounce) package semi-
  sweet chocolate chunks
1 cup pecans or walnuts,
  chopped

Cream butter, gradually add sugars, beating well at medium speed of an electric mixer. Add eggs and vanilla beating well. Combine all-purpose flour, baking powder, and salt. Add to the creamed mixture, mixing well. Stir in the semi-sweet chocolate chunks and nuts. Refrigerate dough at least 1 hour. Drop by teaspoon on ungreased cookie sheet. Bake at 350 degrees for 12 to 15 minutes.
Yield: 4 dozen

Christy Hendrick

Coconut Cookies

¾ cup shortening
⅔ cup brown sugar
⅓ cup corn syrup
2 eggs
½ teaspoon vanilla
2 cups all-purpose flour

1½ teaspoons baking
  powder
½ teaspoon salt
3 tablespoons milk
3 cups coconut, flaked

Cream shortening and brown sugar. Add corn syrup and eggs. Beat well. Pour in vanilla. Stir in flour, baking powder and salt alternately with milk. Add coconut and mix well. Bake at 375 degrees for 12 to 15 minutes.
Yield: 4 dozen

Amanda Statom

Coconut Chews

Crust:
¾ cup shortening
   (or ½ cup butter
   and ¼ cup shortening)

¾ cup confectioners' sugar
1½ cups all-purpose flour

Filling:
2 eggs
1 cup brown sugar
2 tablespoons all-purpose
   flour
½ teaspoon baking powder

½ teaspoon salt
½ teaspoon vanilla
½ cup pecans, chopped
½ cup coconut

Cream shortening and sugar. Blend in 1½ cups flour. Press evenly in bottom of ungreased 9 x 13-inch pan. Bake 12 to 15 minutes at 350 degrees. Beat eggs slightly. Add flour, baking powder, salt and vanilla. Stir in pecans and coconut. Spread over hot crust and bake 20 minutes at 350 degrees. While warm spread with Orange-Lemon Icing. Cool before cutting into bars or squares.

Orange-Lemon Icing:
1½ cups confectioners'
   sugar
2 tablespoons butter,
   melted

3 tablespoons orange juice
1 teaspoon lemon juice

Combine all ingredients and mix until smooth.
Yield: 2½ to 3 dozen

Elaine Redding

285

Fruitcake Cookies

1 cup butter
1 cup light brown sugar, packed
3 eggs
3 cups cake flour
1 teaspoon soda
1 teaspoon cinnamon

½ cup milk
1 pound pineapple, chopped
1 pound cherries, chopped
1 pound dates, chopped
7 cups nuts, chopped

Cream butter and sugar. Add eggs and beat well. Sift flour, soda and cinnamon. Add alternately with milk, mixing well. Add fruit and nuts. Mix. Drop by spoonfuls onto greased cookie sheet. Bake at 300 degrees for 25 minutes.
Yield: 8 dozen

Mary Jo Stone

Giant Fudgies

½ cup butter, softened
¾ cup sugar
1 large egg
1 teaspoon vanilla
1 cup all-purpose flour

½ cup cocoa
½ teaspoon baking soda
1½ cups pecans, chopped
1 (6-ounce) package semi-sweet chocolate chips

Cream butter and sugar. Add egg and vanilla. Combine flour, cocoa and baking soda. Add to creamed mixture. Stir in pecans and chocolate chips. Drop dough by ¼ cupfuls on ungreased cookie sheet 2 inches apart. Flatten dough into 3½-inch rounds. Bake at 375 degrees for 10 minutes until dry to the touch, but still soft. Do not overcook! Let cool on cookie sheet for 2 minutes, then remove to wire rack. Note: These are also great with macadamia nuts and white chocolate pieces.
Yield: 2 dozen

Mary Campagna

Ice Box Cookies

1 cup Crisco
2 cups brown sugar
2 eggs, beaten
3½ cups all-purpose flour
1 teaspoon cream of tartar

1 teaspoon baking soda
½ teaspoon salt
1 teaspoon vanilla
1 cup nuts, chopped

Cream Crisco and sugar. Add eggs, then dry ingredients, vanilla, and nuts. Make four rolls and wrap individually in wax paper. Refrigerate. Slice and place on cookie sheet. Bake in a preheated 350 degree oven until lightly browned.
Yield: 5 dozen

Barbara Hendrick
*Similar recipe submitted by Rhonda Sauls

M & M Cookies

1 cup shortening
½ cup granulated sugar
1 cup brown sugar, packed
2 teaspoons vanilla
2 eggs

2¼ cups all-purpose flour
1 teaspoon baking soda
1 teaspoon salt
1½ cups plain M & M's

Cream shortening, sugars and vanilla. Add eggs and beat. Sift together flour, soda, and salt. Add dry ingredients to creamed mixture. Mix well. Stir in M & M's. Drop by teaspoon on ungreased baking sheet. Bake at 375 degrees for 10 minutes or until golden.
Yield: 6 dozen

This recipe came from Ginna Cooper and was included in the 1981 First Methodist MYF Youth Cookbook.

Lynn Acuff

Mark's Favorite Cookies

3½ cups all-purpose flour
½ teaspoon baking soda
½ teaspoon salt
1 cup butter

2 cups light brown sugar
1 cup nuts, chopped
2 eggs, beaten

Sift flour, soda, and salt together. Mix firm butter and flour mixture together. Add brown sugar, then nuts. Add fluffy, beaten eggs to dough mixture. Knead until smooth. Shape dough into 5 rolls. Wrap in waxed paper and place in refrigerator overnight or until thoroughly chilled. Slice cookies very thin, and place on greased baking sheet. Bake at 350 degrees until light brown.
Yield: 5 to 6 dozen

Judy Mobley

Oatmeal Cookies

2 cups sugar
1 cup margarine or butter
¼ cup Hershey's Cocoa
½ cup milk

2½ cups quick oatmeal
½ cup peanut butter
1 teaspoon vanilla

Mix first 4 ingredients together. Bring to a boil for about 1½ minutes. Add remaining ingredients and mix. Spoon out onto waxed paper. Let cool about 15 minutes. Quick and easy, but must be made on a clear, sunny day.
Yield: 2 dozen

Debbie Brown

Orange Cookies

2 cups all-purpose flour,
   unsifted
2 teaspoons baking powder
1 teaspoon salt
1 cup butter
1 cup sugar

2 eggs, well beaten
¼ cup orange juice
2 tablespoons orange rind,
   grated
2 cups 40% bran flakes,
   slightly crushed

Mix together flour, baking powder and salt. Cream butter, gradually adding sugar, creaming well after each addition. Add eggs, beating thoroughly. Alternately add flour and orange juice, mixing well. Add rind and cereal, mixing thoroughly. Drop by rounded teaspoon onto greased cookie sheets. Bake at 350 degrees for 13 minutes or until lightly browned.
Yield: 5 to 6 dozen

Sandra Plant

Praline Cookies

1 cup butter
1 cup brown sugar
1 cup nuts, chopped

1 package graham crackers
   (⅓ box)

Combine butter, brown sugar and nuts. Cook for 4 minutes. Layer crackers on cookie sheet. Spread cooked mixture over crackers. Place under broiler until bubbly. Remove and cool. Should be crisp.
Yield: 3 dozen

Carol Aguero

Old Fashioned Sugar Cookies

½ cup butter
1 cup sugar
1 egg, well beaten
1 tablespoon milk
½ teaspoon vanilla

1½ cups sifted flour
1 teaspoon baking powder
¼ teaspoon salt
Additional 4X sugar

Cream butter. Beat in sugar, egg, milk and vanilla. Sift flour, baking powder and salt together. Add to butter mixture. Mix well. Cover. Refrigerate 3 to 4 hours or until mixture is firm. Preheat oven to 375 degrees. Roll dough into small balls about ¾ inches in diameter. Place 2 inches apart on lightly greased cookie sheet. Flatten tops lightly with bottom of a glass that has been dipped in sugar. Bake 8 to 10 minutes or until cookies are lightly browned. If desired, brush warm cookies with melted butter and dust with 4X sugar.
Yield: 3 dozen

Jane Tucker
*Similar recipe submitted by Jackie McLean

Toffee Crunch Cookies

½ cup butter, softened
1 package butter recipe
   yellow cake mix with
   pudding
2 large eggs

1 tablespoon water
1 (6-ounce) package Skors
   almond brickle chips
½ to 1 cup pecans, chopped

Beat butter at medium speed with a mixer until creamy. Add cake mix, eggs, and water, beating until blended. Stir in brickle chips and pecans. Drop cookie dough by tablespoonful onto ungreased cookie sheet. Bake at 350 degrees for 8 to 10 minutes or until edges are browned. (Top will look moist.) Transfer to wire racks to cool.
Yield: 4 dozen

Paula Neely

Old Fashioned
Sugar Cookies and Icing

4 cups sifted all-purpose
    flour
1 teaspoon baking powder
½ teaspoon baking soda
½ teaspoon salt
½ teaspoon nutmeg

1 cup butter, softened
1½ cups sugar
1 egg
½ cup sour cream
1 teaspoon vanilla

Sift flour, baking powder, soda, salt and nutmeg. Beat at medium
speed butter, sugar, and egg until light and fluffy. At low speed
beat in sour cream and vanilla. Gradually add flour mixture. Form
dough into 4 balls, wrap in waxed paper and chill overnight. Roll
¼ to ½-inch thick and cut into shapes with cookie cutters. Bake
at 350 degrees for 8 to 9 minutes or until lightly brown. Cool on
wire rack and frost.
Yield: 2 dozen

Icing:
¼ cup butter
4 ounces cream cheese
½ box powdered sugar

½ teaspoon vanilla
½ teaspoon lemon extract
Food coloring (optional)

Beat butter and cream cheese. Add sugar, flavorings, and food
coloring, if desired. Frost cookies. Refrigerate any left-over icing.
Yield: 2 cups

Jane Holman

Polish Tea Cakes

½ cup butter
½ cup sugar
1 egg, separated
½ teaspoon vanilla
1 cup all-purpose flour
½ teaspoon salt

1¼ cups pecans, finely
  chopped or ground
Black or red raspberry
  preserves (optional
  whether seedless or
  with seeds)

Cream butter and sugar until light and fluffy. Add egg yolk, mix well. Add vanilla. Sift flour and salt together, and blend into creamed mixture. Roll dough into small balls. Dip into unbeaten egg white and roll in pecans. Place on buttered baking sheet, and press center of each ball with a thimble. Bake at 325 degrees for 5 minutes. Press center of cookies again with thimble and return to oven for about 10 to 15 minutes. Remove from oven and fill indentations with preserves while cookies are still hot.
Yield: 2 to 2½ dozen

Cherie Anne Whiddon

Tea Cakes From Grandma Dekle

1 cup butter or margarine
2 cups sugar
2 eggs

4 cups self-rising flour
1 tablespoon vanilla

Cream butter and sugar. Add eggs, flour and vanilla. Place dough in refrigerator until chilled. Roll out dough until thin. Cut into shapes. You may also pinch off a small amount, roll it in your hands, drop onto cookie sheet, and mash with fork. Bake at 325 degrees for 10 minutes.
Yield: 8 dozen

Ellen Dekle Alderman

Apple-Nut Crisp

1 (16-ounce) jar applesauce
½ cup brown sugar
½ cup nuts, chopped
½ teaspoon cinnamon

1 cup biscuit mix
½ cup sugar
¼ cup butter

Mix applesauce, brown sugar, nuts, and cinnamon. Pour into a lightly greased 9-inch pie pan. Using two knives, cut together the biscuit mix, sugar, and butter until crumbly. Distribute crumb mixture over applesauce. Bake at 400 degrees for 25 minutes. May be served with a scoop of ice cream over each portion.
Yield: 6 servings

Rhonda Sauls

Piña Colada Trifle

1 (14-ounce) can sweetened
    condensed milk
½ cup cream of coconut
2 cups whipped cream
16 macaroon cookies,
    crumbled

1 (20-ounce) can crushed
    pineapple, well drained
1 (16-ounce) jar cherries,
    drained and cut in half

In a large bowl, combine condensed milk and cream of coconut. Fold in whipped cream. Cover the bottom of a 2½-quart glass serving bowl with macaroon cookie crumbs. Top with ⅓ of the cream mixture, half of the pineapple, and half of the cherries. Repeat layers ending with cream mixture. Cover and chill for 2 to 4 hours. Note: this recipe may be prepared in a 13 x 9-inch pan, using the macaroons as a crust. Top macaroon crumbs with fruit and cover with cream mixture. Freeze at least 6 hours.
Yield: 10 to 12 servings

Connie Mobley

Blueberries in the Snow

½ cup sugar
½ cup milk
1 (8-ounce) package cream
    cheese, softened

1 angel food cake
1 (12-ounce) container Cool
    Whip
1 can Comstock blueberries

Mix sugar, milk, and cream cheese together with hand mixer until smooth. Add Cool Whip. Cut cake into bite-sized pieces and stir into mixture. Spread into 9 x 12-inch Pyrex dish. Top with blueberries. This is also great with strawberries.
Yield: 10 to 12 servings

Polly Boetcher

Brownie Trifle

1 (19.8-ounce) package
    fudge brownie mix
¼ cup praline or coffee-
    flavored liqueur
    (optional)
1 (3.5-ounce) package
    instant chocolate
    mousse mix

8 (1.4-ounce) toffee-flavored
    candy bars, crushed
1 (12-ounce) container
    frozen whipped topping,
    thawed
Chocolate curls for garnish

Prepare brownie mix, and bake according to package directions in a 13 x 9-inch pan. Prick top of warm brownies at 1-inch intervals using a meat fork. Brush with liqueur if desired. Let cool and crumble. Prepare chocolate mousse according to package directions but omit chilling. Place half of crumbled brownies in the bottom of a 3-quart trifle dish. Top with half of mousse, crushed candy bars, and whipped topping. Repeat layer with remaining ingredients ending with whipped topping. Garnish if desired. Chill 8 hours.
Tip: Make shaving by pulling a vegetable peeler across the surface of a square of semi-sweet chocolate.
Yield: 16 to 18 servings

Laura Keith

Chocolate Delight

1¼ cups self-rising flour
1½ sticks butter, melted
1½ cups pecans, chopped
2 small containers Cool
  Whip
1 (8-ounce) package cream
  cheese

1 cup confectioners' sugar
2 packages chocolate
  instant pudding
1 teaspoon vanilla
3½ cups milk
Chocolate shavings for
  garnish (optional)

Combine flour, butter, and pecans. Press into a baking dish. Bake at 350 degrees for 20 to 25 minutes. Cream Cool Whip, cream cheese, and confectioners' sugar together. Spread over cooled crust mixture. Combine pudding, vanilla, and milk, and mix until smooth. Pour over cream cheese layer. Top with a layer of Cool Whip. Garnish with chocolate shavings, if desired. Refrigerate until ready to serve.
Yield: 12 servings

Lynne Stone

Christmas Eve Flan

6 eggs
9 tablespoons sugar
3 cups milk

½ teaspoon salt
½ teaspoon vanilla
2 tablespoons corn starch

Caramel:
1 cup sugar

2 tablespoons water

Beat eggs. Add all ingredients and strain through sieve. Prepare caramel by mixing sugar and water. Cook on medium high heat. Watch carefully. Stir after it turns golden brown. Pour caramel mixture into pie pan or individual molds. Fill with egg mixture. Place in shallow container of hot water and bake at 325 to 350 degrees for 1 hour. Refrigerate and invert to serve.
Yield: 8 servings

Carol Ann Cannon

Chocolate Eclair Cake

1 box Graham crackers	3 cups milk
2 packages French Vanilla instant pudding	1 (9-ounce) carton Cool Whip

Butter 13 x 9-inch pan. Beat pudding mix with milk. Fold in Cool Whip, stirring well. Line bottom of pan with cracker squares. Spread ½ of pudding mix over crackers. Repeat crackers and pudding, ending with crackers on top. Refrigerate, and add frosting when cool.

Frosting:

3 tablespoons cocoa	2 teaspoons light Karo syrup
1 tablespoon oil	1 teaspoon vanilla
3 tablespoons butter	1½ cups (XXX) powdered sugar
3 tablespoons milk	

Combine cocoa and oil, stirring well. Add next four ingredients, pour in saucepan and bring to a boil. Let cool. Add powdered sugar and mix well.
Yield: 12 to 16 servings

Jane Neal

Boiled Custard

1 quart milk	1 cup sugar
4 eggs	1 teaspoon vanilla

Into a double boiler, heat milk, but not boil. Beat eggs together until light. Add sugar to eggs and mix well. Pour a small amount of hot milk into eggs and sugar to warm and thin mixture. Pour slowly into the hot milk. Cook, stirring constantly until it will coat the spoon. Add vanilla. Set aside to get very cold before serving. Use this recipe for homemade ice cream too.
Yield: 8 servings

Rhett Smith

Debbie's Cocoa Ripple Ring

½ cup shortening
¾ cup sugar
2 eggs
½ cup all-purpose flour
¾ teaspoon salt

2 teaspoons baking powder
⅔ cup milk
⅓ cup pre-sweetened
    instant cocoa powder

Cream together shortening, sugar, and eggs until light and fluffy. Sift together flour, salt, and baking powder. Add to creamed mixture alternately with milk. Beat well after each addition. Spoon ⅓ of batter into a buttered 6½-cup ring mold or a 9-inch square pan. Sprinkle half of cocoa powder over batter in pan. Repeat layers ending with batter. Bake at 350 degrees for 35 minutes. Let stand for 5 minutes. Turn out of mold. Serve warm with butter.
Yield: 10 servings

Debbie Cagle

Lemon Bisque

1 can evaporated milk
1 (4-ounce) package lemon
    Jello
1¼ cups boiling water
⅛ teaspoon salt
1 cup sugar

3 tablespoons lemon juice,
    freshly squeezed
2½ cups lemon, chocolate,
    or vanilla wafers,
    crushed
Whipped cream (optional)

Chill milk, bowl and beaters completely. Dissolve Jello in boiling water, then add salt, sugar, and lemon juice. Allow Jello mix to set slightly. Beat milk until stiff in large mixing bowl using high speed. Whip Jello mix into milk until blended. Spray 9 x 13-inch pan with Pam and place ½ of cookie crumbs over pan bottom. Spread Jello and milk mixture over crumbs. Top with remaining crumbs. Refrigerate for a few hours and serve. Top portions with whipped cream if desired.
Yield: 12 servings

Caroline Frizoli

Dessert Crêpes

½ cup cold milk
½ cup cold water
2 eggs
¼ teaspoon salt
2 tablespoons butter,
    melted

1 cup sifted all-purpose
    flour
4 tablespoons powdered
    sugar
1 teaspoon vanilla

Combine milk, water, eggs, and salt in a blender. Blend just to mix. Add flour, butter, powdered sugar, and vanilla. Blend at top speed, scraping sides. Refrigerate at least 2 hours. Cook in a crêpe pan and follow pan directions or lightly grease a 6 to 8-inch skillet. Heat pan until water dropped on surface sizzles. Pour in about 2 tablespoons of batter. Lift the skillet to spread the batter, return to heat and cook on one side only until browned. Loosen crêpe with a small spatula by running it along the edges. Invert pan over paper towel, remove crêpe. Repeat with remaining batter, greasing skillet as needed. Makes 16 to 18 crêpes. Fill crêpes with your favorite filling such as fruits, pie fillings, puddings, or ice cream. Wrap or fold around filling. Top with whipped cream, chocolate, strawberry, blueberry, praline sauces, etc. Use your imagination—you can't go wrong. Crêpes may be frozen between layers of wax paper and used as needed. When filling with ice cream, prepare ahead of time and freeze. Take out when ready to use.
Yield: 16 to 18 servings

Paula Neely

Dessert Pizza

1 (8-ounce) can quick
　　Crescent dinner rolls
1 tablespoon butter or
　　margarine, melted
½ teaspoon almond extract
4 teaspoons sugar
1 (3½-ounce) package
　　vanilla instant pudding

1½ cups milk
1 teaspoon orange peel,
　　grated
½ cup whipping cream,
　　whipped, or 1 cup
　　whipped topping
2 to 2½ cups fresh fruit, cut
　　as desired

Heat oven to 375 degrees. Separate dough into 8 triangles. Place in ungreased 12-inch pizza pan or 13 x 9-inch pan. Press over bottom and ¼-inch up sides to form crust. In small bowl, combine butter and almond extract. Brush crust with butter mixture; sprinkle with sugar. Bake at 375 degrees for 11 to 13 minutes or until golden brown. Cool completely. In medium bowl, combine pudding mix and milk. Beat at low speed for 1 minute. Stir in orange peel. Refrigerate 10 minutes or until set. Fold in whipped cream. To assemble for serving, spoon pudding filling onto crust. Arrange fruit on top. Refrigerate 1 hour before serving. Cut into wedges to serve.
Yield: 8 servings

Farolyn Mobley

Ice Cream

1 cup sugar
2 eggs
1 large can sweetened
　　condensed milk

1 (3½-ounce) package
　　chocolate or vanilla
　　pudding
1 teaspoon vanilla
Enough milk to make 2
　　quarts

Mix ingredients together and beat well. Pour into ice cream churn.
Yield: 12 to 15 servings

Jackie McLean

Lemon Delight

¾ cup sugar
3 tablespoons corn starch
¼ teaspoon salt
¾ cup water
3 eggs, separated
2 tablespoons butter
⅓ cup fresh lemon juice

1 teaspoon lemon zest
¼ teaspoon cream of tartar
⅓ cup sugar
1 angel food cake
Whipping cream and lemon
    slices for garnish

Mix ¾ cup sugar, corn starch, and salt in saucepan. Slowly stir in water. Cook over medium heat, stirring constantly. Boil 1 minute. Beat egg yolks slightly. Add ½ of hot mixture to egg yolks. Stir egg mixture into remaining mixture in saucepan. Cook slowly, stirring constantly until mixture boils. Add butter. Slowly stir in lemon juice and zest. Cool thoroughly. Add cream of tartar to egg whites and beat until foamy. Gradually add ⅓ cup sugar and beat until stiff peaks form. Fold into egg yolk mixture. Cut cake into 4 layers. Spread lemon mixture between layers, on top, and on sides. Chill until ready to serve. Garnish with whipping cream and lemon slices.

Yield: 10 to 12 servings

Sandra Plant

Orange Sherbet

2 cups sugar
2 cups water
1 (9-ounce) can crushed
    pineapple or pineapple
    juice

Juice of 1 lemon
1 bottle of Orange Crush
1 cup whole milk and 1 cup
    cream or 2 cups half and
    half

Cook sugar and water together at boiling point for 5 minutes. Let cool and then add pineapple, lemon juice, and Orange Crush. Freeze to a mush. Add milk and cream. Freeze.

Yield: 1 gallon

Mrs. Love Felton

Peanut Pudding Cake

1 cup all-purpose flour
½ cup margarine
1 cup dry roasted peanuts,
    chopped (divided)
⅓ cup peanut butter
1 (8-ounce) package cream
    cheese
1 cup confectioners' sugar

1 (16-ounce) container
    frozen whipped topping,
    thawed (divided)
1 small package vanilla
    instant pudding
1 small package chocolate
    instant pudding
2¾ cups milk
1 ounce sweet chocolate,
    grated

Layer 1: With pastry cutter, blend flour and margarine. Add ⅔ cup peanuts. Pat evenly into 8 x 12-inch pan. Bake 20 minutes at 350 degrees. Cool thoroughly.

Layer 2: Cream peanut butter and cream cheese together. Add confectioners' sugar and mix well. Fold in 4½ ounces whipped topping. Spread over layer 1.

Layer 3: Using electric mixer or rotary beater, blend pudding mixes with milk. Spread over layer 2.

Layer 4: Top with remaining whipped topping. Then sprinkle with grated chocolate and ⅓ cup peanuts. Chill 2 to 3 hours.
Yield: 10 to 12 servings

Angela Castellow

Pumpkin Supreme

1¾ cups graham cracker
    crumbs
1 cup sugar (divided)
1 stick butter
1 (8-ounce) package cream
    cheese
2 eggs, beaten

2 (3¾-ounce) packages
    vanilla instant pudding
    mix
¾ cup milk
2 cups pumpkin
Dash of cinnamon
1 (8-ounce) container Cool
    Whip
Pecans, chopped

Combine graham cracker crumbs, ¼ cup of sugar, and butter. Press into a 13 x 9-inch pan. Combine cream cheese, remaining sugar, and eggs. Beat until fluffy. Spread over crust and bake at 350 degrees for 20 minutes. Set aside to cool. Combine pudding mix and milk. Beat for 2 minutes. Add pumpkin and cinnamon to the pudding mixture, then stir in 1 cup Cool Whip. Spread the pudding mixture over cream cheese layer, then top with remaining Cool Whip. Sprinkle top with pecans. Store in refrigerator.
Yield: 12 servings

Christy Hendrick

Laura Keith's Frozen Caramel Pies

1 (8-ounce) package cream
    cheese, at room
    temperature
1 can sweetened condensed
    milk
1 (16-ounce) container Cool
    Whip

3 graham cracker pie
    crusts
⅔ cup pecans, toasted
⅔ cup coconut, toasted
Caramel ice cream topping
    for drizzling

Beat cream cheese and condensed milk until smooth. Stir in Cool Whip. Spread half of the mixture between 3 pie shells. Sprinkle half of the nuts and half of the toasted coconut on cheese mixture. Drip caramel all around. Repeat with another layer ending with caramel. Keep frozen until just before serving.
Yield: 3 pies, 6 servings each

Laura Keith

Chocolate Mocha Pie

1 large or 6 small chocolate
    Hershey bars with
    almonds
2 tablespoons strong coffee
1 (16-ounce) container Cool
    Whip

1 Oreo cracker crust
Cool Whip, cherries,
    chocolate shavings for
    garnish

Soften candy bars in microwave. Add coffee, and blend in Cool Whip. Pour in shell. Garnish with Cool Whip, cherries and chocolate shavings. Refrigerate.
Yield: 6 servings

Karen Willis

Mother's Chocolate Pie

1 cup sugar
3 tablespoons flour or corn
   starch
3 egg yolks, reserve whites
   for meringue
3 tablespoons cocoa

1¼ cups milk
Pinch of salt
2 tablespoons butter
3 teaspoons vanilla
Baked pie shell

Meringue:
3 egg whites
Dash of cream of tartar

6 tablespoons sugar

Combine sugar, flour, egg yolks, cocoa, milk, and salt. Cook on medium heat until thick. Add butter and vanilla. Pour into baked pie shell. Beat egg whites, cream of tartar, and sugar until stiff peaks form. Spread over pie. Bake at 350 degrees for 12 to 15 minutes.
Yield: 8 servings

Amanda Statom
*Similar recipe submitted by Marsha McLean

Chocolate Chip Pie

1 cup sugar
½ cup all-purpose flour
1 teaspoon vanilla
2 eggs, beaten
½ cup butter, softened
1 cup chocolate chips

1 cup nuts, chopped
   (optional)
1 unbaked pie shell
Cool Whip or vanilla ice
   cream

Sift flour and sugar together. Mix with remaining ingredients. Pour into unbaked pie shell. Bake at 350 degrees for 30 to 45 minutes. Serve topped with Cool Whip or vanilla ice cream.
Yield: 6 to 8 servings

Lynne Stone

Coconut Pie

1½ cups sugar
½ stick margarine
3 eggs
1 tablespoon vinegar

1 teaspoon vanilla
1 cup coconut
1 unbaked pie shell

Cream sugar and margarine. Add eggs and mix well. Stir in remaining ingredients and mix until well blended. Pour into unbaked pie shell. Bake for 1 hour at 325 degrees. Never fails.
Yield: 8 servings

Joy Matthews

French Silk Chocolate Pie

2 (9-inch) pie shells, baked
    and cooled
1½ cups butter or
    margarine
2 cups sugar
4 (1-ounce) squares
    unsweetened chocolate

3 teaspoons vanilla
4 drops almond extract
6 eggs, chilled
Whipped cream and
    chopped pecans
    (optional)

In large mixing bowl, combine butter and sugar, creaming until light and fluffy. Stir in chocolate and flavorings. Add eggs, two at a time, beating 5 minutes after each addition at medium speed of electric mixer. Spoon into pie shells; freeze. Serve topped with whipped cream and pecans, if desired.
Yield: 2 pies, 6 to 8 servings each

Elaine Redding

French Silk Pie

1 cup vanilla wafer crumbs
¾ cup macadamia nuts,
   finely chopped
⅓ cup butter
1¼ cups sugar
¾ cup butter
3 eggs

3 ounces unsweetened
   chocolate, melted and
   cooled
1½ teaspoons vanilla
Sweetened whipped cream
Chocolate shavings to
   garnish

Combine vanilla wafer crumbs, macadamia nuts, and ⅓ cup butter. Mix well. Press firmly in bottom of 9 or 10-inch springform pan. Bake at 375 degrees for 8 to 10 minutes. Allow to cool. In a medium bowl, combine sugar and remaining butter. Beat until light and fluffy. Add eggs one at a time, beating on medium speed at least 2 minutes after each addition. Blend chocolate and vanilla, and add to mixture. Pour into crust. Refrigerate at least 4 to 5 hours before serving. Serve with whipped cream and garnish with chocolate shavings.
Yield: 10 to 12 servings

Carolyn Lodge

Grasshopper Pie

1¼ cups Oreos, crushed
24 large marshmallows
⅔ cup milk, scalded
¼ cup crème de menthe
2 tablespoons crème de
   cacao

1 cup whipping cream,
   whipped
Slivered almonds, toasted
Fresh mint sprigs

Press Oreos in pie plate and chill. Slowly add marshmallows to milk in double boiler, stirring constantly. Cool to room temperature. Add liqueurs. Fold in whipped cream. Pour into crust. Freeze. To serve, top with almonds and garnish with fresh mint sprigs.
Yield: 6 to 8 servings

Lasse Gammage

Lazy Pie

½ cup butter
1 cup milk
1 cup sugar

1 cup self-rising flour
4 cups fruit (peaches,
    apples, berries, or pears)

Melt butter in a 1½ to 2-quart baking dish. Mix together milk, sugar, and flour. Pour into dish. No need to stir! Pour fruit into dish and do not stir. Bake at 350 degrees for 30 minutes or until firm. *Yield: 6 to 8 servings*

Cherie Anne Whiddon
*Similar recipe submitted by Terrie Moody,
Donna Taylor, and JoAnn M. Caldwell

Peanut Butter Chiffon Pie

1 envelope gelatin
1 cup cold water (divided)
2 egg yolks, well beaten
½ cup sugar or light corn
    syrup (divided)
½ teaspoon salt

½ cup peanut butter
2 egg whites
½ teaspoon vanilla
1 (9-inch) baked pie shell or
    crumb crust

Soften gelatin in ¼ cup water. Combine gelatin, egg yolks, ¼ cup sugar (or corn syrup), ¼ cup water, and salt in top of double boiler. Blend. Cook until slightly thickened and fluffy. Cool. Place peanut butter in a bowl, add remaining water gradually and beat until smooth. Add egg mixture and vanilla; blend with beater. Chill until slightly thickened. Beat egg whites until foamy. Add remaining sugar (or corn syrup) gradually, beating until stiff. Fold into peanut butter mixture. Turn into baked pie shell (or crumb crust). Chill until firm.
Yield: 6 to 8 servings

Anna C. Carlton

Mandarin Orange Pie

1 can sweetened condensed
    milk
½ cup lemon juice
1 (12-ounce) container Cool
    Whip

2 cans mandarin orange
    sections
1 cup pecans, chopped
1 graham cracker crust

Mix ingredients. Pour into crust. Chill.
Yield: 8 servings

Joan V. Stallings

Mince Meat Pie

1 jar mince meat
1 large apple, unpeeled and
    sliced thin

¼ to ½ cup sugar
2 unbaked pie shells

Mix together mince meat, apple slices, and sugar. Put into unbaked
pie shell. Cut remaining pie shell into strips, and make lattice top.
Cook at 325 degrees until crust browns on top.
Yield: 8 servings

Cherie Anne Whiddon

Vinegar Pecan Pie

¾ stick margarine
1 cup sugar
2 eggs, slightly beaten
3 teaspoons vinegar

1 teaspoon vanilla
1 cup pecans
1 unbaked pie shell

Melt margarine in saucepan. Remove pan from heat. Add remaining ingredients in order. Mix and pour into unbaked pie shell. Bake
at 350 degrees for 30 minutes.
Yield: 8 servings

Jeri Clements

Smith's Pecan Pie

1 cup brown sugar
1 cup light corn syrup
½ cup butter, melted
¼ teaspoon salt
4 eggs, beaten slightly

1 teaspoon vanilla
1 (9-inch) unbaked pastry
   shell
1 cup pecan halves

Combine sugar, syrup, butter, and salt. Mix well. Add the eggs and vanilla. Mix well until blended. Pour into unbaked pastry shell. Arrange nuts over top of pie. Bake at 425 degrees for 10 minutes. Reduce heat to 350 degrees and finish baking (about 30 minutes), only until center of filling is just set. Remove from oven as pie will continue to set until it starts to cool. Good served with topping of whipped cream and chopped pecans or ice cream.
Yield: 8 servings

Rhett Smith
*Similar recipe submitted by JoAnn M. Caldwell
and Elaine Redding

Lemon Chess Pie

2 cups sugar
1 tablespoon flour
1 tablespoon plain
   cornmeal
4 eggs
¼ cup butter

¼ cup milk
¼ cup lemon juice
1 tablespoon lemon rind,
   grated
2 unbaked pie shells
Cool Whip

In a large bowl, combine sugar, flour, and cornmeal. Toss lightly with a fork. Beat remaining ingredients together with a rotary or electric mixer and add to sugar mixture. Pour into 2 unbaked pie shells. Bake 10 minutes at 400 degrees, then 30 minutes at 350 degrees. Top with Cool Whip before serving.
Yield: 2 pies, 6 servings each

Christy Hendrick
*Similar recipe submitted by Jane Holman

Fresh Strawberry Pie

2 quarts fresh strawberries
  (divided)
1½ cups sugar
4½ tablespoons corn starch
2 tablespoons lemon juice

½ pint whipping cream,
  whipped
2 tablespoons
  confectioners' sugar
1 (10-inch) pie shell, baked

Reserve a few berries for garnishing. Mash and cook half the berries with sugar, corn starch, and lemon juice. Boil mixture, stirring until thick and clear. When cool, coat the bottom of the pie shell with this mixture. Place the remaining half of washed and drained berries into pie shell. Pour the remaining cooked strawberry mixture on top. Chill. Whip the cream with confectioners' sugar, and spread on top of pie. Garnish with reserved berries.
Yield: 8 servings

Carol Bannister

Strawberry Pie

2 cups water
2 cups sugar
6 tablespoons corn starch
1 (3-ounce) package
  strawberry Jello

Red food coloring
1½ pints strawberries,
  sliced
1 (9-inch) deep dish pie
  shell

Combine water, sugar, and corn starch in saucepan. Heat to boiling point, stirring constantly. When thickened, remove from heat and add strawberry Jello and food coloring. Let cool. Place sliced strawberries on bottom of pie shell. Pour cooled sauce over. Refrigerate and serve when cold.
Yield: 8 servings

Marsha McLean

Beginning Strokes
Children's Section

Beginning Strokes

Children's Section

Creating the Setting

"Basket of Cherries" was submitted by eleven year old Seth Merrill, son of Reverend and Mrs. Pat Merrill of Moultrie. Seth's first interests in drawing were seen as he sketched his father in the pulpit. He has won several drawing contests, including blue ribbon awards at R. B. Wright School, where he is a fifth grader. Seth is enrolled in art classes at the Colquitt County Arts Center under the direction of Kathy Flowers.

Combined for the Setting

Your child's canvas develops from his surroundings; new and full of surprises, waiting to be discovered. Curiosity and creativity are eager to be tapped. Join hands in a delightful discovery of shapes, textures and ingredients found on these next pages. Plan a child's day out by incorporating several of your favorites and inviting over special friends. Don't miss the opportunity to celebrate a holiday, welcome a new season or simply end a busy week with a togetherness project. Smiles make this setting complete.

Alphabet Pretzels

1 package dry yeast
½ cup warm water
4 cups flour
1 tablespoon sugar

1 teaspoon salt
1 egg, beaten
Coarse salt

Dissolve dry yeast in warm water. Mix together flour, sugar, and salt. Combine yeast and dry ingredients. Knead dough on a lightly floured surface for 5 to 7 minutes, adding water as needed to make dough pliable. Divide dough into single portions that can be formed into letters or numbers. Place the resulting shapes on a greased cookie sheet. Brush the tops with egg and sprinkle with coarse salt. Bake at 425 degrees for 25 minutes.

Polly Jackson

Anne's Bread Dough Sculpture

¼ cup salt
6 to 8 tablespoons hot
    water

1 cup plain flour
Acrylic paint
Polyurethane

Dissolve salt as much as possible in hot water. Add flour and mix. Knead dough 10 to 15 minutes until smooth. If dough appears too dry, dip hands into water and work into dough. Mold into desired shape on aluminum foil. Bake in 225 degree oven for 2 to 4 hours, depending on size, until hard. Paint when cooled, then dip in polyurethane 3 to 4 times.

Jane H. Brown

Art Spaghetti

1 box spaghetti
Baggies

Food coloring

Boil spaghetti noodles until cooked. Place a couple of drops of various food colors in baggies. (Different colors per bag.) Place spaghetti in baggies. Shake baggies until spaghetti is colored. Take strands of noodles out and noodles will stick to paper. Pictures can be made with spaghetti noodles. Great art project for young children.

Lorri McCrary

Banana Rounds

4 medium bananas
3 tablespoons honey
⅛ teaspoon nutmeg

⅛ teaspoon cinnamon
¼ cup wheat germ
½ cup yogurt

Peel bananas and slice into rounds. Measure spices, wheat germ, and honey. Mix with yogurt and bananas. Chill.
Yield: 8 servings

Polly Jackson

Bird-Watcher Mix

1 cup popcorn, popped
½ cup Cheerios
¼ cup pretzels

¼ cup raisins
¼ cup nuts

Have your pint-size bird-watchers measure and mix this recipe. Place ingredients listed above into a clean and empty resealable bag. Carefully seal the bag. Shake the contents until thoroughly mixed. Then open the bag and let the nibbling begin!
Yield: 4 servings

Polly Jackson

Blizzard Pie

½ gallon vanilla ice cream   1 bag Oreo cookies
Large container of Cool
   Whip

Soften ice cream. Crumble cookies in ice cream. Add Cool Whip.
Mix well. Pour into a 9 x 13-inch Pyrex dish. Freeze. Cut into
squares and serve. This is great for school parties. Can use any
kind of ice cream and cookies or candy.
Yield: 15 servings

Jan Smith

Bucket of Mud

1 (8-ounce) cream cheese   1 large package Oreo
½ stick butter   cookies, crumbled
2 (3-ounce) packages   1 (12-ounce) container Cool
   instant vanilla pudding   Whip
3½ cups milk   Gummy worms
                         Sand buckets and shovels

Mix cream cheese and butter and sprinkle pudding mix over mixture. Add milk, cookies, and Cool whip. Mix well. Put in sand
buckets. Refrigerate until set. Garnish with gummy worms and
serve with sand shovels.
Yield: 15 servings

*Great for children's summer parties. I use this for end of the year
school parties.*

Jan Smith

Cooking Up Fortunes

Blank paper
1 cup butter, softened
½ cup sugar
1 egg

2½ teaspoons vanilla
   extract
3¼ cups flour
½ teaspoon baking powder

Cut a supply of ¾ x 2-inch strips of blank paper. In advance program each slip with a different message. Then have your youngsters bake a batch of fortune cookies.

Preheat oven to 425 degrees. Mix together butter, sugar, and egg until smooth. Add remaining ingredients. Mix together to form a ball of dough. On a lightly floured surface, roll out half of the dough to ⅛-inch thickness. Cut dough into 2½-inch circles. On each circle of dough, lay a "fortune" slightly off center. Fold the cutout in half vertically. Fold in half horizontally. Pinch the open edges closed. Place on an ungreased cookie sheet. Repeat the process with the remaining half of the dough. Reroll all the dough scraps. Repeat the process a third time. Bake the cookies for about 10 minutes or until they are lightly browned. Serve when cool.
Yield: 25 cookies

Polly Jackson

Crazy Popcorn

6 cups popcorn, popped
   (no salt or butter)
1 cup dry-roasted nuts
1 cup marshmallows

1 cup raisins
½ cup peanut butter
2 tablespoons margarine

Mix the popcorn, nuts, marshmallows and raisins together. Melt the peanut butter and margarine over low heat. Toss with popcorn mixture. Store in an airtight canister.
Yield: 15 servings

Jan Smith

Edible Play Dough

1 cup peanut butter
1 cup corn syrup
1¼ cups nonfat dry milk

1¼ cups confectioners'
    sugar

Mix, then knead the ingredients. Let your children create yummy sculptures then "dig in" and gobble 'em up!

Jane H. Brown
Similar recipes submitted by Polly Jackson and Donna Taylor

"Fried" Ice Cream

Vanilla ice cream
Frosted Flakes

Chocolate syrup

Dip 1 to 2 scoops vanilla ice cream. Roll in Frosted Flakes. Place in bowl. Top with chocolate syrup.

Erica and Jonathon Stallings

Ice Cream Cone Cakes

Any flavor cake mix
2 dozen flat-bottomed
    waffle ice cream cones

Any flavor frosting

Make batter for cupcakes as directed on the cake mix package. Pour scant ¼ cup batter into ice cream cones, filling ½ full. Set on pan and bake for 15 to 18 minutes at 400 degrees. Cool and frost.
Yield: 2 dozen

Donna Taylor

A Fishy Treat

1 package blue gelatin   **Gummy fish or fruit sharks**

This tasty snack is a cool compliment to a fish or summertime theme. Prepare gelatin according to package directions. Refrigerate the mixture so that it solidifies just slightly (about 5 to 10 minutes). Stir in gummy fish or fruit sharks. Refrigerate the gelatin for a couple of hours. Serve this fishy treat while you read aloud a favorite fish tale.
Yield: 4 to 6 servings

Jan Smith

Fish Cookies

Sugar cookie dough   **M&M candies**

For each cookie, cut a circle shape from sugar cookie dough. Cut a triangle from the circle. Attach the tip of the triangle to the opposite side of the circle. Press an M&M candy into the dough for an eye. Bake the cookies according to the sugar cookie recipe. Great recipe for preschool age children when talking about shapes.

Jan Smith

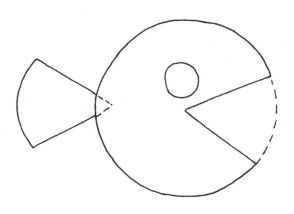

Gingerbread House

8 squares of graham
   crackers
½ pint size milk carton,
   washed and dried
1 pound confectioner's
   sugar

3 egg whites
½ teaspoon cream of tartar
Candy to decorate
Marshmallows
Dry cereal
Gummy Bears

Mix sugar, egg whites and cream of tartar in a bowl with an electric mixer at low speed. Increase the speed to high and beat for seven minutes, until stiff peaks form. Keep this frosting covered or in the refrigerator until ready to use. It will become hard as it dries. Dab a tablespoon of frosting on the bottom of the milk carton. Place in the middle of a sturdy paper plate. Dab a tablespoon of frosting to the back of four squares of graham crackers. Press each one on the sides of the carton. Dab frosting on the back of two more squares of crackers and place on the top of the milk carton to form the roof. Cut triangular shapes from the last two graham cracker squares and attach with frosting to cover the eaves of the house. Now prepare to decorate! Spread the roof with frosting. Place candy, dry cereal shapes or white or multicolored marshmallows in rows onto the frosting before it dries. Frost each area of the house and decorate, creating doors, windows, chimney and a path to the door. Small graham cracker bears or gummy bears can stand in front of the house by placing a small amount of frosting at their bases. To save, wrap tightly in a plastic bag.
Yield: 1 house

Paula Neely

Martin's Microwave Playdough

2 cups all purpose flour,
   sifted
2 cups water
1 cup salt
4 teaspoons cream of tartar
2 tablespoons oil

Food coloring
Ziploc bags
Flavoring (spearmint,
   peppermint, etc., just
   for scent)

In a large bowl, mix all ingredients together. Cook on high in microwave for 3 to 5 minutes, stirring every minute. Time may vary depending on microwave oven. When it gets to the right consistency, place in a Ziploc bag, and add food coloring and scent. Zip it up and mash through the bag to spread the color. This keeps from staining your hands. You may want to divide the dough up and make 2 or 3 colors.

Polly Jackson
*Similar recipes submitted by Carol Bannister,
Jan Smith and Donna Taylor

Mini Pizza

2 English muffins, sliced
1 small jar Zesty spaghetti
   or pizza sauce
Parmesan cheese
Onion, chopped

Ground beef or sausage,
   cooked and crumbled
Mushrooms
Mozzarella cheese
Anything you desire!

Slice the muffins, and spread spaghetti sauce on them. Top with Parmesan cheese, onion, beef, mushrooms and mozzarella cheese or additional toppings of your choice. Bake at 375 degrees for 15 minutes or until top is cooked.
Yield: 4 servings

Jan Smith
*Similar recipe submitted by Carol Bannister

Moon Cookies

2 sticks butter, softened
2 cups sugar
6 eggs

1 teaspoon vanilla
2 cups flour

Topping:
½ cup sugar   ½ cup nuts, chopped

Preheat oven to 350 degrees. Cream butter and sugar. Add eggs one at a time. Stir in vanilla and add flour. Mix until well blended. Pour batter into greased jellyroll pan. For topping, mix together sugar and nuts. Sprinkle the mixture atop the cookie batter. Bake for 10 to 15 minutes. Cool slightly. Cut into moon shapes. To do this, first cut out a circle of cookie using a round cookie cutter. Set this cookie aside. Then, working from the resulting opening, use the cookie cutter to cut out a variety of moon shapes.
Yield: 8 dozen

Polly Jackson

Orange Snowballs

3 large oranges   ⅔ cup sugar
2½ cups water

Cut oranges in half. In a bowl, squeeze out all the juice. Clean out the inside of the oranges, so that you can use them for bowls. You won't need the pulp. Mix water and sugar, boil for 5 minutes. Remove from heat and let cool for about 20 minutes. Mix in orange juice. Fill each orange bowl with mixture. Place in freezer for not more than 3 hours. Stir mixture once or twice during freezing. This is really yummy on a hot day!
Yield: 6 servings

Children, make this slushy treat with your favorite grown-up!
Jan Smith

Paintbrush Cookies

⅓ cup soft shortening
⅓ cup sugar
1 egg
⅔ cup honey

1 teaspoon vanilla
2¾ cups flour, sifted
1 teaspoon soda
1 teaspoon salt

Mix the shortening, sugar, egg, honey, and vanilla together. Stir in the flour, soda and salt. Chill the mixture. Preheat oven to 375 degrees. Roll dough out on a floured pastry cloth, using floured covered rolling pin. Roll to ¼-inch thickness. Cut in different shapes. Set on greased baking sheet. Paint designs with Egg Yolk Paint (see following). Bake 8 to 10 minutes. For clear colors, do not let cookies brown.
Yield: 5 dozen (2½-inch) cookies

Egg Yolk Paint:
1 egg yolk
¼ teaspoon water

Food coloring
Paintbrushes

Blend well egg yolk and water. Divide mixture among several small custard cups. Add a different food coloring to each cup to make bright colors. Paint designs on cookies with small paintbrushes. If egg yolk paint thickens on standing, add a few drops of water.

Donna Taylor

Play Dough

2 cups flour
1 cup salt
4 teaspoons cream of tartar
2 teaspoons oil

2 cups boiling water
2 packages unsweetened
  Kool-Aid mix

Mix first three ingredients. Add Kool-Aid to water and add oil. Then mix flour mixture and colored water. Knead, cool, PLAY and SMELL!

Jan Smith

"Cooky" Cookie Cutters

Make your own "cooky" cookie cutters! Draw or copy the pattern you desire on heavy cardboard. Cut out each one and grease it. Lay pattern greased side down on dough and cut around it with a sharp knife. Lift onto baking sheet with wide spatula. Try some of these designs first.

Donna Taylor

Peanut Butter Energy Balls

2 tablespoons peanut
   butter
1 teaspoon honey
2 tablespoons raisins

2 tablespoons uncooked
   oatmeal
2 teaspoons chopped apple

Mix together peanut butter and honey. Stir in raisins, oatmeal and apple. Roll into a ball. Chill for approximately one hour. Eat and enjoy!
Yield: 1 to 2 servings

Do your children need an energy boost? Here's a snack that just might do the trick!

Polly Jackson

Sidewalk Chalk

5 cups Plaster of Paris
10 (10-ounce) plastic cups
Wax paper
Newspaper
Oil
Napkins

5 cups tempera paint,
 colors of your choice
10 toilet paper tubes
10 craft sticks
Water

Place ½ cup of plaster of Paris in each plastic cup. Tear off a piece of wax paper for each child to work on. Cover work area with newspaper. Pour small amount of oil onto napkin and rub oil on the inside of cardboard tube. Choose paint color. Add ½ cup of powdered tempera paint to plaster in cup. Use craft stick to stir contents in cup. Add two tablespoons of water to mixture. Stir until it looks like thick pudding. Add a little more water if mixture is too dry. Place end of cardboard tube on wax paper. Pour mixture into tube, almost to the top. Allow at least 4 to 5 hours for chalk to dry. Once chalk is dry, tear tube away from chalk. Use chalk to draw on pavement. Erase with water.
Yield: 10 pieces of chalk

Angela Castellow

"Worms" By Knox Gelatine

4 envelopes Knox
 Unflavored Gelatine

3 packages (4-serving size
 each) flavored gelatin or
 sugar-free
4 cups boiling water

In a 13 x 9-inch baking dish, mix all the gelatins; add boiling water. Stir until completely dissolved. Chill until firm. Cut in long, narrow, wavy strips - lengthwise in the pan. Then cut across into thirds, and use spatula to remove to Ziploc bag. These will keep a fairly long time unrefrigerated.

Jane H. Brown

324

Old Fashioned Molasses Taffy

⅔ cup molasses
⅓ cup light corn syrup
1½ cups firmly packed
   brown sugar
1½ tablespoons vinegar

½ cup water
¼ teaspoon salt
⅛ teaspoon soda
¼ cup butter

Combine molasses, syrup, brown sugar, vinegar, water, and salt in a large, heavy saucepan. Stir over low heat until sugar dissolves. Cook, stirring occasionally, until mixture reaches 265 degrees on candy thermometer. Remove from heat and stir in soda and butter. Pour into buttered large shallow pan and let cool until it can be handled - about 15 minutes. Turn edges in to center as it cools. Butter your fingertips. Cut off pieces of candy and pull and twist until candy changes color, to bronze. Twist in shapes or cut into 1-inch pieces with scissors dipped in cold water. Wrap in plastic paper.

Yield: 150 pieces

Notes: 1. If you don't boil molasses long enough, it won't harden like it should. 2. Boiled down syrup is unmercifully hot! It quickly and severely burns anything it touches. 3. If the taffy is to turn out white instead of gray, hands that pull it must be very clean.

Donna Taylor

Pretzel Bird Nests

Pretzel twists
Wax paper

White almond bark
Pastel M&M's

Place a pretzel twist atop a slightly larger piece of waxed paper. Spoon melted white almond bark into each of the pretzel's enclosed spaces; then place a pastel-colored M&M candy into each one. When the project has cooled and the almond bark has hardened, peel the nest from the paper and indulge.

Polly Jackson

Have-A-Heart Sandwiches

Heart shaped cookie cutter
Whole wheat bread
White bread

Strawberries
Cream cheese, softened

Use the cookie cutter to cut hearts out of the bread. Wash the berries and mash them into the cream cheese with a fork. It's okay if the berries are lumpy. Spread a white-bread heart with strawberry cream cheese. Top it with a whole-wheat bread heart. Serve on a pretty plate with a few strawberries.

Angela Castellow

Green Eggs and Ham

1 to 2 eggs
2 drops green food coloring

1 tablespoon margarine, melted
Cubes of ham

Beat eggs and food coloring. Scramble eggs in margarine over medium heat. Top with ham to serve.
Yield: 1 serving

A St. Patrick's Day Treat!

Carol Bannister

Easter Rabbit Salad

Lettuce leaf	**Almonds**
Pear half	**Raisins**
Cottage cheese	**Cherry**

Make your own Easter rabbits! Place lettuce leaf on plate, and add pear half. A drop of cottage cheese makes the tail; almonds for the ears; raisins for the eyes; and a cherry makes the nose!

Jan Smith

Easter Garden

Fill a flat dish with pebbles and moss. Put halved egg shells amongst them which are cleaned out and filled with earth. (I like to use colored egg shells.) Sow seed in them - wheat, millet, birdseed, or marigolds. In between the shells, you may want to put chicks or the Easter bunny. Prepare all this well over a week before Easter, so that you can see the new shoots on Easter morning.

Angela Castellow

Pumpkin Pancakes

2 cups flour
1 teaspoon baking soda
2 teaspoons baking powder
½ teaspoon salt
1 teaspoon cinnamon
¼ teaspoon ginger
¼ teaspoon nutmeg
2 eggs

¼ cup shortening
¼ cup water
2 cups buttermilk
1 cup pumpkin
Confectioners' sugar
Candy corn
Raisins

Mix flour, baking soda, baking powder, salt, cinnamon, ginger, and nutmeg in a large bowl. Beat eggs in a separate bowl. Add shortening, water, buttermilk, and pumpkin to eggs. Mix thoroughly. Gradually add the flour mixture to the egg mixture and blend well. Heat a griddle to a temperature setting appropriate for cooking pancakes. Coat the griddle with shortening. Drop spoonfuls of batter onto the griddle. Turn pancakes after small bubbles appear in the batter and the edges of the pancakes start to turn brown. When the pancakes are golden brown on both sides, remove them from the griddle. Sprinkle the pancakes with confectioners' sugar. Have children decorate their pancakes with candy corn, raisins or other edibles to resemble jack-o'-lanterns.

Polly Jackson

Crunchy Pumpkin Seeds

Vegetable oil
Salt

Pumpkin seeds from 1
pumpkin

Wash and dry seeds. Spread them out on a cookie sheet and lightly coat with oil. Sprinkle with salt. Roast seeds in 300 degree oven for 30 to 45 minutes or until crispy and golden brown.

Polly Jackson

Halloween Spider Cookies

1 (12-ounce) bag semi-sweet
   chocolate morsels
1 (6-ounce) bag
   butterscotch morsels

1 (3-ounce) can chow mein
   noodles
1 (7-ounce) can peanuts

Melt chocolate and butterscotch morsels in a saucepan over very low heat. Quickly stir in peanuts and chow mein noodles. Drop by spoonfuls onto waxed paper and refrigerate until hard.
Yield: 3 dozen

> *Polly Jackson*
> **Similar recipe submitted by Jan Smith*

Thanksgiving Turkey

Oreos
1 can chocolate icing
Candy corn

Chocolate malt balls
Cinnamon drops

Open Oreo and spread frosting on inside of each side. Hold at a 90 degree angle, like an open clam. On one side of Oreo, press in 5 to 6 pieces of candy corn in a fan pattern for tail feathers. On other half of Oreo, anchor 1 malt ball for body/head. Put a dot of frosting on 1 cinnamon drop and stick to the malt ball for waddle. Gobble, Gobble!

> *Polly Jackson*

 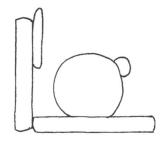

Christmas Gumdrop Wreath

4 (9-ounce) packages of
  gumdrops
12-inch Styrofoam wreath
Round wooden toothpicks

Fabric or ribbon bow
Florist's pick
Wire

Sort the gumdrops by color to help you remember to use all colors around the wreath. Wrap a wire to make a loop for hanging. Break toothpicks in half. Push one end of the half of toothpick into the Styrofoam wreath. Press a gumdrop on the pick. Add more gumdrops. Place the gumdrops so close together that they touch. Cover wreath with gumdrops. Wrap the wire of the florist's pick around the bow. Push the pick into the wreath.

Make this yummy wreath just for the fun of it, and don't be surprised if you find bits of it missing during the holidays.

Jan Smith

Christmas Holly Wreaths

60 large marshmallows
1 cup margarine
1 (1-ounce) bottle green
  food coloring

6 cups crispy rice cereal or
  cornflakes
Red cinnamon candies

Combine marshmallows and margarine in large saucepan. Cook, stirring over low heat until melted. Remove from heat. Stir in food coloring until well blended. Add cereal; stir well. With buttered fingers, pinch off small pieces of cereal mixture and shape into wreaths. Place on waxed paper. Decorate with candies. Leave on paper 24 hours.
Yield: 4 to 6 dozen

Carol Bannister
*Similar recipe submitted by Donna Taylor

Christmas Tree Cones

1 can of white frosting
Green food coloring

Candy pieces (M&M's, red
hots, sprinkles, etc.)
Pointed ice cream cones

Mix a few drops of food coloring with the frosting. Stand cones inverted, on wax paper. Spread frosting all over cones with a butter knife. Leave tops bare so children can turn cones while trimming. Decorate with candy. Spread frosting on the tops.

Polly Jackson

Cinnamon Ornaments

1 can of cinnamon plus
extra for dusting
Applesauce
Wax paper

Paint, buttons, beads, etc.
for decoration
Ribbon

Pour the can of cinnamon into a bowl. Add several tablespoons of applesauce to make a dough texture. Shape the dough into a ball. Dust a piece of waxed paper and the rolling pin with cinnamon. Place the ball of dough in the center of the paper. Flatten the ball with your hand and then roll it out with the pin until it is ¼-inch thick. Use any cookie cutter, cut out shapes. Gently lift and place on a clean piece of waxed paper. Make a hole at the top of your ornament with a toothpick. Let dry for at least 24 hours, turning them often. When completely dry, use an emery board to smooth out rough corners. Decorate with slick paint, buttons, beads, fabric scraps, etc. Use a ribbon for hangers. These are for decorations only. Do not eat!

These make a sweet smelling ornament to hang on a tree or for giving as gifts.

Paula Neely
*Similar recipe submitted by Jan Smith
and Sabrina Faison Odom

Jar Toppers

Any size glass jars with metal lid
4 cups flour

1 cup salt
1½ cups water

Mix the flour, salt and water until mixture clings together. Knead dough on floured surface until smooth. Divide the dough according to the size lids you have. Shape the dough into a ball then shape each ball over a lid. Keep the dough thin. Keeping in mind if it's a special holiday season, use a knife, spoon, fork or toothpick to make decorative holes and cuts on the dough-covered lids. Using extra dough make small cut-outs with small cookie cutters. Stick the shapes on by moistening the bottom of dough shape with water and placing on top of lid. To help air escape while baking, poke several holes in dough. Place dough lids on cookie sheet, and bake at 250 degrees for 2 to 3 hours or until dough hardens. Remove from oven and let lids cool. After lids have cooled, try some other decorating ideas:

Color cut-outs with markers; glue seasonal candy or painted pastas to lid; glue on tiny ornaments; spray lid with clear acrylic spray and add candy sprinkles or paper confetti.

(Continued on next page)

(Jar Toppers, continued)

After decorating, spray jar lid with acrylic and let dry. Fill jar with goodies and top off with a colorful ribbon around rim of jar.

This craft can be used for any holiday season. The jar lids can be decorated with Valentine hearts, Easter bunnies, Halloween pumpkins and / or Christmas trees. Once you have decorated your jar, fill it with matching seasonal candies.

Paula Neely

Handprinted Christmas Wrapping Paper

White shelf paper   **Large paintbrush**
Tempera paint (red and
   green)

Unroll the paper to be painted. Work with only one paint at a time, so that colors are not muddied. Have the child hold up both hands while parent brushes paint over each hand. Each time the hands are painted, the child holds his fingers apart and presses down firmly to make a handprint. When enough of one color has been done, then begin on the next. Let the paper dry, and wash up!

Here is a Christmas wrapping paper that children delight in painting... and chances are that Grandmother will carefully save it, cherishing the little hands that made it.

Jan Smith

Edible Snowflakes

Flour tortillas
Oil

Powdered sugar

Let it snow! Let it snow! Let it snow! To make these edible snowflakes, each child folds a flour tortilla in half twice. Then using a pair of sterilized scissors, he cuts a snowflake design for his tortilla just as if it were paper. While children observe from a safe distance, heat a small amount of oil in electric frying pan and lightly fry each snowflake. Place the "flakes" on paper towels to drain. Let each child sprinkle his creation with powdered sugar. Snow is definitely in the forecast.

Polly Jackson

Index

Index

D

E

F

Index

Index

Moultrie Service League
P.O. Box 1365
Moultrie, GA 31776

Please send ____ copy(ies) of *Southern Settings*   @ $17.95 each _____
Postage and handling   @   3.00 each _____
Georgia residents add sales tax   @   1.08 each _____
TOTAL _____

Name _____

Address _____

City _____ State _____ Zip _____

Please make checks payable to *Moultrie Service League.*

- -

Moultrie Service League
P.O. Box 1365
Moultrie, GA 31776

Please send ____ copy(ies) of *Southern Settings*   @ $17.95 each _____
Postage and handling   @   3.00 each _____
Georgia residents add sales tax   @   1.08 each _____
TOTAL _____

Name _____

Address _____

City _____ State _____ Zip _____

Please make checks payable to *Moultrie Service League.*

- -

Moultrie Service League
P.O. Box 1365
Moultrie, GA 31776

Please send ____ copy(ies) of *Southern Settings*   @ $17.95 each _____
Postage and handling   @   3.00 each _____
Georgia residents add sales tax   @   1.08 each _____
TOTAL _____

Name _____

Address _____

City _____ State _____ Zip _____

Please make checks payable to *Moultrie Service League.*

Reorder Additional Copies